Colour for
Architecture Today

Colour
for
Architecture
Today

edited by

Tom Porter and
Byron Mikellides

Taylor & Francis
Taylor & Francis Group

First published 2009 by Taylor & Francis
2 Park Square, Milton Park, Abingdon, Oxon, OX14 4RN

Simultaneously published in the USA and Canada by Taylor & Francis
270 Madison Avenue, New York, NY10016

Taylor & Francis is an imprint of the Taylor & Francis Group, an informa business

Design concept by Karen Willcox for aleatoria.com
Designed and typeset in Helvetica by Alex Lazarou, Surbiton
Printed and bound in India by Replika Press Pvt. Ltd, Sonepat, Haryana

British Library Cataloguing in Publication Data
A catalogue record for this book is available from the British Library

Library of Congress Cataloging- in-Publication Data
A catalog record for this book has been requested

ISBN10 0-415-43814-4 (hbk)
ISBN10 0-415-43815-2 (pbk)

ISBN13 978-0-415-43814-8 (hbk)
ISBN13 978-0-415-43815-5 (pbk)

Contents

Foreword by Sir Terry Farrell

I must thank the publishers for providing me with the opportunity to read this book and give some time aside to thinking about colour and architecture; always so worthwhile and particularly so at the present time when it seems architecture is well into its stride in an era of colour renaissance after over 100 years of what John Outram calls in his essay 'chromatic deprivation'. We have been living through an era of deep suspicion of colour; a time almost of 'chromaphobia'.

Many of these essays touch on the cultural swings and changes behind this twentieth-century rejection of colour – the perceived excesses of the Victorians, the counterbalance of Ruskin and his followers with eventually a rigorous, reductivist puritanism emerging at the outset of the twentieth century, to the point where the followers of Corbusier (if not perhaps the complex, contradictory master himself) saw whiteness as a 'moral' issue. And it wasn't just the forward-looking practitioner designers who embraced this ethos; even the historians restoring the Elgin Marbles saw fit to radically erase all traces of colour from these glorious Parthenon sculptures; pure form, whiteness and no colour were how the past and the future were to be perceived.

More interesting is why everything has swung back in recent times and these excellent essays are brought together partly with the aim, as the editors put it, of encouraging a 'more colourful and exciting built environment', as well as gathering the thoughts of those dedicated to studying the phenomenon of colour in these much more open, enlightened and adventurous times. There has been a recent, accompanying explosion of technological possibilities which has brought about a vast array of colouring and lighting techniques. 'Fabric engineering' – the engineering of the very clothes that dress our buildings – has progressed rapidly in both technical and creative terms, with a new accompanying psychological mindset change where human clothing fabrics (the most primitive and earliest form of built environment!) are seen as an inspiration and kindred spirit in terms of pattern, texture, surface and, of course, colour. There has also been a liberation of connectivity within the widest range of artistic endeavour, such that

Sauerbruch Hutton can describe their building as an 'inhabited painting' and Will Alsop can initiate the building design process by the act of painting itself.

One reason these artistic connections work so well is that those artists, painters and sculptors who now enthusiastically engage in architecture have discovered the joy of scale and permanence, and also the very public exposure that architecture naturally brings. The artist, Liam Gillick, when collaborating with me on the new Home Office headquarters in London, was enormously stimulated by the sheer size and scale of the multi-coloured canopy overhang he was helping to create – 90 x 6 metres and six storeys in the air above the roof tops in central London. What sculptor outside the world of buildings, he asked, has such opportunities? We live in times when, not only can architects liberate the inner artist in themselves, but (particularly with computer technology supplanting much of the technical and bureaucratic drudgery of detailing and specification writing) artists like Thomas Heatherwick and Michael Craig-Martin can now readily become architects/building designers, sidestepping seven years of so called 'professional' training.

Colour is such a powerful design tool that it is hard to comprehend its suppression (as part of twentieth-century baggage along with ornament, one of Adolf Loo's modernist 'crimes'). It is hard too to reconnect and reintegrate with a world of sensibility, delight and articulation that we have made available to ourselves once more. It seems that we have reopened a long-sealed treasure box of sublime potentialities, which always were, and still are, as primitively fundamental as form and space themselves. The better understanding of the psychological power and meaning of colour, colour's ability to help the communication and mapping of modern life's complexities, and the scientific analysis of colour creation and colour effects upon the eye all add strength and potential to our era's liberation. It is as though we have finally allowed ourselves to travel with Dorothy to find the Wizard of Oz and have only in the last decade or so triumphantly arrived (but with a large dose of wide-eyed, bewildered astonishment) from a land of black and white to a wonderful new world; a world that is in colour.

Acknowledgements

Contributors

Grateful thanks are due to: Anne Barnaby, Charles Bear, Marisa Benabib, Berit Bergström, Wakefield Carter, Roderick Coyne, Emma Davies, Susan Dunsmore, Tonya Gronin, Astrid Harel, Cécilia Hurstel, Jennifer Benz Joy, Andy King, Ian Korn, Caroline Mallinder, Sharon Matney, Henk Mihl, Katherine Morton, Bob Pomfret, Keith Reeves III, Silvia Rizzo, Marjorie Rodney-Goodin, Pascale Scheurer, Antonio Venturini, Kim Victoria, Elizabeth Walker, Fem Windhorst and Caroline Wolf.

Special thanks are due to Jean-Philippe Lenclos for his enthusiasm and valued input in the development of this book.

The editors would also like to express their sincere gratitude to the contributors who have graciously prepared material and statements for inclusion in this book.

Will Alsop
Principal, SMC Alsop, London.

Alain Bony
Artist, Paris.

Giovanni Brino
Architect and Professor of Architecture, Turin Polytechnic, Turin, Italy.

Kristina Enberg
Architect and colour designer, Stockholm, Sweden.

Karin Fridell Anter
Architect and Lecturer at the Royal Institute of Technology, Stockholm.

Paul Green-Armytage
Architect and Adjunct Research Fellow, Curtin University, Australia.

Anders Hård
Colour scientist, founder of the Scandinavian Colour Centre and inventor of the current version of the NCS (Natural Color System).

Maud Hårleman
Lecturer, Royal Institute of Technology, Stockholm, Sweden.

Nicholas Humphrey
Writer, broadcaster, Professor at London School of Economics, London.

Louise Hutton and Matthias Sauerbruch
Principals, Sauerbruch Hutton Architects, Berlin.

Jan Janssens
Architect and Associate Professor, Lund University, Sweden.

Andrew Jones
    Student, Department of Architecture, Oxford Brookes University.

Peter Jones
    Artist, Cwmni Colourscape, Ceredigion, Wales.

Yann Kersalé
    Artist, Vincennes.

Rikard Küller
    Emeritus Professor in Environmental Psychology, Lund University, Sweden.

Ricardo Legorreta
    Principal-founder, Legorreta + Legorreta, Mexico.

Jean-Philippe Lenclos
    Colourist, Paris.

Mark Major
    Principal, Spiers and Major, Lighting Architects, London.

Niall McLaughlin
    Principal, Niall McLaughlin Architects, London.

Byron Mikellides
    Emeritus Professor in Architectural Psychology, Oxford Brookes University.

Anne Militello
    President and Principal Designer, Vortex Lighting Inc., Hollywood, California.

Zena O'Connor
    Design researcher, the University of Sydney, Melbourne, Australia.

Roy Osborne
    Artist and author, London.

John Outram
    Principal, John Outram Architects, London.

Tom Porter
    Visiting Fellow, Oxford Brookes University.

Michiel Riedijk
    Principal, Neutelings Riedijk Architects, Rotterdam.

Grete Smedal
    Interior architect and Emeritus Professor, Bergen National Academy of the Arts, Norway.

Peter F. Smith
    Emeritus Professor of Architecture, Leeds Metropolitan University and Special Professor in Sustainable Energy at Nottingham University.

Werner Spillmann
    Former Professor of Architecture, Winterthur Polytechnic, Switzerland.

Lois Swirnoff
    Painter, photographer and visual logician, Brookline, Massachusetts, USA.

For
Andreé and Sarah

Introduction

Tom Porter and Byron Mikellides

'What colour has Paradise?' was a playful and rhetorical enquiry following a lecture promoting Colour in Architecture presented in Sweden in 1984 by a Swiss academic. The questioner prefaced this by suggesting that when architects attempt to represent Eternity in their built work, they invariably employ pure geometrical form. Indeed, in order to realize the essential purity of form, architects such as Étienne-Louis Boullée and Claude-Nicolas Ledoux, expunged colour as a perceptual hindrance of their abstracted plastic forms. In proposing his own answer to the question, the interlocutor further suggested that art and literature usually depict Paradise in terms of achromatics or as pure white – concluding that when Dante, guided by his beloved Beatrice, ascended to the utmost chamber, 'all was white'. Meanwhile, it seems, when seen in the visions of painters, such as Hieronymus Bosch, Purgatory is a far more colourful place.

Firmly established at the beginning of the twentieth century, the myth of a Modernist 'whiteness' and an abstinence of any architectural polychromy continued well into the latter half of the twentieth century. This is partly explained by the dearth of colour printing at the time which meant that Modernist buildings, such as those by Le Corbusier – whose huge body of work included just one building without colour – were initially disseminated to his followers in monochrome and thus visualized in the architectural psyche as white or grey. This misconception was also compounded by the austerity and the greyness of a pervading concrete used in the ensuing and hurried post-war rebuilding programme. This greyness is epitomized by a book published in Germany in 1960 and entitled *Colour and Architecture* which contained not a single colour plate – relying instead on descriptive captions to explain the unseen colour in the photographs. The upshot has been a deep suspicion of colour – a form of chromophobia as outlined in David Batchelor's book of the same name in which he accounts for a kind of Daltonism that sees colour as paradoxical – as historically subdued or subordinated and to be considered as something 'other'.[1]

The precursor of this book – *Colour for Architecture* – entered this debate in 1976. Its aim was to bring together the ideas of leading architectural colour practitioners of the time together with artists and psychologists whose work exhibited an attitude to the built environment and to illustrate their work in full colour. The intention was to deal directly with the issue of colour in the built environment. It opened with the thoughts of the Op artist, the late Victor Vasarely, who offered two conceptions of the Parthenon: one of a beautifully proportioned, pristine Pentellic marble temple and another of the same temple completely painted in lime-wash and embellished with gilded and brightly coloured statuary. Vasarely argued that while the former perception is one that remained misunderstood in the mind's eye of architects as an icon of architectural perfection and purity, the latter was the reality – the more colourful Parthenon not only symbolizing purity in the minds of the ancient Greeks but also being built two thousand years before the quattrocento, when painters, sculptors and architects became separated into their respective disciplines.

Colour for Architecture also included several influential contributions published in English for the first time, including the regional colour mapping methodology of the French colourist Jean-Philippe Lenclos that provides a logical design tool for establishing closer links between a building and its setting. Another was the documentation of the innovative NCS (Natural Color System) of Anders Hård, then Director of the Swedish Colour Centre in Stockholm. This is a system that annotates hue in terms of our colour perception, that is, directly in the eye and brain, as well as providing a sophisticated yet easy-to-use research tool that brings insight to our understanding of colour while dispelling many of its associated myths. Indeed, the exposure of the NCS in English in *Colour for Architecture* directly led to its eventual adoption in the UK under the trade-name of 'Colour Dimensions'.

Although several of the original selection of international contributors, such as Sir Hugh Casson, Victor Pasmore, Oscar Newman, Joe Esherick and Faber Birren have sadly died in the three-decade interim since the first publication, the editors are intensely proud to have had the opportunity to publish their work and ideas. However, thirty years later, the story of colour in the built environment now comes with a new twist. New technologies have brought innovative ways of bringing colour to urban space; façades can now change colour depending upon the perceptual point of view, they can thermochromically colour-react to daytime and seasonal temperature-shift, be chromatically animated by sensors, by light-projection systems or by plasma screen. Such innovations have caused a paradigm shift. Indeed, the advent of sophisticated and energy efficient LED lighting, buildings – albeit assuming a completely new persona – now find a night-time life and an around-the-clock urban presence. What was once achieved with the painted surface is now subject to other forms of colour treatment, for example, the advent of the fascination with image, user interaction, illusive and ephemeral surface-effects and a nocturnal presence in the light of coloured illumination – causing some to proclaim that 'the painted wall is dead'.

To form a deeper understanding of the colour experience, we retain our mix of architects, artists who collaborate with architects, scientists and researchers in order to present a comprehensive picture of the current 'state of the art'. To do so, we have invited contributions from leading authorities from the world of architecture and art and from eminent researchers who work in experimental and architectural psychology, science and biology. All have been selected because of their contributions to a more colourful and exciting built environment or their dedicated study of this phenomenon in relation to the human experience.

The noted American colour authority, Lois Swirnoff, is author of *The Color of Cities* (2000) and *Dimensional Color* (2003). A prominent student of Albers, she is a painter, photographer and visual logician. She presents two contributions: the first explores the links between a culture's distinctive character and how colour choice is rooted in the geophysical and determined by how colours originate in – and are modified by – the angle of the sun's rays; the second describes the nature and spatial function of colour in architecture.

Professor Nicholas Humphrey is a distinguished British psychologist whose work on evolutionary psychology and aesthetics, the evolution of consciousness, cognition and sensory perception has contributed greatly to our knowledge of the subject. As a researcher, writer, TV and radio broadcaster, he has received many accolades and awards, including the British Psychological Society first book award in 1993 for *The History of the Mind*. Other books include *Consciousness Regained* (1983), *Inner Eye* (1986) and *Seeing Red: A Study of Consciousness* (2006). Humphrey provides us with a fascinating account of how and why colour vision has evolved and how it contributes to our biological survival as a species.

Roy Osborne is a practising artist, writer, and educator and past President of the Colour Group (Great Britain). His books include *Lights and Pigments* (1980), *Color Influencing Form* (2004) and *Books on Colour 1500–2000* (2004). Osborne (with Byron Mikellides) considers the relationship between light, surface and colour phenomena and the various theories of colour perception.

Architect and researcher Peter F. Smith explores the basic human drives in relation to the modern environment. His books include *The Dynamics of Urbanism* (1975), *The Dynamics of Delight* (2003) and *Architecture in a New Climate of Change* (2007). They examine urbanism, architecture and psychology and offer a glimpse of how a new kind of dialogue between architects and psychologists can inform the environmental design process. He is Emeritus Professor of Architecture and past Vice-President of the RIBA, and is currently Special Professor in Sustainable Energy at Nottingham University.

More an architect and urban planner than a colourist, Giovanni Brino is internationally recognized for his heroic reconstruction and installation of over 10,000 façades in his native Turin following the discovery of the 1850 Turin Colour Archives. His approach to the colour plans for over 50 historic cities and monuments across Italy and beyond derive from an essentially traditional restoration methodology but applied at the city scale. He is the author of several books, including *Crystal Palace: Cronaca di un'avventura progettuale* (1995) and *Carlo Mollino: Architecture as Autobiography* (2005).

In his analysis and application of colour in industrial products, environment and particularly architecture, Jean-Philippe Lenclos is widely regarded as the world's foremost colourist. From his Atelier 3D Couleur in Paris came the much-imitated methodology for documenting an architectural colour vocabulary. Rehearsed in France and then further developed in Japan, his process of colour analysis, trademarked under 'The Geography of Colour', has taken him to all the continents of the world. This epic undertaking has resulted in three award-winning books co-written with his wife, Dominique and published by Moniteur, Paris: *Couleurs de la France* (1982), *Couleurs de l'Europe* (1995) and *Couleurs du Monde* (1999).

Academic and colour consultant, Werner Spillmann is former Professor of Architecture at Winterthur Polytechnic in Switzerland. He has lectured extensively on architectural colour throughout the world and has assembled a significant archive of colour-order system publications which include many of the seminal works in their original form. He writes here about his largest urban project – the colouration of Kirchsteigfeld new town in Potsdam, Germany.

Zena O'Connor conducts research in environmental assessment and aesthetics as well as building performance and post-occupancy evaluation. Trained as a designer, her doctoral research conducted at the University of Sydney examined aesthetic response to façade colour within the context of planning policy in Sydney, Australia, and here explains her shadowing of Jean-Philippe Lenclos' environmental colour mapping methodology in a case study using a digital technology.

When the eminent scientist Anders Hård first introduced the NCS (Natural Color System) in the English language in the first edition of *Colour for Architecture* in 1976, there was no Atlas of colour notation for practitioners and researchers to use. Since then and in the past 30 years that the Atlas has been produced, the NCS has been adopted as national standard, not only in Sweden and Norway but also in Spain and South Africa. In Chapter 9, Anders Hård and Kristina Enberg introduce the latest version of the system followed by others who have applied it in both research and practice.

Karin Fridell Anter and Maud Hårleman are Swedish colour researchers who hail from Uppsala and Stockholm respectively. Based on their individual investigations, both demonstrate how inherent colour (the actual colour of an object) and its perceived colour (the appearance of the same colour when seen at a distance) are perceived differently. While Fridell Anter explores this phenomenon on the colour of external façades, Hårleman – an interior designer and researcher at the Royal Institute of Technology – studies it in rooms, comparing walls with north and south orientations.

A member of the faculty of the Department of Design at Curtin University of Technology in Western Australia, Paul Green-Armytage's research interests are in colour and other aspects of appearance. He has served as a member of the AIC (Association Internationale de la Couleur) Executive Committee and is a past President of the Colour Society of Australia. Green-Armytage discusses how different specialist fields claim to own the study of colour and, drawing on the various disciplines, proposes definitions for seven kinds of colour.

Professor Rikard Küller, of the University of Lund, has been the most prolific researcher in architectural psychology over the past 40 years in Sweden. He was the first elected President of the International Association for People Environment Studies (IAPS) and Chairman of the Technical Committee of Psychobiology of the International Commission on Illumination (CIE). He has received many awards for his pioneering research on the importance of light and colour on psychological mood. Küller considers the importance that light has on our health and well being and the psycho-physiological problems related to SAD (Seasonal Affective Disorder).

Jan Janssens is an architect and researcher at the University of Lund. Working with Rikard Küller and using sophisticated colour simulation experiments of building façades in the laboratory and in the field, he considers whether colour aesthetic judgements and colour preference studies apply in the context of buildings.

Grete Smedal combines her interior architect practice with teaching colour design at the National Academy of the Arts in Bergen, Norway. Her various colour design projects deal with architecture of different types and scale, from single buildings to large-scale settlements – including her acclaimed longitudinal Longyearbyen project at Spitsbergen which is the subject of her chapter.

Also included is a chapter by Andrew Jones, a third-year architecture student at the Oxford Brookes University. He writes from personal experience on the subject of colour synaesthesia.

Louisa Hutton and Matthias Sauerbruch are the principals behind the prize-winning practice of Sauerbruch Hutton Architects, founded in Berlin in 1989. Celebrated internationally for a design approach that combines the enjoyment of sensuality of space with a pragmatic approach to construction and technology, they are also distinguished by another aspect of their work – their exciting approach to architectural colour being documented here in a chapter modified from a lecture presented at the Gottfried Semper (1803–1879): Greece and Contemporary Architecture Symposium, Athens, October 2003.

The architectural practice of John Outram has a considerable reputation for innovative and inventive use of traditional materials. It has received accolades from both the Royal Fine Arts Commission and the Ancient Monuments Society. Outram's coloured surface techniques using castings of smashed bricks in coloured concrete progressed to colour concrete designs inlaid into rubber moulds, followed by laser-copy monoprinting onto plaster and, most recently, computer-driven printing into fabric. He describes his colour philosophy and the inspiration for his work.

The design approach of Will Alsop is unorthodox as it involves colour from the very outset. His architectural process derives not from the conventional paper trail of architectural drawings but from an initial investigation of concepts expressed through the liquidity of paint on huge canvases. Often considered a maverick or labelled 'avant-garde' by the architectural fraternity, his resulting modernist buildings are invariably distinguished by their vibrant use of bright colour and unusual forms; always thought-provoking and controversial, they have won criticism and high praise in equal measure – his Peckham Library, London, winning the 2003 Stirling Prize.

Other architects who contribute material include Ricardo Legorreta of the Mexico City and California-based offices of Legorreta + Legorreta and Michiel Riedijk of Neuterlings Riedijk Architecten in Rotterdam, Holland, together with the young London practice headed by Niall McLaughlin (Niall McLaughlin Architects). Their respective contributions contrast traditional colour approaches with radically new and novel thinking in the deployment and material in the creation of an ephemeral architectural colour.

Fascinated by the illusory nature of the painted surface, Alain Bony is an artist who has collaborated with Jean Nouvel for over 20 years. His ground-breaking approach taps into the 'poetry' of a building with remarkable installations and perceptual effects transforming the architectural surface while attempting to unashamedly create a monumental work of art. Apart from installations for other architects including the Peking Opera House with Paul Andreu, the Nouvel collaboration has seen his intervention on a significant series of his iconic buildings; notably, the Lycée Dhuoda, Nîmes, the publicity agency CLM/BBDO, Issy-les-Moulineaux and the Kultur und Kongresscentrum in Lucerne.

Artist Peter Jones has been designing, building and exhibiting Colourscapes for the past 50 years. Unlike spaces coloured by pigment and coloured light, when one enters a Colourscape, it is as if one experiences another dimension, like breathing or being inside colour. Generated feelings of well-being and healing, both stimulating and relaxing, change as one moves from one coloured chamber to another, while colour phenomena, such as additive colour mixture, appear in different colour combinations to be experienced full-on by the eyes and the body.

Anne Militello is President and Principal Designer of Vortex Lighting Inc. in Hollywood, California. She is one of the pioneer exponents of the nocturnal colouration of buildings, her seminal New 42nd Street, near Times Square, New York, for Manhattan architects Platt Byard Dovell White, provides a simulated and apparent interactive urban colour experience and a pulsating exemplar for others to follow.

Mark Major is a principal of the award-winning Spiers & Major Associates – lighting architects who have worked on projects including the interior of St Paul's Cathedral, Kew Gardens, the Millennium Dome, Gateshead Bridge, and the Burj Al Arab Tower in Dubai. Major discusses their sources of inspiration in employing cutting-edge technologies and materials in their projects – from nature, theatre and entertainment, the rock-'n'-roll industry's revolutionary moving-head colour projector and LED, TFT, LCD technologies, plus the introduction of the RGB system that could, while being energy-efficient and sustainable, colour whole environments with an intensity of hues not previously possible.

Finally, Yann Kersalé is internationally recognized as the foremost lighting artist. He has hundreds of experimental installations, which he calls 'Expéditions-Lumière', and in situ projects to his credit. Apart from heroic installations for Coop Himmelblau, Daniel Libeskind and Patrick Bouchain, these include the nocturnal lighting of the Sony Centre in Berlin and the airports at Chicago and Bangkok for Helmut Jahn, and Jean Nouvel's Lyons Opera House, Quai Branly Museum in Paris and the Agbar Tower in Barcelona.

Colour for
Architecture Today

1

PART 1 WHY AND HOW WE SEE COLOUR

Visual perception is a creative act; each time we visually survey the world around us, data are transferred via the optic nerve to the visual cortex in the brain where the image in view is instantly reconstructed and its meaning determined. However, an important dimension of this perception is that it is also seen in colour – colour vision also being an integral part of the creative act of seeing.

This results from electro-chemical processes taking place in the brain. The fact that colour is an experience within us – that is, within the viewer rather than what is viewed – is demonstrated by our experience of afterimages, when, beyond the initial sensation, colour continues to be experienced in the eye and brain. This is further qualified when we witness colour in our dreams or, with closed eyes, when we can mentally conjure up colour in our mind's eye.

Part 1 examines some basic facts and theories concerning colour vision. Our perception of colour is influenced by the spectral distribution of the light source, the characteristic of the object in terms of absorption reflection and transmission, what goes on in the eye and brain and, finally, our personal experiences in terms of age, gender and psychological make-up. Various colour phenomena and experiences related to the above factors are discussed, such as complementary colours, colour constancy, adaptation and contrast as well as colour blindness and attempts to classify colour. Both the Trichromatic theory proposed by Thomas Young and Hering's Opponent theory are discussed, as well as theories based on recent discoveries of 'double opponent' neurons beyond the retina and thalamus. These neurons cover more opponent combinations that reflect the probability distributions of ambiguous retinal light spectra. As technological innovations in neuroscience become more and more sophisticated, our understanding of what happens in the eye and brain becomes clearer but not yet sufficiently understood. Perhaps the best verdict to date of this theorizing comes from the distinguished scientist Richard Gregory: 'There is a conflict between designing experiments simple enough for analysis and sufficiently complex to reveal the full richness of phenomena. So science is an art. However, like the arts, it is not completely mastered.'[1]

In Chapter 3, Professor Peter F. Smith considers the vital role that colour plays in both our appreciation of beauty and as an essential component of sustainability in the twenty-first century. Buildings and townscapes can only be truly sustainable if they also display the quality of beauty. Referring to the historical and psychological literature on aesthetics, he proposes that the same principles governing proportion and harmony also apply in the realm of colour.

However, the opening chapter by Nicholas Humphrey describes the evolution of colour vision and its crucial function as part of our biological survival kit. Humphrey reminds the reader of our good fortune in being able to see colour, and how and why it contributes to our survival and well-being. His fascinating account of the significance that people attach to the colour red by reference to psychological, physiological, medical and anthropological studies is a further testimony of the importance of colour in so many different contexts. For the designer who is becoming more and more responsible for colouring and lighting our internal and external spaces, he poses the challenge of either using colour in an arbitrary way or building upon our biological predispositions and study how colour is used in nature.

1

The Colour Currency of Nature

Nicholas Humphrey

Mankind as a species has little reason to boast about his sensory capacities. A dog's sense of smell, a bat's hearing, a hawk's visual acuity are all superior to our own. But in one respect we may justifiably be vain: our ability to see colours is a match for any other animal. In this respect we have, in fact, surprisingly few rivals. Among mammals, only our nearest relatives, the monkeys and apes, share our ability – all others are nearly or completely colourblind. In the animal kingdom as a whole, colour vision occurs only in some fishes, reptiles, insects and birds.

No one reading this book can doubt mankind's good fortune. The world seen in monochrome would be altogether a drearier, less attractive place to live in. But Nature did not grant colour vision to human beings and other animals simply to indulge their aesthetic sensibilities. The ability to see colour can only have evolved because it contributes to biological survival.

The question of how colour vision has evolved is – or should be – an important issue for psychologists (and for designers). If we were to understand how the seeing of natural colour has in the distant past contributed to our ancestors' lives we might be better placed to appreciate what colour in 'artificial' situations means to us today. Yet this is not in fact an issue which has been much explored. Indeed, few psychologists, for all their obsession with the physiological mechanism of colour vision, have asked what to an evolutionary biologist must seem the obvious question: where – and why – does colour occur in nature?

It may seem odd to tack 'why?' on to the question 'where?' But the question why is crucial, for the evolution of colour vision is intimately linked to the evolution of colour on the surface of the Earth. It may go without saying that in a world without colour, animals would have no use for colour vision; but it does need saying that in a world without animals possessing colour vision there would in fact be very little colour. The variegated colours which characterize the Earth's surface (and make the Earth perhaps the most colourful planet of the universe) are in the main organic colours, carried by the tissues of plants and animals – and most of these

life-born colours have been designed in the course of evolution to be seen.

There are, of course, exceptions. Before life evolved, the drab landscape of the Earth may have been relieved occasionally by, say, a volcanic fire, a rainbow, a sunset, perhaps some tinted crystals on the ground. And before colour vision evolved, some living tissues were already 'fortuitously' coloured – blood was red, foliage green, although the redness of haemoglobin and the greenness of chlorophyll are wholly incidental to their biochemical roles. But the most striking colours of nature, those of flowers and fruits, the plumage of birds, the gaudy fishes of a coral reef, are all 'deliberate' evolutionary creations which have been selected to act as visual signals carrying messages to those who have the eyes to see them. The pigments which impart visible colour to the petals of a dandelion or a robin's breast are there for no other purpose.

We may presume that colour vision has not evolved to see the rare colours of inorganic nature, since rainbows and sunsets have no importance to survival. Nor is it likely to have evolved to see simply the greenness of grass or the redness of raw flesh, since those animals which feed chiefly on grass or on flesh are colour-blind. It can and almost surely has evolved alongside signal colouration to enable animals to detect and interpret nature's colour-coded messages.

The messages conveyed by signal colouration are of many kinds. Sometimes the message is simple: 'come here' addressed to an ally (the colour of a flower serving to attract a pollinating insect, the colour of a fruit to attract a seed-dispersing bird), or 'keep away' addressed to an enemy (the colour of a stinging insect or a poisonous toadstool serving to deter a potential predator). Sometimes the message is more complex, as when colour is used for communication in a social context in courtship or aggressive encounters (a peacock displaying his fan, a monkey flashing his coloured genitalia). Whatever the level of the message, signal colours commonly have three functions: they catch attention, they transmit information, and they directly affect the emotions of the viewer – an orange arouses appetite in a monkey, a yellow wasp fear in a fly-catcher, the red lips of a young woman passion in a man.

Primates came on the scene relatively late in evolutionary history, and the surface of the Earth must already have been given much of its colour through the interaction of plants, insects, reptiles and birds. The early tree-dwelling primates moved in on an ecological niche previously occupied by birds: they picked the same fruits, caught the same insects, and they were in danger of being harmed by the same stings and the same poisons. To compete effectively with birds, primates needed to evolve colour vision of the same order. It is for that reason, I suspect, that the trichromatic colour vision of most primates (including humans) is in fact so similar to that, say, of a pigeon (although, as it happens, the selectivity of the three types of colour receptor is achieved by quite different physiological mechanisms in primates and birds). Once primates had joined the colour vision club, however, they too must have played their part in the progressive evolution of natural colour, influencing through selection the colours both of themselves and of other plants and animals.

Then, not far back in history, the emergence of *homo sapiens* marked a turning point in the use of colour. For human beings hit on a new and unique skill – the ability to apply colour in places where it did not grow. Most probably they first used artificial colour to adorn their own bodies, painting their skins, investing themselves with jewels and feathers, dressing in coloured clothes. But in time they went further and began to apply colour to objects around them, especially to things which they themselves had made … until the use of colour became eventually almost a trademark of the human species.

In the early stages, humans probably continued the natural tradition of using colour primarily for its signal function, to indicate maybe status or value. And to some extent this tradition has continued to the present day, as testified, for instance, in the use we make of colour in ceremonial dress, traffic signals, political emblems, or the rosettes awarded to horses at a show. But at the same time the advent of modern technology has brought with it a debasement of the colour currency. Today almost every object that rolls off the factory production line, from motor cars to pencils, is given a distinctive colour – and for the most part these colours are meaningless. As I look around the room I'm working in, man-made colour shouts back at me from every surface: books, cushions, a rug on the floor, a coffee cup, a box of staples – bright blues, reds, yellows, greens. There is as much colour here as in any tropical forest. Yet whilst almost every colour in the forest would be meaningful, here in my study almost nothing is. Colour anarchy has taken over.

The indiscriminate use of colour has no doubt dulled modern humans' biological response to it. From the first moment that a baby is given a string of multi-coloured – but otherwise identical – beads to play with, she is unwittingly being taught to ignore colour as a signal. Yet I do not believe that our long involvement with colour as a signal in the course of evolution can be quite forgotten. Even though the modern use of colour may frequently be arbitrary, humans' response to it surely continues to show traces of their evolutionary heritage. So people persist in seeking meaning from colour even where no meaning is intended, they find colour attention-catching, they expect colour to carry information and to some extent at least they tend to be emotionally aroused.

The most striking illustration of human beings' deep evolutionary involvement with colour is the significance that people still attach to the colour red. I was first alerted to the peculiar psychological importance of red by some experiments not on humans but on rhesus monkeys.[1] For some years I had been studying the visual preferences of monkeys, using the apparatus shown here (Figure 1.1).

The monkey sits in a dark testing chamber with a screen at one end onto which one of two alternative slides can be projected. The monkey controls the presentation of the slides by pressing a button, each press producing one or the other slide in strict alternation: thus when he likes what he sees he must hold the button down, when he wants a change he must release and press again. I examined 'colour preference' in this situation by letting the monkeys choose between two plain fields of coloured light. All the monkeys that were tested showed strong and consistent preferences. When given a choice between, for instance, red and blue,

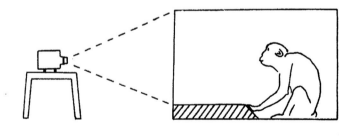

1.1 Rhesus monkey in testing chamber.

they tended to spend three or four times as long with the blue as the red. Overall, the rank order of colours in order of preference was blue, green, yellow, orange, red. When each of the colours was separately paired with a 'neutral' white field, red and orange stood out as strongly aversive, blue and green as mildly attractive. Direct observation of the monkeys in the testing situation indicated that they were considerably upset by the red light. When I deliberately added to their stress by playing loud and unpleasant background noise throughout the test, the aversion to red light became even more extreme. Further experiments showed that they were reacting to the red light exactly as if it was inducing fear.[2]

This aversion to red light is not unique to rhesus monkeys. The same thing has been found with baboons and also, more surprisingly, with pigeons. But what about humans? Experiments on colour preference in humans have given results which appear at first sight to be at odds with those in other primates. When people are asked to rank colours according to how much they 'like' them, red often comes high if not top of the list, although there is a wide variation between individuals depending among other things on personality, age, sex and culture. However, I am inclined to give little weight to such findings for two reasons. First, as Tom Porter has emphasized, the choice of a 'favourite' colour may be heavily biased by changes in fashion; indeed, when Porter tested people from social backgrounds where fashion probably has relatively little influence – African children, on the one hand, the residents of an Oxford old people's home, on the other – he found that both groups ranked colours in much the same way as did my monkeys, consistently preferring the blue end of the spectrum to the red.[3] Second, and more important, there is a methodological problem with most of the preference experiments, for the question 'Which do you like best?' is really much too simple a question to ask of a human subject: people may say they 'like' a colour for a host of different reasons depending both on the context in which they imagine the colour occurring and on how they construe the term 'like'. It would be manifestly foolish to ask people the abstract question 'Do you like better to be excited or to be soothed?', and it may perhaps be equally foolish to ask 'Do you like red more than blue?' To discover the significance of colours to human beings we must look to rather more specific studies.

I shall briefly list some of the particular evidence which demonstrates how, in a variety of contexts, red seems to have a very special significance for humans:

1 Large fields of red light induce physiological symptoms of emotional arousal – changes in heart rate, skin resistance and the electrical activity of the brain.[4]

2 In patients suffering from certain pathological disorders, for instance, cerebellar palsy, these physiological effects become exaggerated – in cerebellar patients red light may cause intolerable distress, exacerbating the disorders of posture and movement, lowering pain thresholds and causing a general disruption of thought and skilled behaviour.[5]

3 When the affective value of colours is measured by a technique, the 'semantic differential', which is far subtler than a simple preference test, people rate red as a 'heavy', 'powerful', 'active', 'hot' colour.[6]

4 When the 'apparent weight' of colours is measured directly by asking people to find the balance point between two discs of colour, red is consistently judged to be the heaviest.[7]

5 In the evolution of human languages, red is without exception the first colour word to enter the vocabulary – in a study of 96 languages, Berlin and Kay found 30 in which the only colour word (apart from black and white) was red.[8]

6 In the development of a child's language, red again usually comes first, and when adults are asked simply to reel off colour words as fast as they can, they show a very strong tendency to start with red.[9]

7 When colour vision is impaired by central brain lesions, red vision is most resistant to loss and quickest to recover.[10]

These disparate facts all point the same way, to the conclusion that humans as a species find red both a uniquely impressive colour and at times a uniquely disturbing one. Why should it be so? What special place does the colour red have in nature's scheme of colour signals?

The explanation of red's psychological impact must surely be that red is by far the most common colour signal in nature. There are two good reasons why red should be chosen to send signals. First, by virtue of the contrast it provides, red stands out peculiarly well against a background of green foliage or blue sky. Second, red happens to be the colour most readily available to animals for colouring their bodies because, by pure chance, it is the colour of blood. So an animal can create an effective signal simply by bringing to the surface of its body the pigment already flowing through its arteries: witness the cock's comb, the red bottom of a monkey in heat, the blush of a woman's cheek.

The reason why red should be in certain situations so disturbing is more obscure. If red was always used as a warning signal, there would be no problem. But it is not, it is used as often to attract as to repel. My guess is that its potential to disturb lies in this very ambiguity as a signal colour. Red toadstools, red ladybirds, red poppies are dangerous to eat, but red tomatoes, red strawberries, red apples are good. The open red mouth of an aggressive monkey is threatening, but the red bottom of a sexually receptive female is appealing. The flushed cheeks of a man or woman may indicate anger, but they may equally indicate pleasure. Thus the colour red, of itself, can do no more than alert the viewer, preparing him to receive a potentially important message; the content of the message can be interpreted only when the context of the redness is defined. When red occurs in an unfamiliar context, it becomes therefore a highly risky colour. The viewer is thrown into conflict as to what to do. All his instincts tell him to do something, but he has no means of knowing what that something ought to be. No wonder that my monkeys, confronted by a bright red screen, became tense and panicky: the screen shouts at them 'This is important', but without a framework for interpretation they are unable to assess what the import is.[11] And no wonder that human subjects in the artificial, contextless situation of a psychological laboratory may react in a similar way. A West African tribe, the Ndembu, state the dilemma explicitly, 'red acts both for good and evil'.[12] It all depends.

I have tried to show how an evolutionary approach can help throw light on human beings' response to colour. Whether this approach can be helpful to the practice of design remains an open question. In many areas of our lives we already overrule and nullify our natural tendencies. But I believe we should try to be 'conservationists' as much on behalf of ourselves as we are learning to be on behalf of other species, and that we should try where possible to make our style of life conform to the style to which our ancestors were biologically adapted. Designers, who are now more than anyone responsible for colouring our world, have a choice before them. They can continue to devalue colour by using it in an arbitrary, non-natural way, or they can recognize and build on humans' biological predisposition to treat colour as a signal. If they choose the latter, bolder course they might do well to study how colour is used in nature. Nature has, after all, been in the business of design for over a hundred million years.[13]

2

Seeing Colours

Byron Mikellides and Roy Osborne

While we often take our perception of colour for granted, it takes a highly complex visual mechanism to make it possible. The system is still not fully understood and as yet there exists no single scientific theory to account for all of it. Richard Gregory observed as recently as 2005 that over 50 theories were put forward by 50 scientists at a meeting on the subject![1] We do know certain basic facts, however, which are the result of decades of scientific investigation by physicists, biochemists, physiologists and psychologists. Colour is a subjective sensation caused by light and is not properly a quality inherent in the object itself. In general terms, colour does not exist without light, which is radiant energy that manifests itself in the form of the visible spectrum of sunlight. Without the eye and brain of an observer, these rays do not in themselves constitute colour. As Sir Isaac Newton explained in his *Opticks* (1704), 'The rays are not coloured. In them there is nothing else than a power to stir up a sensation of this or that colour.'[2]

In short, the perception of colour depends upon three essential factors: (1) the spectral energy distribution of the light (including the conditions under which the colour is perceived); (2) the spectral characteristics of the object, with respect to absorption, reflection and transmission of light; and (3) the activity and sensitivity of the eye and brain (Figure 2.1).

The light source

In physical terms, light is simply the name given to a narrow band of the energy constantly radiating from the sun. Newton, by placing a glass prism in the path of a beam of sunlight, observed how the beam divided itself into the band of colours he called the spectrum. We now know that the colours of the spectrum vary in wavelength (the distance between the crest of one energy wave and the next) and that the visible range of wavelengths extends from about 400 to 750 nanometres (billionths of a metre).

Using a second prism, in 1665, Newton demonstrated that white light is obtained when all the colours of the spectrum are recombined into a single beam. Observers such as Thomas Young (1807) later found that white light could be obtained by mixing red, green and blue beams only, and that all other colours could be obtained by mixing these three lights in different proportions. This became the basis of the theory of vision proposed by Young[3] and later developed by Helmholtz (1856)[4] that there are only three kinds of colour receptors in the human eye, corresponding to the dominant wavelengths of red, green and blue, and that all other colours can be sensed by them; the sensation of yellow, for example, occurs when both red and green sets of retinal cells are stimulated. This is the celebrated Trichromatic theory of colour vision.

Light emitted by a tungsten filament lamp is deficient in energy at the blue end of the spectrum (towards 400 nm) and relatively high at the red end (towards 700 nm) – hence its colour-rendering capacity will emphasize the orange-redness of an object (by making it lighter and brighter) and minimize its blue-greenness. In the case of fluorescent tubes (usually mercury-vapour discharge lamps), the

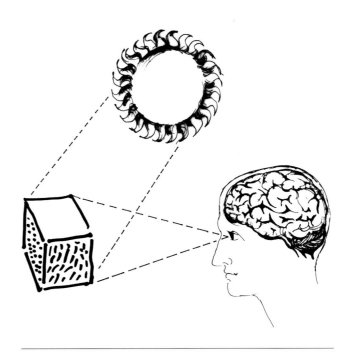

2.1 Light, object, brain

bulk of radiant energy is concentrated in narrow spectral bands. Although such lamps can be made to emit energy throughout the spectrum by the use of fluorescent phosphors (sprayed on the inside of the tubes), their peaks of energy still conform to mercury's spectral lines and, therefore, the colour rendering of these lights will differ from both tungsten-filament light and daylight (which might be considered 'normal'). An ideal standard source for measuring radiation, a so-called 'black body', consists of a small furnace that can be heated to different temperatures. It becomes 'red hot' at about 500 degrees and becomes increasingly white as it approaches 6000 degrees (the surface temperature of the sun). As the heat increases, so the amount of light emitted at the red end of the spectrum decreases in proportion to that emitted at the blue end. Hence light emitted by a light source can be expressed in terms of its 'colour temperature', and this offers a convenient method for specifying the energy distribution of both artificial and natural light sources, including daylight.

The spectral energy distribution of all light sources used by architects, such as the sun, filament lamps, metal-vapour office lighting and gas-discharge street lighting, inevitably affects the perception of the colours of surfaces lit by them. Hence we always need to consider what will be the most appropriate light source to use. In a self-service restaurant it is important to make the food appear appetizing, for instance. The colour of meat (and most cooked food) is generally enhanced by the orange-red bias of tungsten light, but might appear greyer and less appetizing seen under 'cooler' fluorescent tubes.

Optical dimensions of colour

In the world of colour, it is estimated that we can discriminate between some 300,000 tints and shades through differences in the purity and tonality of colours. If, for example, we add grey paint to red paint, its chromatic strength is weakened or desaturated; in fact, if we add any contrasting colour to another, its purity (sometimes called chroma) will diminish and its tonality will also usually darken. The 'neutral colours', black, grey and white, are sometimes referred to as achromatic, as they lack both an identifiable hue and variation in colour saturation. Colour or hue is the most obvious way that colours differ in appearance, and the third way can be defined in terms of their brightness, which corresponds to the amount of physical energy apparent in a light source or reflected from the surface of an object.

The process of mixing beams of coloured light (as in Newton's prism experiments) is called additive colour mixture and should not be confused with the subtractive colour mixture that occurs when coloured substances are intermixed as paints, inks or dyes – which always involves a degree of subtraction or absorption of light. An 'in-between' way of mixing colours which is additive in principle is seen when spinning a coloured disc fast enough that the colours visually 'fuse'. When mixed in this way, contrasting pairs of colours, such as blue and yellow, will produce grey. Colours of maximum contrast are called complementary and commonly placed diagonally opposite each other on the artists' colour wheel. The fusion effect is also observed in the interwoven threads of cloths or in static mosaics (seen from a distance) as on a colour television or computer screen.

Psychologists have attempted to explain our perception of colour using simple graphic models. Most of these representations have deliberately ignored the physical composition of light in terms of its wavelength, and have concentrated instead on psychological and phenomenological aspects of colour. Attempts to classify or specify individual colours by dividing, scaling and numbering each of the three dimensions above have resulted in useful methods of colour notation offered for example by the Munsell System (1905),[5] the Ostwald system (1916),[6] and the Natural Color System (NCS, 1979). The NCS colour solid is illustrated in Figure 9.2 on p. 55. The hues along the periphery of the colour circle represent the colours of the spectrum (with red and violet linked by a non-spectral purple), with complementary colours appearing approximately opposite each other. The colour dimension of saturation (called chromaticness in the NCS) is represented by the relative distance of each fully saturated colour on the periphery from the achromatic grey at the centre. The remaining colour dimension of brightness or tonality can be visualized as a vertical axis cutting through the grey and extending from white at the top of the model to black at the bottom. Though this particular system is measured in terms of colour content, black content and white content, the above-mentioned dimensions of hue, saturation and brightness can be represented by its three-dimensional colour solid.

The object

We live in a spatial world and convert information from our environment from two-dimensional retinal images into three-dimensional experience. Our brains seem to 'reconstruct' space by taking into consideration distance, depth and solidity. Space without content is meaningless; space is defined by objects which act as visual agents having perceptual properties of their own, such as size, shape, texture and colour.

In a strict sense, objects have no intrinsic colour because we only see them if they reflect light; only light sources are able to emit their own light. We do, however, take into consideration changes in natural and artificial illumination during daytime and seasonal cycles and have learnt to compensate for these changes through what psychologists call 'colour constancy'. This is a sophisticated perceptual process in which objects seem to retain stable colouring – or what artists call their 'local colour' – despite changes in light, shade and texture. However, when we take changing light for granted, we generally consider colour as a property of objects in so far as it is the physical and chemical composition of the objects which determine how much light they absorb, reflect or transmit.

Most of the colours we see around us in our daily lives occur by a process of selective absorption. A red object looks red because it has the property of absorbing or subtracting from the white light it receives everything except primarily for the colour component it reflects. A pigment or dye has the quality of absorbing some parts of the light and the colour it appears results from the remainder of the light which remains available for reflection. In sunlight, a bright red table will absorb most wavelengths except for those in the 650 nm region of the spectrum, for example. A white object will reflect roughly the same amounts of all wavelengths which our visual system ingeniously mixes together to give a single sensation of white. A black object, on the other hand, will absorb all wavelengths and hence appear black.

The eye and the brain

The retina possesses two sets of sensing cells, the rods and cones. Whereas the cones sense full colour in daylight, the rods operate only at low levels of illumination and are effectively 'colour blind'. Hence, no colour appears by moonlight, as there is a threshold of illumination below which colour cannot be seen, though there may be enough light to allow the perception of shape, movement and the size of objects. This can be demonstrated if we imagine red lettering painted on a black building. The lettering is illegible

by moonlight but, as night turns into day, we are gradually able to read the letters, though the daylight has to increase considerably before the letters are fully perceived as red. Correct colour rendering requires the right balance of light – preferably daylight, which contains the full solar spectrum.

The sensory information reaching our eyes is not experienced as colour (or light) until it reaches the brain. The idea that colour is 'seen' in our brain is therefore correct in this sense. A blind man, able to regain his sight and see for the first time, would have to learn which colour is called red or blue or green. Just like sensations of sound, taste, smell and touch, visual sensations are initially experienced entirely in the brain and can exist without light or the need for a coloured object. We may well experience colour in dreams and it can even be induced consciously with our eyes closed by pressing on the eyeball. Colour responses can also be induced from black-and-white patterns, as when viewing Benham's top – a white disc patterned with irregular black shapes which, when spun fast, elicits sensations of colour.

The light-sensitive nerve cells known as rods are closely packed on the retina but are absent at its centre, which features a small depression known as the fovea, which is exclusively populated by cone cells. The rods are sensitive to light and tonality but not to colour, and hence unable to distinguish red, yellow, green or blue. They are active in very low levels of illumination and cease to react at high levels. Even so, the rods are very sensitive and would enable us to see, for example, a match being lit one and a half miles away. The cone-cell colour receptors are very closely packed in the small, rod-free fovea. This is an area a little larger than one square millimetre and contains in the region of 100,000 cones, although some seven million are distributed across the whole retina.

Another part of the retina, known as the 'blind spot' has neither rods nor cones and this is the point at which the optic nerve connects and sends messages to visual projection areas in the brain. From there, neural activity spreads to other parts of the brain, such as the 'visual association region'. As the cone colour-receptors are very tightly packed in the fovea, it means that our best colour discrimination (and focusing of form) are limited to a small, central area of our field of vision, and at wider angles our critical judgement of colour declines, as the cones are sparser. The quality of perceived colour therefore depends on the part of the retina stimulated. If we keep our eyes fixed on a point in front of us, a coloured object entering our visual field from the side would progressively change as it approached our fixation point. At the edge of our visual field, the object would appear colourless; then, as it moved across, its colour will appear modified and its red and green characteristics appear only when the object approaches the centre of our field of vision. The area of the complementary pair of blue and yellow is much larger than the respective area of red and green. Christine Ladd-Franklin's Evolutionary theory of colour vision (1929) springs from this observation.[7] She suggests that originally the primitive eye was entirely made up of rods which perceived only a grey world. Then, as the eye evolved, the rods split into the blue–yellow sensitive cones and, finally, the yellow sensitive cones subdivided into the red and green receptors. The Ladd-Franklin Evolutionary theory appeals to the incidence of anomalous colour vision in that total 'colour blindness' is very rare; this is followed by the yellow–blue visual deficiency of less than 1 per cent of the population and, finally, to the most common colour defect of red–green deficiency, which coincides with the central colours in the indirect vision experiments (10 per cent of the male population has anomalous colour vision, whereas it is very rare in females – about one in 200).

A further example of our psychological experience of colour is *adaptation*. By staring continuously at a colour, such as yellow, often in no more than a few seconds a change in colour is apparent, as the yellow gradually loses intensity and appears greyer. Another experience of adaptation occurs as our eyes adjust to a darkened environment after being exposed to strong sunlight, for instance, or adjusts to artificial illumination when we switch on a light. This can be a particularly important consideration when the architect is designing spaces for use under widely different illumination levels. Contrast is another way in which the appearance of colours can vary. In general, there is a tendency for our visual system to exaggerate differences between colours either in space or time. This phenomenon is called simultaneous colour contrast (if spatial) or successive colour contrast (if temporal). Simultaneous contrast occurs when colours are placed edge to edge and viewed at the same time. Successive contrast also relates to the complementary nature of colour mentioned previously and with respect to afterimages. A negative afterimage is experienced by staring at a coloured object for half a minute or so and then directing our gaze elsewhere. The colour complementary to the surface of the object is then seen. The same negative afterimage can be experienced from black-and-white objects and a common example is the 'lingering' image on a television screen perceived immediately

after the set has been switched off. Not all afterimages are negative, however, and a positive afterimage – of the same hue as the original sensation – is sometimes seen after a short exposure to a very bright colour. Contrast effects influence the perception of space and the legibility of images, and so awareness of them is important in graphic reproduction, interior design, art, printing and textile design – as well as in architecture and three-dimensional design – and is a subjective response common to all observers.

This psychological experience of colour interaction, as in the case of negative afterimages, is affected by the complementary nature of colours and relates back to the colour-pair zones identified in the indirect vision experiments. Evidence from our psychological experience of colour phenomena, together with colours seen in indirect vision, indicates that we are not simply dealing with three primary colours but with pairs of double-acting colour receptors and processes. For example, in the case of negative afterimages, if a blue stimulus is removed from the field of vision, the blue processing stops and the opposite process begins – inducing a yellow perception. Such observations were taken as the basis of Ewald Hering's theory and known as the Opponent colour theory. Hering (1878) postulated that there are three pairs of processes, each consisting of two opposite colours (red–green, blue–yellow and white–black).[8] As the colour members of each pair are opponents, we cannot experience them simultaneously so one would not normally speak of 'reddish green' or 'bluish yellow'. If both members of the pair are equally stimulated, they cancel each other out and we see grey. Hurvich and Jameson proposed a modernized version of this theory in the late 1950s which offered a quantitative and mathematical explanation for most of the facts of colour vision, such as colour mixture, colour blindness and various colour phenomena.

In other neurophysiological work, support is given to both the Young–Helmholtz Trichromatic theory and Hering's Opponent colour theory at the two different levels of the eye and brain. Rushton (1962) developed a technique for identifying single cone pigments in the human eye by measuring light reflected from the back of the retina; the quality of this reflected light was affected by any visual pigment it passed through. In these experiments he confirmed that there are three different types of cone pigment, corresponding to the green, red and blue 'additive' primaries.[9] His experiments were followed by formidable work by MacNichol in the United States using an instrument called a microspectrophotometer with which the absorption of light in single cones could be studied. By passing monochromatic light through photo pigment contained in a cone, he measured the amount of light absorbed by the pigment at different wavelengths. His results supported Rushton's, since he also found three cone pigments responding to red, green and blue lights.

These revealing experiments offer strong support to the Young–Helmholtz Trichromatic theory at the retinal level. However, further electrophysiological experiments behind the retina, along the optic nerve and in the higher nervous system of the brain, indicate activity consistent with Hering's Opponent colour theory; that is, there are brain cells (neurons) responding in an 'on–off' fashion to either blue and yellow or to red and green. The Swedish psychologist Svaetichin discovered two opponent pairs of colour – precisely those suggested by Hering: red–green and yellow–blue. By stimulating a single neuron with red light, he found it responded in one direction, and that the same neuron subjected to green light responded in the opposite direction; this same neuron, however, did not respond to any other colour. He also established that another neuron responded in the 'on–off' fashion to blue and yellow light. The North American neurologist De Valois has also shown that there are neurons in the brains of monkeys that 'fire' when red light is shone on the retina but these are inhibited when green light is used.

Further research by Scheir and Desimore (1990) and Komatsu (1998) is cited by Purves and Lotto (2003)[10] and proposes that beyond the thalamus, 'the neuronal receptive fields of spectrally sensitive cells are even more complex including "double opponent" neurons that cover a much larger range of opponent combinations than those evident in retinal or thalamic neurons'. Purves and Lotto concluded that:

> The phenomenology of colour perception suggests that the purpose of spectral processing at successive stages in the primary visual pathway is to generate colour percepts that reflect the probability distributions of possible sources of the inevitably ambiguous retinal activity initiated by the interaction of light spectra with the three cone opsins.[11]

There are still many colour phenomena that cannot be explained in a single theory. Edwin Land (1977), inventor of the Polaroid camera, was able to exhibit many colours in an image while employing only one red filter, rather than the three colour filters used in Young's and Maxwell's early experiments.[12] The perception of colour also depends not only on its wavelength but also of differences of intensities of adjacent regions. The meaningfulness of the object, prior knowledge and expectation all play a role in the colours we perceive. According to Gregory: 'Any simple account of colour vision is doomed to failure.'[13]

In general terms, the Young–Helmholtz theory offers an understanding of the visual processing of colour by the eye and the Hering theory appears to be the most satisfactory explanation of our higher perception of colour in the brain. It accounts for most of the colour phenomena discussed so far at the phenomenological level of our experience of colour. For this reason, in Part 3, we present an explanation of the NCS, which is based on Hering's theory, devised by Sven Hesselgren and developed by Anders Hård, the founder of the Swedish Colour Centre. It is a basic and easy system for the designer to comprehend and communicate colour appearance, as can be seen from its various applications in research and practice (see Chapter 9).

The meaning assigned to visual messages after they are relayed from the back of the brain to the visual association region and beyond is a complex affair that neurophysiologists have not yet resolved. We still do not fully comprehend how what we experience, learn from and associate with different colours comes into contact and interplay with our genetic predisposition. Whether our ultimate response is owing to the physical energy of the colour itself or to its associations and symbolic meaning is yet another question involving the 'nature–nurture' controversy. As these psychological factors are of basic importance to the way we emotionally respond to colour, they will be dealt with in more detail and included in the presentations on colour research and architectural psychology that appear later in Part 5.

The Dynamics of Colour

Peter F. Smith

There is general dissatisfaction with the uniformity of cities as so much economic growth is channelled into buildings. At the same time, there is a groundswell of concern about sustainability issues. These tend to focus on climate change and security of energy. However, sustainability also encompasses the aesthetic quality of the built environment. It is the buildings and townscapes of rich diversity of form and colour within the boundaries of harmony which endure. How to plan and design within this component of sustainability is the challenge for the twenty-first century.

In the years following the Second World War, there was a tidal wave of redevelopment across much of Europe thanks to the clearances in Allied countries managed by the Luftwaffe. In Britain, design and planning philosophy was dominated, first by the Corbusian urban dream and second, by an austere concept of harmony. The architectural critic Jonathan Glancey wrote in the *Guardian*: 'Architects were once their own worst enemy when they delighted in buildings conceived as purely functional objects. But one of those functions must be to provide beauty.'[1] To many of the immediate post-war generation of architects and planners, such a statement would have been anathema.

So, what went wrong with post-war planning? It stemmed from a misperception of the meaning of harmony. Then, it was equated with orderliness and uniformity. Minimum variation was allowed between buildings within the streetscape in terms of form, materials, storey heights, colour and scale. Variety was suppressed in favour of tedious conformity. What post-war planners failed to realise was that harmony depends upon disequilibrium. Fundamentally it concerns a clash between dissimilar entities within a single logical frame of reference.

So, what is the real essence of harmony? Gerard Manley Hopkins hit the spot: 'likeness tempered with difference';[2] order spiced with complexity. In other words, a precondition of harmony is the existence of tension. Donald Berlyne sums it up: 'The aim of all pursuits, including science, philosophy and art (including the art of building well) is to seek unity in the midst of diversity or order in the midst of complexity.'[3]

If there is to be a basis for discussing aesthetic perception in other than a subjective way, it has to have its foundations in deep structure value systems common to humanity. This is dangerous territory since many resent the idea that beauty is anything other than a property of the eye of the beholder. To suggest that our perception of beauty can originate in deep structures of the mind is to violate human individuality.

Humans are complex biological systems and the most complex organ in all higher animals is the brain. It is logical to believe that certain ground rules in Nature affect our perceptions and value judgements, including the concept of harmony.

In the forerunner of this book, my contribution went to some length to describe the current thinking concerning the division of the cerebral cortex into right and left hemispheres. They were said to have very different information processing functions. Since then, it has been found that the relationship between the hemispheres is more complex. However, it is still orthodox neuroscience to believe that 'the left hemisphere has a bias towards detail, the right a more holistic outlook'.[4] Roger Lewin's assertion made in the 1970s still holds true: 'Sequential information processing occurs in the left hemisphere and simultaneous processing in the right.'[5] Since the first edition there has also been a significant development in the nature of the aesthetic response. In 2004, neuroscientists in the United States identified the location in the brain of the 'eureka' moment which is often associated with aesthetic perception. The left hemisphere concentrates on identification and classification of data; the right on searching for pattern. When a pattern suddenly jumps into focus, it is the anterior superior temporal gyrus of the right lobe which generates the eureka experience: the aesthetic emotional response.[6]

So, it is still scientifically credible that the right hemisphere has a dominant role in processing abstract information like pattern and colour. It may also be the case that high saturation colours with strong symbolic links activate the limbic brain whereas subtle tones are processed in the cerebral cortex, creating a further opportunity for cortical dynamics.

This provides a framework for understanding how the brain analyses, say, an Impressionist painting. The left hemisphere attributes names to the contents and the possible overall meaning of the picture. The right side analyses patterns of form and colour and is particularly sensitive to colour relationships. In architecture, say, a

Greek temple or Palladian mansion, the left hemisphere analyses the cognitive meaning of the individual elements, classifying them against stored data. The right reassembles the data into a unified whole, making it capable of being judged against aesthetic criteria. Both functions contribute to the full perceptual experience.

If Noam Chomsky was right to claim that there are certain collective deep structures underpinning language, then why should this not also be true of apprehension of harmony whether in sound, shape or colour?

Chomsky concluded that there are certain collective 'deep structures' forming archetypal rules of language.[7] Developmental psychologists have demonstrated that even newborn infants have a degree of perceptual ability which can have no basis in experience. One such deep structure that determines how we organise information has been suggested by social biologists Lumsden and Wilson: 'In many instances the possible routes to a solution are legion but the mind reduces the options to a binary choice.' The mind 'chunks information into binary alternatives'.[8]

A basic binary figure is a rectangle. It is widely regarded as a yardstick of good proportion when it conforms to the proportions of the golden ratio: 1 to 1.618, denoted by the Greek letter phi. This is the golden section rectangle which has been the subject of innumerable experiments (Figure 3.1). To have endured as the epitome of perfect proportion from the Pythagoreans to Bela Bartók suggests that the appeal of the golden ratio is not an accident.

This is where we encounter the link between the human brain and the wider realm of Nature. The golden section ratio is the product of a mathematical series associated with Leonardo of Pisa known as Fibonacci. It is a series in which each number is the sum of the two previous numbers in the progression: 1.1.2.3.5.8.13.21 … Any pair of numbers comprises the golden section ratio to higher levels of accuracy the higher the value of the paired numbers. It is only relatively recently that the Fibonacci series has been recognised as being a generative feature in a wide range of systems in Nature thanks to mathematicians like Ian Stewart. Its presence can be seen in the number of petals of flowers like geraniums, the packing of florets in the centre of sunflowers, in generating the spirals in shells and the spacing of branches from a trunk and the venation of leaves. This is not some mystical design principle designed to offer aesthetic satisfaction but a method whereby plants achieve the most efficient pattern of growth and stability.

In architecture, phi has played a prominent role ever since it defined the limits of the front elevation of the Parthenon and is said to be one of the main reasons for its status as perhaps the world's most perfectly proportioned building. The relationship of height to width is a perfect example of tensile harmony. However, most buildings are more complex such as a typical Palladian mansion which embodies two contrasting elements: the domestic and the ceremonial represented by the portico (Figure 3.2). When there are two such features within a composition, the mind automatically 'weighs' them against each other to discover if there is a stable relationship.

3.1 (above) Gustav Fechner preference graph
3.2 (right) Priory Park, Bath: binary divide

There are two kinds of stability: symmetry and harmony. The former is where one element is the mirror image of the other. Generally the mind dismisses symmetry as posing an insufficient challenge to the problem-solving demand of the brain. Harmony, on the other hand, involves a contest between dissimilar features which poses a challenge to the mind to discover if the outcome is stability or uncertainty. In extreme cases that latter is defined as ugliness. Stability stemming from a clash of dissimilars is a definition of harmony.

In the Palladian mansion, the domestic and ceremonial each represent a quantum of complexity. The aesthetic ideal is when quantum A outweighs B, but only by so much that dominance is clearly established but not crushingly so. The dominant is the portico due to its higher density of visual information and symbolic associations with status, religion and history. The domestic element is physically larger but embodies a much lower density of information. The outcome is a clear-cut case of counterpoint between opposites: order embodying difference. The domestic and ceremonial elements coalesce in the Palladian mansion. It is aesthetically rewarding when that clash is close to the limits of stability, that is, just before our perception reaches the tipping point of disorder.[9] As post-war planners failed to realise, harmony depends upon disequilibrium.

How can the mansion be judged against the yardstick of the golden ratio? Obviously this is mathematically impossible. However, if it is considered in terms of information or complexity, then it has the potential to be judged as an analogy of the golden ratio; a complex extension of the two axes of the phi rectangle. Two dissimilar quanta of information are juxtaposed to assess if there is an overall outcome which reconciles the opposites. If there is a clear dominant but also a robust subordinate, the result is a tensile but stable situation resulting in the satisfaction of certainty born of tension. In other words, the aesthetic experience. If this is true of the elements of buildings, it should also apply to the realm of colour.

Since the first edition of this book, inhibitions about the use of colour in townscape have considerably weakened. So, it is desirable to consider how colour makes its contribution to third millennium townscape. One answer is to apply the principles of harmony discussed above in relation to built form.

Also in the first edition, Nicholas Humphrey suggested that 'Painters consciously manipulate the apparent weight of colours, and their paintings are often said to have a centre of gravity which is possibly determined by colour juxtaposition.'[10] The idea of perceptual weight is a matter of the relative complexity of a colour within the colour spectrum.

The components of chromatic complexity are hue, saturation and brightness. As regards hue, relative complexity was indicated in experiments by Humphrey *et al.* showing that there is a 'statistically significant order of apparent weight' from heavy to light ranging from red to yellow. In red, for example, this not only reflects the neuronal activity generated by the colour but also symbolic associations with primal features like blood and fire.

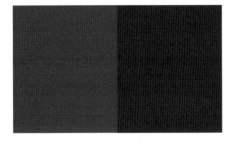

3.3 Red and green

Saturation involves the chromatic strength or purity of a colour. Certain colour combinations at maximum saturation are classed as discordant, most notably red and green (Figure 3.3).

Green has less dominant strength than red but the difference is not enough to establish a clear dominant to subordinate relationship. Arguably this is because there is no synchronicity between wave profiles. Colour pairs deemed to be harmonic may feature respective wave profiles in which the rate of synchronicity outweighs wave clash at or near the limits of stability. In other words, there is tension between the principles of order and difference, with order winning the contest, but only by a margin that just avoids visual dissonance: another analogy of phi.

However, sometimes the areas of colour are adjusted so that the red, for example, forms a small part of the visual field and green the remainder. The human brain responds most intensely to red, to such an extent that focussing on this colour for any length of time can cause the visual field to break up. This is one reason why following fog lights in bad road conditions can rapidly induce fatigue. However, in Nature the bright reds of, say, roses within a sea of green are a delight. The red dominates but is sufficiently counterbalanced by the much greater area of green to create natural harmony.

Another route to harmony is to reduce the chromatic strength of one of the components so that there is a significant difference in saturation between the two. This is achieved by adding grey which can be manipulated to create a sufficient discrepancy between rates of complexity to produce harmony. Even red and green can echo phi. Surface texture can moderate chromatic strength with a pattern of highlights and shadows. This can add variety to large surfaces which might otherwise be excessive expanses of flat colour.

Today architects have an arsenal of materials, finishes and colours at their disposal. The art is to deploy them with economy and sensitivity. Colour can bring places to life or it can be an aggressive statement of corporate hubris.

Finally, there is a role for colour as entertainment. Even a city renowned for its prestigious buildings and imperial past can sometimes drop its guard. Thus did Vienna when it succumbed to the advances of Friedensreich Hundertwasser. Not only were apartments given the Hundertwasser treatment, his *tour de force* was

3.4 Friedensreich Hundertwasser's Heat and Power plant in Vienna

the city's incinerator. He transformed a utilitarian pile into a fairground folly that cannot fail to raise a smile, proving that colour and humour can go together. It is a fitting monument to the artist and an appropriate addition to a city that was home to Sigmund Freud (Figure 3.4).

Climate change is understandably now dominating the design agenda. However, towns may have all the attributes to make them 'green', but they will only be truly sustainable if they also display the quality of beauty.

More than ever there is a need for the built environment to engage the mind through form and colour to experience the creative synthesis between the various mental levels involved in perception. However, we not only need to be involved in sensory perception *per se*, we also seek the mental rewards that accompany the apprehension of harmony either in proportion or pattern. At its most basic, aesthetic experience is a way of exercising the mind in its archetypal mission of imposing orderliness upon chaos. When colour is present, it enables the mind to exploit the full richness of its perceptual apparatus to this end. In the first edition of this book, I described this as nothing less than a kind of therapy. It still is.

2

PART 2 COLOUR MAPPING: COLOUR AT THE CITY SCALE

The colour of the traditional city is an aspect of its history. Until the early nineteenth century, European towns and cities developed by a slow process of organic growth, generally employing materials indigenous to their regions. Architectural styles evolved within the limitations of available materials and this disciplined the form of the buildings, which were related to human scale. The constant use of local materials produced an urban setting with visual harmony despite a diversity of forms. As part of this process, colour decisions were disciplined simply by the cheapness of applying local deposits of coloured earth or employing them to tint or stain distemper and lime-wash. This process created architectural 'colour maps' in which certain colours became identified with particular regions. However, these local colour maps were always tempered by the diversity of imported pigments – for those who could afford the protection of oil-based paints for exposed woodwork, the more 'foreign' hues could bring status. However, today, the designer can select colours for external use from a huge palette of similarly priced and reasonably stable paint colours, but this was not the case in the past when pigments varied wildly in cost and quality. For example, in the early nineteenth century, the association of the brighter colours with wealth stemmed from the fact that blues, organic yellows and reds and some greens were ten times, and often as much as one hundred times, the price of the common mineral pigments.

The shift from a restrictive colour choice controlled by cost and accessibility to the availability in the twentieth century of 'any colour and all at the same price' came to erode and disrupt traditional environmental colour palettes – a situation that from the mid-twentieth century led to legislative control of chromatic identity in cities such as Lyons, Vienna and Venice.

The subject of architectural colour in the traditional and modern urban and industrial landscape is essentially concerned with the visual quality of architecture, and the shift from limited to extensive colour pigments brought with it a degree of concern. The exterior of a building occupies a unique position as the public face of architecture and is within our collective domain; any change in it concerns us all and cannot be left to the whim or fancy of arbitrary choice or of sweeping decisions, whatever the motive. This concern came to evolve a new breed of designer involved in the built environment – namely, the colourist. Initially, during the 1970s, the mainstream colourist movement had remained firmly rooted in France, but the widely exhibited and published methodology of Jean-Philippe Lenclos and his Atelier 3D Couleur came to promulgate the colourist discipline in France and in other European centres.

Lenclos' methodology emanates from a country with extreme diversities in climate, from Mediterranean to Nordic, and a corresponding variety of building materials adapted to the local weather conditions. Lenclos' thesis is simple: a traditional architecture is usually built from the geological substrate on which it stands, with clay-based areas generating brick-built towns and stone-based areas generating towns built in masonry. A further observation was made by Lenclos during a revelatory drive through Picardy between Soissons and St. Quentin, when he noticed that residents of these respective settlements react quite differently in their choice of paints for doors, shutters and trims, etc. For example, in the ashlar-based Soissons, colours are monochromatic, apparently faded, pale and muted, while less than 50 kilometres away in the brick-built St. Quentin, colours are richer, more saturated and variegated. Realizing that he had recognized the basis of an architectural colour language, Lenclos embarked on his celebrated 'geography of colour' research which aims to provide logical colour design tool for both an existing and a future architecture.

Simultaneously, in northern Italy's Piedmont region, the original colour plan for the city of Turin had been discovered by architect Giovanni Brino, and this led to its reconstruction on an epic scale. Although Brino does not consider himself a colourist, his restoration research, involving the revival of the fresco technique and the *trompe l'œil* skills of architectural surface embellishment, is not dissimilar to Lenclos in that his use of natural mineral pigments are essentially local. In other words, the colours used in his restoration are derived from nearby, indigenous building materials – the very materials they aim to simulate.

As environmental colour provides one of the clearest noticeable differences in terms of our perception, and as it is also one of a number of attributes that contribute to urban design aesthetics, we now turn to urban colour mapping. In Part 2, both Brino and Lenclos explain their respective methodologies and colour philosophies. Their contributions are accompanied by one by Werner Spillmann and his realized colouration of a Kirchsteigfeld – a new town in Potsdam, Germany; another a digital case-study conducted by Zena O'Connor in Berry's Bay, Sydney, Australia. It opens with a chapter by the noted American colour theorist Lois Swirnoff, who explores links between a culture's distinctive character and how colour choice is rooted in the geophysical and determined by how colours originate in – and are modified by – the angle of the sun's rays.

Light, Locale and the Color of Cities

Lois Swirnoff

For much of the world's population, color is a vivid expression of their culture. Attributed to 'traditions', distinctions are observable in the built environment of towns, cities, districts and *nations* over the globe, in their use of color: signatures for native groups, of their very identity. Color preferences are part of a local vernacular, almost as spoken languages are, perhaps as their visual equivalents.

Modern cities, on the other hand, are cosmopolitan, comprised increasingly of migrating populations. Many bring their traditional color preferences with them, embellishing a host city's district, which they populate, with colors of their geographic origins – with mixed results.

Some parts of the world are brighter, geophysically speaking, than others. In New York City, for example, the brightly colored façades in streets of Manhattan's Lower East Side quickly identify the district as Mexican or Central American. While exuberance of highly saturated color is marvellous in those geographical regions, exported to North America, the same colors can appear oddly depressing.

What accounts for this? Essentially, context and light. Color juxtapositions interact, whether they appear together on the surface of a page or an artist's canvas, or on the surfaces of a city street. Their contrasts can become factors of integration, as well as dissonance. Hence, amidst the neutrality of a modern city's surrounds, saturated colors can grate on the nerves and disturb the eye, as much as the noise of urban cacophony hurts the ear.

But more fundamentally, the light of a given environment has a pronounced influence on the visual system – the eye and brain. In some sense, I think, we are shaped by light. In traditional cultures that have been stable over long periods of time, a color sense seems to arise in their human populations, which becomes universally preferable – a collective, vernacular sense of color. But while vernacular choices evolve collectively, over time, contemporary color usage would have to be affected by conscious design.

Geophysically, the Earth is illuminated by the Sun in predictable pathways. At the circumference of the Equator, its angle of incidence is prevalent at 90 degrees – a direct hit. At this angle, the Earth reflects sunlight with maximum reflectivity. Concurrent with this physical fact, the psychological response of human populations to this stimulus is a preference for highly saturated colors. Bright color confronts brilliant light, as brilliant light reflects all wavelengths. Made visible in the vernacular of color choices in Africa, Mesoamerica, or the Caribbean, the influence of light seems to be twofold: it influences how we see color, and it may also influence how we shape it (Figure 4.1).

Nearer the Arctic Circle, in Scandinavia, for instance, the angle of incidence is acute. Skimming the surface of the Earth in midsummer, sunlight shines all night. Observing light and its complement, shadow, in these environments, one can see yellow reflected from buildings' surfaces, while a blue/violet hue imbues its shadows – a complementary split of 'white' light. In New England in midwinter, the Sun appears lower, nearer the horizon than it does in the other seasons, but less acutely there, than how it is reflected in Norway (Figure 4.2). Sun rakes the heavy grey of the Atlantic Ocean with amber light at dusk in this season, a redder, longer wavelength.

In Japan, a landmass comprising a series of islands is surrounded by the sea; low lying clouds pervade the atmosphere, in turn lowering environmental luminosity. The color preferences in Japan, expressed in their color systems as well as in built environments, are generally subtle, mixed and subdued. The sense of color is evident in their film emulsions: Fuji film is balanced toward blues and violet, calibrated to the prevailing atmospheric light of its environmental source, and the perceptions of its people.

In Japanese traditions, bright colors were relegated to ceremonial garments and artefacts. In this manner, an essential distinction is made between a restrained and limited use of color in their dwellings and garments, and an acknowledgment of occasions of special purpose, effected by brilliant primary colors, in textiles and ritual objects. With the exportation of American Pop culture to Japan, some younger artists, influenced by cartoon-inspired graphic imagery, seem to revel in denying traditional color sensibility by their indulgence in the blatant use of tacky colors.

Global position, relative to the Sun, seems to have had a profound influence on human responses to light that are related to their

4.1 (top) Levels of color and quality of light in Oaxaca, Mexico

4.2 (left) Levels of color and quality of light in Bergen, Norway

geographic locales. Cultural reactions, however, are predictable, and cannot be considered as determined by location alone.

Ceremonial color prevails in traditional Persian architecture, for example, where blue-tiled domes make reference to Heaven, or by contrast, gold heightens reflections of its light. Arab neighborhoods in Jerusalem make use of blue surrounding doorways, a fragmentary symbolic reminder of orientation toward Mecca – and beyond. Color symbolism, prevalent in many cultures, travels and prevails beyond their place of origins.

But for contemporary culture the cosmopolitan city, with its complex populations, and in its mixed use, corporate neutrality in buildings is not necessarily the only option. Grey uniformity, an expression of caution and timidity, has not always been the choice, nor was 'decoration' eliminated in the early twentieth century. Modernists like Le Corbusier advocated color in architecture, but restricted its hues to the 'pure' primaries. Architects practicing in the International Style advocated the tenet of universality, and the red, yellow and blue of Dutch 'de Stijl' is evident in the buildings of van Doesburg and the paintings of Mondrian. Even if the idea of globalization, which now permeates political discourse, has displaced the concept of 'universality' of Modernist aesthetics, contemporary architecture need not bow to the tribalism of 'cultural identity'.

Buildings are constructed site-specifically all over the world. Given an understanding of the perceptual effects of light, the color of new architecture would enable the variety and diversity we witness in the vernacular. This, however, would require preliminary analyses.

Our studies of color dimension included perceptual analyses of light and shadow.[1] In experiments with geometric solids, we found that ratios of lightness/darkness are made by the human visual system, the eye and brain. Ratios underlying the experience of *chiaro e oscuro* were not known in Italy, but they were noted by their use in the frescos of ancient Rome, and named as such in the Renaissance, by the observing eye of Leonardo da Vinci.

If color is applied to a volumetric surface, these underlying ratios persist and mix with the hues selected. We found that the most significant factor describing volumetric light/dark scales was the direction of the angle of incidence of light. Building models, we succeeded in causing a pyramidal structure to appear flattened when calibrated greys were applied to all its four faces. Whether in the studio indoors, or seen outdoors in sunlight situating the model relative to each light source – the same ratios prevailed under vastly different degrees of light intensity.[2] Thus, the siting of a building at the onset of its conception would be a significant influence on how it is perceived, and would influence the siting and selection of its color as well.

Most architectural modeling exists in an environmental vacuum. Forms in the environment, however, are perceived, rather than conceptualized. Nature's complex environments, a feast of forms and their variations, are to the eye a combination of contrasts in reflected colors and their gradients of light, distinguished by the visual system as forms or shapes against backgrounds. Sight begins with light and color.

To use color in the built environment, devoid of guides of tradition and culture, the visual analysis of place would be an essential starting point. Geographical location would be the underlying factor. Bright color does not work well in subdued environments. In fact, under conditions of low luminosity, the shorter wavelengths (the saturated blues and violets) appear light, middle greens appear more saturated, and dark or deep reds work better than brighter ones. Under these conditions, then, less color is more. In areas of the world where altitude, latitude or meteorological conditions cause environmental brightness, the use of highly saturated color is highly effective. In Mexico, the architecture of Luis Barragan shows an intrinsic relationship between form and color – he 'builds' with color. But his palette would not work in England, nor in the north-eastern United States, while it could in its south-west.

The orientation of building masses might also be considered a factor in appearance, and at the same time, in energy conservation. The diurnal pattern of the sun and shadow fluctuates, of course, seasonally. But the cardinal points on the Earth's surface are still relevant to city location. The expression of orientation by color to the prevalent angle of incidence of sunlight is an aesthetic possibility. It may surprise us, but the cities we build, as the essential artefacts of human activity, the repositories of our culture and of our conscious aspirations, are still subject to the forces of nature.

The light of Manhattan is influenced by the position of its slender landscape, its southern tip jutting out into the expanse of the Atlantic Ocean, and surrounded by rivers. There is a great deal of reflected light from these bodies of water which bounce and scatter from the surfaces of New York's skyscrapers, now crowded as urban patterns. In earlier days of the skyscrapers' dominance, the shadows cast by their heights were studied and controlled as part of the process of urban development. Some architects in New York at present are inventing ingenious structures that permit daylight to permeate the interior spaces of office buildings. A creative solution to energy conservation, the expansion of natural light over artificial resources, is at the same time a healthier, more humane option.

For new cities, the global challenge is how to adapt these visual and technological possibilities to specific locations. Presented as a new challenge, basic analyses of the patterns of light would have to be included at the onset of the design process. Color decisions made then, rather than added at the end, would change the function of color from surface embellishment to color structure – a component of building itself – thus greatly enhancing architectural expression, and its effects on human beings.

Italian City Colour Plans (1978–2007)

Giovanni Brino

In the field of colour plans of historical city centres, the Colour Plan of Turin was the first to appear in Italy. Its restoration was directed by the writer between 1978 and 1983 – the ensuing period seeing its continuation under the auspices of the Municipality of Turin.

In reality, Turin's Colour Plan is not new. It results from meticulous research in the City Archives which contain evidence of an existing historical colour plan carried out by the Conseil des Ediles (Council of Builders) between 1800 and 1850. This colour plan, in turn, originated in the Baroque period during the reign of Victor Amadeus II – the King of Sardinia and the founder of the Baroque city in the second half of the seventeenth century.[1] Just as Louis

XIV had recreated Paris and Versailles to promote his own image – thus providing a model for other kings in Europe during the same period – Victor Amadeus similarly conceived the City of Turin as the Theatrum Sabaudiae, a sort of self-aggrandizing, multi-sensory happening for its own celebration. In fact, this Theatrum, with its aspiring triumphal arches, castles, palaces, hunting lodges and arcaded streets, with its colour and light, and even with its music, represented an idealized 'stage set' on which to perform political, religious and military displays (Figure 5.1).

However, due to the intervention of war and pestilence, the Baroque Turin City Colour Plan was never fully implemented. Indeed, we know from paintings and colour prints of the period that up until the end of the eighteenth century it was confined to the more important streets and squares (Figure 5.2). At the beginning of the nineteenth century and lasting for a period of 50 years, the Conseil des Ediles not only painstakingly recovered and restored the remains of the Baroque colours but also extended the colour plan to those streets

5.1 Piazza Castello as Theatrum Sabaudiae. Anonymous engraving, 1682

MAPPA CROMATICA

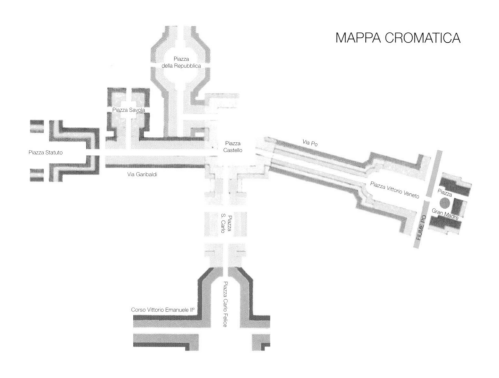

Piazza della Repubblica

Piazza Savoia

Piazza Statuto

Piazza Castello

Via Garibaldi

Via Po

Piazza Vittorio Veneto

FIUME PO

Piazza Gran Madre

Piazza

Piazza S. Carlo

Piazza Carlo Felice

Corso Vittorio Emanuele II°

5.2 (left) The Turin Colour Plan showing central processional routes and associated colours

5.3 (below) Turin's restored ideal centre, the Piazza Castello

TAVOLOZZA DEI COLORI

(2.5 yr 8/4)	(n 8.5)	(7.5 y 6/2)	(5 y 8/1)	(10 yr 6/8)	(2.5 y 6/2)	(2.5 yr 5/6)	(5 yr 6/6)
GIALLO MOLERA ( ) Rif. Munsell	BIGIO CINERICCIO	MALANAGGIO VERDASTRO	BIGIO CERULEO	NANCHINO OSCURO	TERRA OMBRA NATURALE	ROSSO PERSIGHINO	FOGLIA MORTA

and squares whose façades were not stuccoed together with the new streets and squares resulting from urban sprawl.

By 1850, the colour plan, involving environmental standards with surprisingly sophisticated specifications, had been set out by the Conseil for the whole city. The concept was to invest principal streets and squares characterized by a uniform architecture with colours according to a co-ordinated system. The Conseil devised a series of chromatic pathways founded upon popular city colours – coloured routes which followed the major processional approaches to Turin's ideal centre – the Piazza Castello (Figure 5.3). The major routes were interconnected by a network of smaller streets and squares for which secondary and more variegated colour sequences were prescribed. The basic scheme enlisted a palette of around 80 hues which, first being displayed for public approval on the north wall of City Hall, was deployed to form a continuous and, at the same time, changing progression of chromatic experience.

The main Turin palette of hues imitated the noble building materials: marble, granite, terracotta and brick. While pigments such as 'Giallo Molassa', 'Verdastro' and 'Bigio Ceruleo' imitated local stone, taken from the Casale, Malanaggio and Sarizzo quarries respectively, 'Grigio Chiaro' imitated the light-coloured local marble, and so on. It should be understood that Turin, just as 'Genua Picta', i.e., Genoa to the south in the same period, was an impoverished regional capital attempting to attract status using poor, stuccoed façades dressed with mineral pigments that acted as a simulacrum for a more expensive range of building material. However, the difference between Turin and Genoa was that while the latter façades involved flat colour, Turin appeared three-dimensional in that pigments perfectly colour-matched the noble materials and often involved a sophisticated decorative finish applied by skilled artisans including the painted insertion of trompe l'œil sham windows, fake shutters, etc.

After surviving a series of bureaucratic changes, the Conseil was abolished in 1845. No one knows just how long the original colour scheme survived, but it existed as one of Turin's distinguishing features, praised by illustrious visitors such as Friedrich Nietzsche in the late nineteenth century. What is known is that the Conseil was replaced by a bureaucrat who in the ensuing seven years proceeded to erode and systematically obliterate the sophisticated polychrome city concept under a monotone layer of 'Giallo Molassa' (Molasses Yellow). This particular colour is a dull yellow

that does not require admixture with expensive pigments; it is a natural, waterproof lime-wash of hydraulic lime from Casale – a city linked at the time to Turin by the railway. Gradually the yellow spread in all directions until it became known as 'Turin Yellow' – a colour that not only lasted for more than a century but also had become identified in the collective imagination as the original City colour.

However, it was fortunate that the Conseil had accurately documented their fantastic colour plan in the City Archives in sufficient detail to enable its reconstruction – the restoration being achieved with patience and passion by the author and his team over a period of six years.[2] But this was not without some difficulty as one intriguing problem concerned the reconstruction of a colour palette founded on obsolete colour terms. During this period, the Turin Municipal Administration strongly supported the notion of restoring city centre streets and squares in their entirety and this has been done following the Conseil's original plan. In order to reinstate the use of traditional lime-wash colours – often difficult to achieve – a series of façade restorations have been accomplished with the help of the National Association of Craftsmen (CAN). To date, all the most important squares and streets of the city centre have been restored following the colour plan guidelines; the restoration is on-going, encompassing around 10,000 façades.

At this point it would be useful to say something about the difference between the quality of acrylic paints (which can unfortunately be found in many restoration projects) and the traditional mineral pigments. The reason why lime-wash and lime stuccoes should be used in traditional façades is simple, they are entirely compatible with the nature of the wall. For example, the mortar used for the original stucco ('intonaco') was made with slaked lime and sand and, even if these tints appear 'softer' than acrylic paints, they make a perfect bond while allowing the wall to remain permeable to moisture travelling from inside to outside. Conversely, acrylic colours form a barrier and, thus preventing the movement of moisture and over a decade or so, tend to become fissured and ultimately detach.

Following the Turin experience, the concept of colour plans rapidly spread across Italy. But not before a vigorous debate between professional restorers and town planners who, up until the publication of the first book on the Turin Colour Plan with a reproduction of the City Archive documents, were not convinced of its validity. However, by the beginning of the 1990s, several regions of Italy had sponsored the development of colour plans, and two of them – Piedmont and Liguria – have established rigorous ground-rules for the use of their historical colours and promoted them through exhibitions and publications. Indeed, the Liguria region in particular has endorsed systematic research into the traditional façade colours used in *trompe l'œil* decoration and commissioned the writer to devise a pilot colour plan in the typical seaside town of Noli, near Savona.[3] This project also included the trial restoration of a *trompe l'œil* façade in lime-wash and natural pigments. More recently, the Liguria region has also fostered several further colour projects, including the ongoing façade restoration in Sassello – albeit on a small scale – another version of the 'Genua Picta' experience, in which the writer was directly involved (Figure 5.4).

Since 1978, nearly 50 colour plans have been directed by the author in many regions of Italy, in other European countries and beyond. Each of these ensuing colour plans represents a specificity due to the size, history and geology, etc. of each settlement. Such an example is Marseilles in France, whose colour plan was directed for 17 years, from 1988 to 2005. An historical town with an important port, Marseilles comprises many different city districts and once-independent suburban villages. For instance, one such annexed coastal settlement is L'Estaque, which attracted the famous colony

5.4 Restoration of a Sassello façade in the Liguria region using traditional techniques and mineral pigments

of painters; there is also St André, where the famous bricks and tiles were produced, and architecturally in ovidence, and other villages occupied by Italian immigrants which express the painted façades of their native Neapolitan or Sicilian villages. For each of these city districts and suburban villages it was necessary to devise a discrete colour plan in order to account for their variety and the particular pattern of façade treatments. These are sometimes conceived in natural stone, brick or in *trompe l'œil* decorated stucco, artificial stone (Marseilles being one of the nineteenth-century centres of the cement industry), or ornamented with majolica tiles or, indeed, all mixed together. Consequently, when compared with the more homogenous palettes of Italian cities, the case of Marseilles is far more complicated. Unlike cities like Turin, Genoa, Rome and Sienna, etc., which, as I have mentioned, derive their pigments directly from local building materials to achieve a likeness of those materials, Marseilles is a city composed of many architectural and polychromatic personalities – and it provides an intriguing problem (Figure 5.5).

The development of these city colour plans developed almost by chance. They began in Turin at a time when the writer was involved in research for the architectural and structural restoration of the House of Alessandro Antonelli – the most important Italian architect of the nineteenth century.[4] Working in collaboration with Franco Rosso, the eminent specialist on Antonelli's architecture, evidence of its original 1851 polychromy was discovered in the City Archives. Prior to its restoration the façade had been completely painted over with the pervading monochrome 'Turin Yellow' but in its original state we discovered that Antonelli's intention consisted of three primary colours: 'Molasses Yellow', imitating limestone for structural elements such as pillars and arches; 'Brick Red' to simulate the appearance of typical Turin brickwork (used inside the arcades), and 'Blue Stone' for the ornaments and cornices. When the façade restoration was completed, and Antonelli's colours correctly re-established, the scaffolding was removed. The initial reaction of the City of Turin Administration was to order that the colours be removed and returned to a 'traditional Turin Yellow' – an order unfulfilled because, of course, we could demonstrate its authenticity using the documented evidence found in the City Archives (Figure 5.6).

Coincidentally, parallel to the Antonelli restoration, the writer had also been involved in research into Joseph Paxton's Crystal Palace for London's International Exhibition of 1851, and in particular the

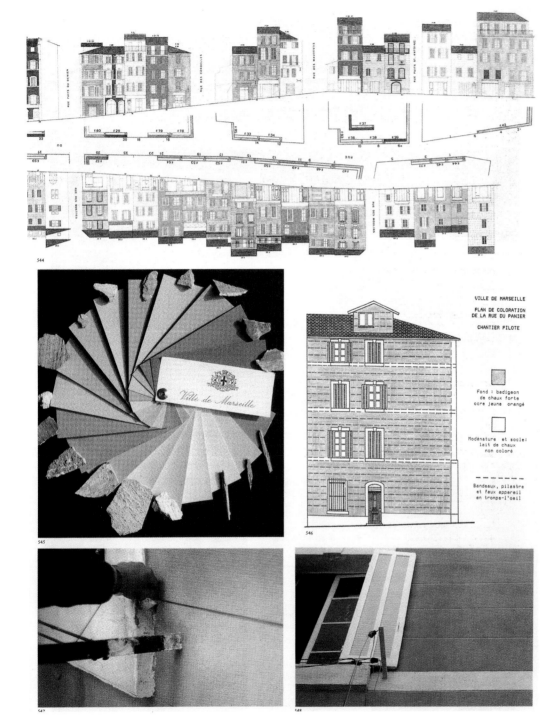

5.5 Part of Giovanni Brino's 17-year survey of urban colour in Marseilles, in this case, the quartier du Panier district

5.6 The Antonelli House (left) in its found state; (middle) as Allesandro Antonelli originally intended it; and (right) after Brino's restoration in 1970

colour plan made by Owen Jones.[5] As is well known, Jones' colour plan was based on the three primary colours: blue, yellow and red. Jones deployed these hues to visually underline its structural form – composed of steel, cast iron and wood – following the chromatic laws of M.E. Chevreul, the French scientist and authority on colour who, still living at that time, had his Cercle Chromatique exhibited in the French Court section of the Great Exhibition in Hyde Park. Furthermore, he also had connections with Turin in that the Turin dyer, G. G. Arnaudon, had visited the Great Exhibition and was so impressed by Chevreul's colour circle that he moved to Paris to work with Chevreul for ten years. It is curious and but perhaps no coincidence that Antonelli had used the same three hues, adapted to his masonry structure, with the same chromatic principles.

Stimulated by the colour experiences of Alessandro Antonelli and Owen Jones, I was charged to found the 'Course for Decoration' at the Turin School of Architecture, and later commissioned by the City Administration to restore the Turin Colour Plan. Without the subsequent teaching and research activity conducted at university level – together with the assistance of Franco Rossi and the help of students – the Turin Colour Plan and the rigorous methodology of its restoration would not exist. However, the Turin Plan was set up at a time when the scientific methodology of façade restoration

– derived from the methodology of mural restoration established by the Istituto Centrale del Restauro di Roma was not yet fully focused. Furthermore, traditional materials such as slaked lime, lime-wash and mineral pigments – from which the stucco and the colours for façade restoration were prepared – had at the time all but disappeared in favour of cement and acrylic paint. Craftsmen skilled in the restoration of the historical façade had also disappeared, some of them transferring to new construction during the economic boom of the 1950s and 1960s without transmitting their knowledge to a new generation. Therefore, in order to solve the technical problems associated with the restoration of historical façades plus the correct execution of colour plans, a revival of mineral pigment production and the old skills of restoration had to be implemented. To do so, an ad hoc institution, the Turin School of Urban Restoration was, with the help of several surviving skilled craftsmen, founded in 1982 and directed by the writer until 1992. A 'mobile workshop' was also created that enabled restorations to be made in all parts of Italy, France and Switzerland.[6]

The continuous research process in the Turin Archives into the colours and materials relating to the restoration of historical façades, together with the proliferation of European colour plans, has necessitated the setting up of a 'Colour Data Bank'. Initiated for the Turin Colour Plan, this now encompasses all the above-mentioned plans plus the colour plans at regional level, such as those in Piedmont and Liguria together with many others. A more particular version is represented by the 'Colour Dictionary', an ongoing data bank established to identify the original mineral pigment recipes related to the colour names found in the archives of the Conseil des Ediles. This contains more than 15,000 colour names together with their history, their Munsell and NCS colour notation and their colour designation in the ISCC.NCS system.

6

Unity in Diversity at Kirchsteigfeld, Potsdam

Werner Spillmann

Built between 1994 and 1997, as part of Germany's reunification programme, Kirchsteigfeld is a new district of Potsdam housing 7,500 residents around a central cluster of shops and civic buildings. Master-planned by the Berlin-based urban design practice of Rob Krier and Christoph Kohl, the original design credo for this new town, although driven by the idealized slogan 'unity in diversity', did not initially involve a comprehensive colour expression; rather a reliance upon each of the 25 architectural firms who would individually design and colour its buildings. However, it was the realization that, subject to the nature of architectural education and the realities of competitions and commissions the modern architect operates as a 'lone wolf' which, together with the apparent demise of local, regional and the timeless sets of rules that would induce harmony and result in unity, led to a different strategy. As opposed to the danger of an unbridled or superficial colouration imposed by the pressure of such a huge construction site, and realizing that Kirchsteigfeld provided an outstanding opportunity to orchestrate building on an urban scale as an ensemble of form, space and colour, the proposal for the systematic creation of a homogenous colour plan was first initiated by Potsdam's far-sighted City Building Director, Richard Rohrbein.

Consequently, I was first approached in 1994 to devise the basic guidelines for a colour concept and then subsequently commissioned by the general contractor Groth & Graalfs in Berlin to coordinate its implementation. Echoing the theme of 'unity in diversity', its aim was to simultaneously create chromatic homogenization and differentiation, that is, on the one hand, to consolidate the larger urban relationships while, on the other hand, provide a colour-intensive discrimination between streets and squares, public spaces, semi-public courtyards and private spaces. This led to the development of a colour palette involving a series of six colour-families. These consist of particular ranges of red, yellow, blue, grey and variations of white which became assembled into a colour fan comprising approximately 65 hues (Figure 6.1). When developing the colour plan, the conscious decision was made not to include green. This stems from the fact that Kirchsteigfeld is characterized by widespread landscaping of shrubs and trees – their greenery providing a lively interaction with the selected architectural hues. Meanwhile, the yellow ochre hues are typical of those found in traditional Potsdam – the seat of Frederick the Great, with its famous Sans Souci Castle, while the oxide reds reflect those in Old Potsdam – namely, the brick houses of the so-called 'Dutch Quarter'. However, while the strategy involved the extension of existing local architectural colour, the intention was not to mimic its historical use but to chromatically deploy the palette in order to clarify the structure of urban space in the spirit of our own time.

My basic concept for Kirchsteigfeld's colour plan assigned the oxide-red range to the district's spacious central area with its market square and recreational area. From this red core, hues gradually lighten, that is, moving through yellow ochre to the paler, whitish colours on the periphery of the settlement at the ring road (Figure 6.2). The distinct colour shift from subtle chromatics to achromatics of this radial strategy was deliberate. It was conceived to obviate any sense of edge, that is, any separation from surroundings or visual enclosure around the urban fringe. Moreover, the yellowish

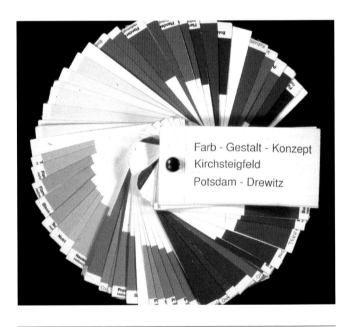

Farb - Gestalt - Konzept
Kirchsteigfeld
Potsdam - Drewitz

6.1 The architectural palette formulated by Werner Spillmann for Kirchsteigfeld, Potsdam

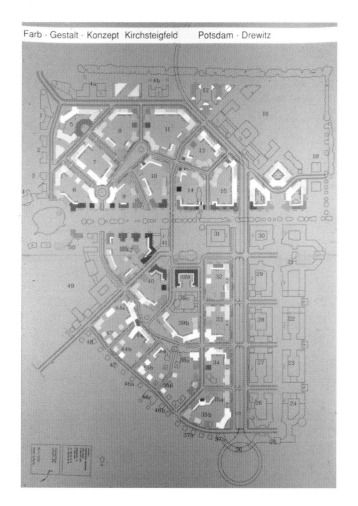

Farb - Gestalt - Konzept Kirchsteigfeld   Potsdam - Drewitz

6.2 (above) The Kirchsteigfeld new town colour plan

6.3 (top right) A corner at Kirchsteigfeld representing the reddish coloured central zone

6.4 (right middle & right) Here the Kirchsteigfeld blue zone meets the reddish-yellowish sector

colours would, even on overcast days, offer a bright, 'sunny' appearance to intermediate streets while the reds at the heart of the new town would induce a sense of arrival, plus a feeling of activity and arousal.

Further decisions affected the semi-public courtyards which, leading from the yellow ochre residential streets, became designated in nuances of white. This choice not only indicated a transition from public to the semi-private domain but also induced a space-expanding illusion as well as allowing a neutral frame on which inhabitants could create personalized accents. Also, in the red centre of Kirchsteigfeld, public buildings, such as the administrative centre, shopping centre and church, etc., are contrasted in the white and grey ranges while two school buildings situated at the periphery of the central area are built in reddish brick. Finally, the blue range was reserved as an accent hue for use – especially on prominent projecting elements – against the broader architectural fields of red, yellow and white. Variations of blue are also deployed on the small urban villas, the so-called 'cube houses' located at some corners of the plan and at points where the sequence of façades open up to reveal their courtyards.

The general colour concept for the Kirchsteigfeld plan plus its colour fan was then delivered to the architectural teams in 1995 which, incidentally, included SOM (Skidmore, Owings & Merrill), KPF (Kohn Pedersen Fox) and Neumüller Architekten, Krier + Kohl, plus many others. During my attendance at the four ensuing and deliberative meetings with the architectural teams, the colours were finally selected and architecturally designated. However, during this process an important rule had to be observed: to optimize a subtle and continuing variation the architects could use a façade colour and secondary hue only once along any sequence of row houses. In terms of colour selection for subordinate elements, the architects were free to make their own choices. This freedom allowed them not only to colour structure their buildings according to their complexity and sculptural form but, in the context of the plan, it also instilled an additional variation without impinging on the coherence of the whole (Figures 6.3 and 6.4).

The aim of the colour strategy at Kirchsteigfeld was to imbue a new architecture with contrast and diversity while simultaneously encouraging a visually comprehensible and chromatic continuity.

7

The Geography of Colour

Jean-Philippe Lenclos

The revelation of the concept of a 'geography of colour' came to me in the surprising confrontation between two diverse cultures: the culture of my childhood in northern France and my extended stay in Japan from 1961 as a young architecture student in Kyoto. Indeed, I had left the humidity of Pas-de-Calais, birthplace of Matisse, with its orange tiles and brick-red façades that contrasted in a Fauvist manner with the intense green of its vegetation and now found myself under different skies. I was now steeped in a different climate and a different universe of colour dominated by grey terracotta roofs over the darkly toned patina of wood walls with the dramatically contrasting white *shojis* (sliding rice paper screens) of traditional Japanese houses. It was in Japan that I suddenly realized that each country, each region, each settlement expressed specific colours unique to their settings. Due to diverse factors such as geography, geology and light, to which we may add the socio-cultural behaviours of inhabitants, these colours appeared to determine and contribute to the affirmation of a national, regional or local identity.

There was also a further revelation that was to profoundly affect my future work. This was my exposure to Japanese calligraphy in which, like Chinese painting, the interaction between the white of the paper represents not unoccupied or negative space but an entity that is as materially occupied and significant as the black ink flourishes of the calligrapher's brush. Ever-present in Zen and Taoist philosophies, and evident in the Western pictorial languages of, for example, Mondrian and Malevich, this Yin–Yang relationship comes together in the duality of solid and void and positive and negative as expressed in the gestural rhythm of the line of the ideogram; at once a sign and a pictogram. Indeed, this complementary yet harmonious tension of black and white, in which so-called 'negative space' is as supercharged as its positive counterpart, is the source of all writing and the genesis of all colour; it suggests a whole range of becoming.

Back in France in 1965, my process for analysing, documenting and comparing the chromatic features of architecture began to evolve. During this time I was commissioned to prepare a paint colour guide, a design tool for architects, for which I initiated a systematic survey of the traditional colours of architecture across 15 regions in France, where there is an extreme diversity of climates, from Mediterranean to Nordic, and a corresponding variety of building materials adapted to the local weather conditions. This research became a point of departure for a more ambitious global study, the first of which was commissioned in 1970 by the Colour Planning Centre in Tokyo. The subsequent exhibition of my work at the Ichiban Kan Gallery in 1972 was apt because, of course, Japan had been precisely the origin of my discovery of the reality of the geography of colour. With ensuing and major exhibitions of my colour research appearing at London's Design Centre in 1974 and at the Georges Pompidou Centre, Paris, in 1977, Japan represented the first foreign country where I had the opportunity to develop and publicize my research.

The analysis

The subject of architectural colour in the modern landscape is essentially concerned with the visual quality of architecture, whether the environment is natural, urban, or industrial. The environment is our collective domain; any change in it concerns us all and cannot be left to the whim or fancy of arbitrary choice or of sweeping decisions. Consequently, my regional analysis aims to identify the predominating characteristics and chromatic detail of the existing architecture in a given area, both in general and in detailed form. In order to select subjects for analysis, individual houses or groups of buildings are chosen as being representative, i.e., embodying typical architectural and colour qualities in keeping with their setting.

First phase:
the methodological examination of the site

Our method at this initial stage of the study is to rely, as far as possible, on the objective evidence provided by the architecture and its environment in the form of sample fragments taken directly from the architecture and the site. It proceeds with a meticulous examination of the area and a careful study of the various materials that constitute its chromatic existence in terms of earth (ground plane), walls, roofs, doors, shutters, etc. (Figure 7.1).

7.1 Lenclos' investigation essentially consists of assembling the existing architectural spectrum of an area with building materials and natural elements collected from the site in question

When a sample is impossible to obtain, colours are annotated with the help of paint and coating manufacturers' colour fans, by making a hand-painted colour match on the spot, or using various colour notation systems, such as NCS (Natural Color System), Pantone Professional Color Selector or RAL Design System. Also, residual to our ongoing research, is an extensive colour reference system archived in our workshop, but it has to be said that, even with several thousand colours at our disposal, in some cases this vast colour-matching resource is not always sufficient. When we have recourse to make hand-painted colour samples, these are made with the aid of a spectrocolorimeter, and the data placed on an electronic database.

Of course, colour is not static but subject to the geographical, diurnal and seasonal dynamic of the natural landscape and the fading and renovation of surfaces and materials – all augmented by the constant change of light. There is also the architectural incidence of impermanent colours that affect the chromatic physiognomy of façades, such as a parasitic foliage, mosses and lichens, to which can be added window boxes, curtains, awnings and even passers-by who, albeit temporarily, counterpoint the more constant character of architecture and hold the potential of bringing bright and accidental hues to a setting. Knowing their importance, these elements factor into our analysis.

7.2 The next phase sees the collected site samples back in the atelier for their conversion into meticulously colour matched painted colour ranges

Second phase: the synthesis of collected data

The chromatic information thus obtained from a site is then assembled in the studio for a long and meticulous process of synthesis. All the collected samples are examined and translated into painted gouache colour plates which faithfully reproduce the original colours (Figure 7.2). However, when dealing with physical material samples, it is not always possible to represent them in a single hue. Indeed, materials or flakes of paint are rarely monochromatic – a fragment of brick, stone or coating acquiring a patina over time is often expressed by an infinite number of nuances that are difficult to reproduce in a single colour. When confronted with this situation we can employ two strategies: either reconstituting the chromatic feel of the material by making a composition of coloured marks or, if a simplified register is required, reproducing the sample's dominant hue as seen from a distance.

Once this production of colour plates is complete, these are then classified and re-grouped into a series of panels which produce a colour synthesis of both a region and of its architectural elements.

Third phase: systems of chromatic conceptualization

The result of our site study and studio synthesis is the presentation of an applied colour vocabulary appropriate to a particular site. General and selective colour palettes can be developed which are co-ordinated so that they can combine to offer harmony and variety in their application to existing or proposed future building projects. Colour palettes can take different forms. For instance, a basic format for communicating the qualitative (tonality, clarity and saturation) and quantitative relationships of a site's architectural polychromy is to produce tables comprising same-sized colour samples systematically arranged along a scale of brightness, lightness or tonality. Here we show the colours of walls, shutters, window framework and doors found in Viviers in the southern region of France (Figures 7.3 and 7.4).

However, another version of our synthesis can focus more on dimensional colour relationships as governed by the structure of buildings. In this case, we offer three colour charts: (1) the

7.3 (below) The painted colour samples are then reassembled into a series of discrete colour palettes, in this case representing the precise colours of (a) walls; (b) shutters; (c) windows and doors

7.4 (facing) A final classification sees the colour samples regrouped into colour ranges that synthesize the predominating hues of related architectural elements. This illustrates Lenclos' chromatic proposals for the town of Viviers

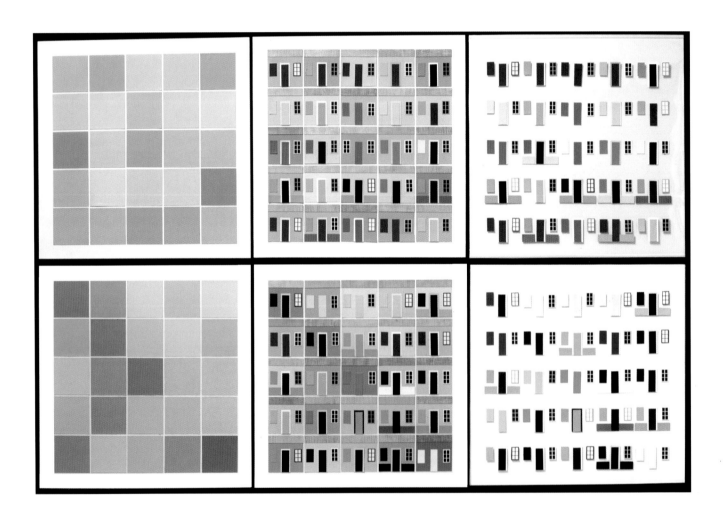

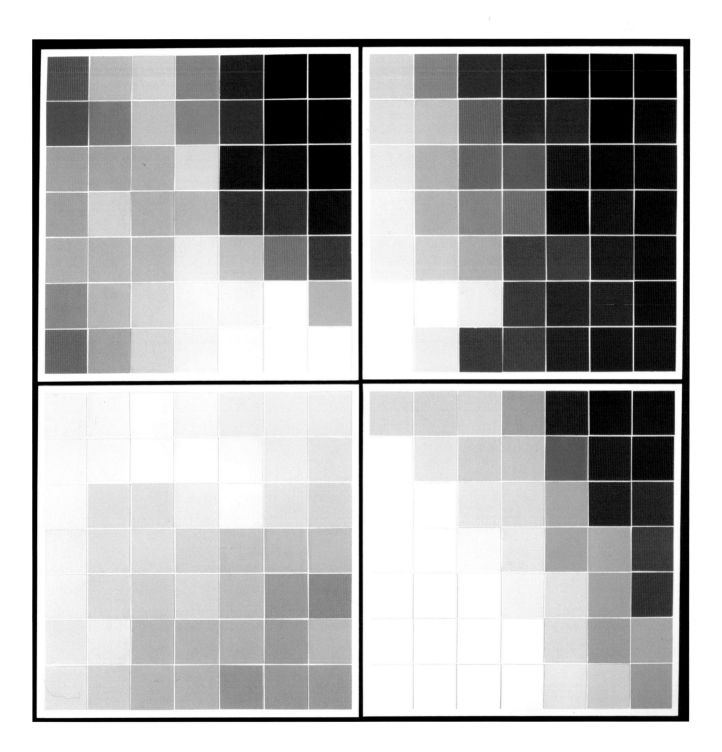

general colours of façades and roofs as registered from outside the settlement; (2) a selective palette that catalogues the predominant and proportional incidence of the colours of doors, windows, shutters, framework and plinths, etc.; and (3) a chart that superimposes the elements of the selective palette on to the general palette. It is this final synthesizing chart that captures the historical and geographical notation of an architectural site's polychromatic mode at a given point in time.

Present-day architecture no longer responds sympathetically to the natural landscape but, by its breadth and scale, creates its own landscape and its own environment. Industrially produced materials have become less connected to the site; synthetic materials of every kind and origin are distributed and indifferently employed anywhere with an ever-growing risk of neutralizing what was once the original and essential visual quality of the architecture in different regions and countries.

Colour in modern architecture can, therefore, be conceived in new terms: the simultaneous construction of large-scale complexes which, as out of context with nature, create new urban landscapes. The dimensions of the modern town or city, particularly where there are high-rise buildings, make it difficult to introduce the natural elements which act as an important link with, and symbol of, living nature. Certainly, colour is no remedy for this irreplaceable link but by its plastic and rhythmical powers of expression it is able to release a poetic dimension which complements the man-made environment. Here, colour in material, structure, rhythm, contrast, can be a new plastic language whose riches are offered to the city of tomorrow.

Digital Colour Mapping

Zena O'Connor

Environmental colour mapping is a process in which the colour characteristics of natural and artificial elements within an environment are identified and documented. Developing over the past three decades environmental colour mapping has provided a basis for identifying architectural colour palettes as one of a number of indicators of regional and local identity. Outcomes of this process have been used to assess the role of façade colour, address the issue of 'colour pollution' in existing settlements and facilitate chromatic cohesion and continuity in terms of new settlements within existing communities. Generally speaking, the result of the process is a database of colour specifications that informs subsequent evaluation, analysis and review, especially in terms of planning decisions. Colour mapping procedures, such as that pioneered by Jean-Philippe Lenclos in Japan and France, have previously been conducted manually, that is, perceptually by eye.

A survey of those methodologies devised for environmental colour mapping in urban and landscape settlements[1] reveals four main stages: (1) definition of the environment to be colour mapped; (2) identification and collection of samples of natural and/or artificial elements; (3) colour matching of elements to an existing colour notation system; and (4) creation of a database of environmental

8.1 Apartment building in Berry's Bay, Sydney, Australia – the site of Zena O'Connor's experimental digital colour survey

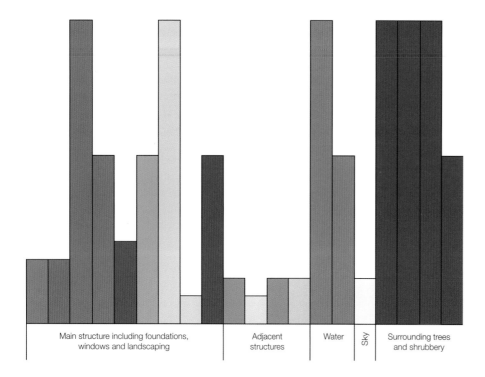

Main structure including foundations, windows and landscaping

Adjacent structures

Water

Sky

Surrounding trees and shrubbery

colour characteristics. However, if one shadows this methodology while applying digital technologies, we find that they can be introduced to all but the second stage.

A small apartment building on Berry's Bay in Sydney was selected as the subject of the case study – its digital image being captured at the highest setting (JPEG at 2592 x 1944 pixels per image) of a Pentax Optio 550 camera. The downloaded image was then processed in Photoshop 7.0 computer software and stored as a JPEG file (Figure 8.1).

As Photoshop 7.0 does not provide a tool for the process, the ensuing task of determining the major colour areas was conducted perceptually by the researcher. To do so, two assumptions were made: first, façade colours that appeared similar in the digital image were deemed to be identical; second, surrounding areas of foliage that seemed similar were also treated as identical. As a consequence, 14 areas were identified as being 'major' areas of colour.

The next task of colour-matching the major colour areas was carried out by the computer Photoshop 7.0 picker tool. This tool can ascertain the hue within an individual or group of pixels for its identification by a variety of colour notation systems. A grid was superimposed on the master image and its format reduced by 75 per cent. Each individual colour area within each grid segment was then identified and tallied, thereby building a database of colour specifications.

The resulting colour characteristics represent the environmental colour map of the building and its setting. Having been annotated – in this case to NCS (Natural Color System) co-ordinates – and collated digitally, data can be reformatted in any number of configurations. For example, as illustrated, the data have been grouped into five main categories: main structure, adjacent structures, water, sky and surrounding trees and shrubbery (Figure 8.2).

From this study, it can be seen that the digital colour mapping process embodies a number of advantages as well as some limitations.

For example, while digital images can capture a huge amount of information, they cannot capture 100 per cent of this information. Moreover, subject to seasonal and diurnal cycles, environments are constantly in a state of temporal change. Indeed, unless conducted longitudinally, both manual and digital studies are limited in this respect. There is also the question of the degradation of digital images during processing, compression and transference – the current convention being to avoid multiple file transfers and editing.[2]

Although only general conclusions can be drawn, digital technology does appear to provide a number of benefits, such as its colour matching function not relying upon the perceptual prowess of the observer/researcher, and the resulting colour data being easily translated into various colour systems. Colour maps can be created, stored, re-formatted and transported across a number of different Microsoft applications; they can also be easily printed and disseminated over the Internet. However, certain limitations impact on the process and further studies using digital technology will bring fresh insights to the effectiveness of applying this technology to the environmental colour mapping process.

3

PART 3 THE NCS (NATURAL COLOR SYSTEM) AND RESEARCH APPLICATIONS

Many designers and architects have shadowed the 'geography of colour' methodology established by Jean-Philippe Lenclos, not least the editors of this book. For example, Byron Mikellides worked on a colour plan for Savannah, Georgia, while Tom Porter was commissioned by the Oslo School of Architecture and the Institutt for Romkunst to direct a postgraduate student group in the colour mapping of that traditionally colourful city adapting Lenclos' principles. A more recent project commissioned by Roger Evans Associates was conducted on the greenfield site for Newhall – a new town extension to Harlow in Essex currently under construction – to provide coordinated colour palettes for all façade components together with floorscape treatments. However, while these projects involved hand-painted colour-matched samples, a similar experiment using a digital technology to that initiated by Zena O'Connor in Australia, was conducted in 2007 with fifth-year architecture students at Montana State University in Bozeman. Two nineteenth-century settlements in the Rocky Mountains were subject to a comparative study: the Main Street of the university town of Bozeman and the centre of the historic district of Butte – a copper-mining town situated 90 miles to the north-west (see figure on pp. 52–3).

All the students used digital cameras to collect the data. For example, the figure presented here was taken with an Olympus C-4000 Zoom camera. The detailed images of façade and trim colours were shot with the same settings to obtain colour consistency between all the images. The aperture value was set at f/3.5, with a shutter-speed of 1/200, an ISO of 200, and an average focal length of 12.7mm. The white balance was preset to 'Cloudy Weather' due to the fact that the detailed images were taken under partially overcast conditions. As a back-up to the colour-matching process, many physical samples of actual materials and paint fragments were collected and used in calibrating the hues. In order to accurately match the fragments taken from the site, Adobe Photoshop was used to import all the images before being tweaked. Furthermore, the monitor was set to the colour profile of ICC-sRGB 1EC61966-2.1 which was found to provide the most accurate results to the colour plotter.

The need for a universal system of colour notation and studies into other related aspects of our experience of colour in the built environment has been the subject of an ongoing research programme based in Scandinavia, particularly at the Swedish Colour Centre. It is to this research and its applications that we now turn.

In the 1930s, the Swedish physicist Tryggve Johansson introduced his version of Ewald Hering's Opponent-colour theory, discussed in Chapter 2; he called it the 'Natural Color System'. In 1952, the architect Sven Hesselgren produced the first Colour Atlas in Sweden. Later the Swedish Colour Centre was established under the directorship of the eminent scientist Anders Hård, and produced a refined version of the NCS. Hård first introduced the NCS into the English language in the first edition of *Colour for Architecture* in 1976, and in the 30 years since the NCS Atlas was published it has been widely adopted, and used as a national standard in Sweden and Norway and also in Spain and South Africa.

The NCS has proved to be practical and beneficial in simplifying the communication, specification and notation of colour appearance in the practice of architecture and design as well as in conducting serious research. In Chapter 9, Anders Hård and Kristina Enberg introduce the latest version of the system followed by others who have applied it in both research and practice.

Chapter 10 by Karin Fridell Anter considers the difficulties facing architects and designers who have chosen colours using colour samples alone. She shows that it is possible to survey and map out what colours people perceive on façades observed under different conditions of illumination, distance and surrounding colours. Fridell Anter coined two simple terms to show the differences between 'perceived' and 'inherent' colour. Consistent variations in perceived colour can be of practical use, and some probable explanations are discussed.

In Chapter 11, Paul Green-Armytage develops the distinction between 'perceived' and 'inherent' colour, and discusses the kinds of colour that exist among different disciplines, each of which approaches the study of colour in its own way. Understanding the obstacles produced in these potentially confusing methodologies could increase communication between these disciplines and improve the education of the designer in the art, science and technology of colour.

In Chapter 12, Maud Hårleman, an interior designer based at the University of Stockholm, considers the influence of daylight on ambience and colour choice in two rooms, one facing north and the other facing south. Using a consistent methodology, in an extensive empirical study employing more than 23 colours and ten experiments, she found that there are significant shifts in perceived colours, not only in terms of hue but also in nuance (lightness and chromaticness).

Finally, in Chapter 13, Grete Smedal explains her approach and methodology of the longest ongoing project in Longyearbyen, close to the North Pole, in the Spitsbergen archipelago. Smedal had the opportunity to develop, evaluate and monitor the overall colour scheme chosen by her, in collaboration with clients, local authorities and residents in different types of buildings, ranging from public and municipal houses, the harbour, to private dwellings. This project presents us with a unique opportunity and first-hand knowledge to observe the development of her ideas using the NCS as the communicative and research tool at all stages of design and practice. The ever-changing, extreme and dramatic landscape not only confronted the designer with difficult decisions but offered a good opportunity to explore the potency of colour, its combinations and contrast, and the interaction of colour and nature.

Montana State University architecture student Brady Ernst shadows Jean-Philippe Lenclos'
methodology in the comparative digital colour mapping of 'historic district' streets in Butte (on
the left) and Bozeman (on the right), Montana

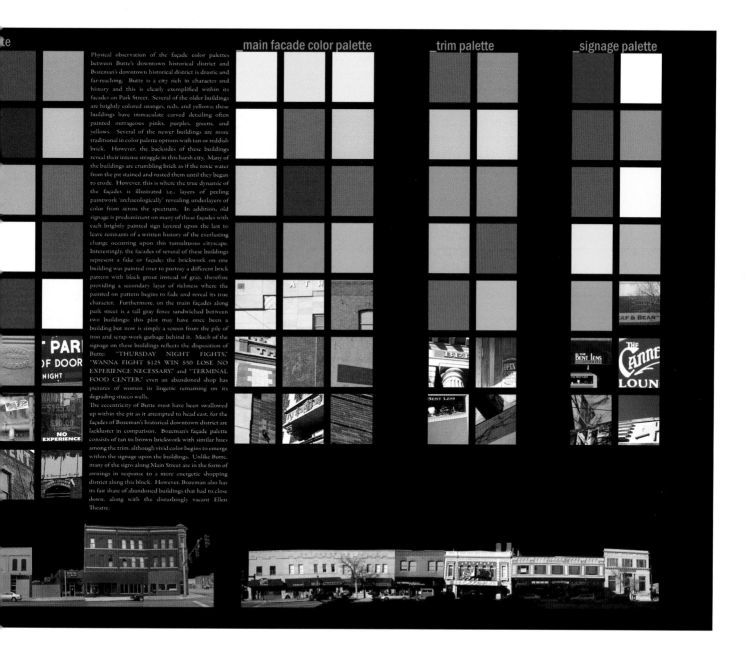

Physical observation of the façade color palettes between Butte's downtown historical district and Bozeman's downtown historical district is drastic and far-reaching. Butte is a city rich in character and history and this is clearly exemplified within its facades on Park Street. Several of the older buildings are brightly colored oranges, reds, and yellows; these buildings have immaculate carved detailing often painted outrageous pinks, purples, greens, and yellows. Several of the newer buildings are more traditional in color palette options with tan or reddish brick. However, the backsides of these buildings reveal their intense struggle in this harsh city. Many of the buildings are crumbling brick as if the toxic water from the pit stained and rusted them until they began to erode. However, this is where the true dynamic of the façades is illustrated i.e., layers of peeling paintwork 'archaeologically' revealing underlayers of color from across the spectrum. In addition, old signage is predominant on many of these façades with each brightly painted sign layered upon the last to leave remnants of a written history of the everlasting change occurring upon this tumultuous cityscape. Interestingly, the facades of several of these buildings represent a fake or façade; the brickwork on one building was painted over to portray a different brick pattern with black grout instead of gray, therefore providing a secondary layer of richness where the painted on pattern begins to fade and reveal its true character. Furthermore, on the main façades along park street is a tall gray fence sandwiched between two buildings; this plot may have once been a building but now is simply a screen from the pile of iron and scrap-work garbage behind it. Much of the signage on these buildings reflects the disposition of Butte: "THURSDAY NIGHT FIGHTS," "WANNA FIGHT $125 WIN $50 LOSE NO EXPERIENCE NECESSARY," and "TERMINAL FOOD CENTER," even an abandoned shop has pictures of women in lingerie remaining on its degrading stucco walls.

The eccentricity of Butte must have been swallowed up within the pit as it attempted to head east, for the façades of Bozeman's historical downtown district are lackluster in comparison. Bozeman's façade palette consists of tan to brown brickwork with similar hues among the trim, although vivid color begins to emerge within the signage upon the buildings. Unlike Butte, many of the signs along Main Street are in the form of awnings in response to a more energetic shopping district along this block. However, Bozeman also has its fair share of abandoned buildings that had to close down, along with the disturbingly vacant Ellen Theatre.

NCS – The Natural Color System for the Denotation of Colour

Anders Hård and Kristina Enberg

When discussing colour as an environmental factor, it is essential to bear in mind that we are concerned with both the process in which human beings perceive colour, as well as the effect of coloured pigments and materials on environmental perception. A true knowledge of the interaction between colour perception and man is imperative if we are to formulate human requirements in environmental design. In its wider implications, this study is essential to the creators of our environment and to those industries which market coloured materials. However, under the pressure of production, technology and physical science, colour has mainly been approached as a physical entity in spite of the fact that physics can only describe and specify spectral energy distribution with the help of measuring instruments, but does not measure what we *see*. Energy radiation is the stimulus correlated to colour perception but it is not the same as the colour experience.

Under technological influences, many so-called colour order systems have been developed as a means of measuring the colour stimulus and setting physical tolerances for the production of coloured materials. Both are essential in our technologically well-developed culture but they are little concerned with our perception of environmental colour or reactions and behaviour in a coloured world.

It is not only the physicist who has contributed to the confusion between colour as perceived and colour stimuli as emitted (the same problem seems to exist when discussing light, sound, texture, etc.). Psychologists involved in psychophysical studies have also, very often, used physical approaches as the basis for perceptual investigations. Thus, the perceptual structure has been formed and biased by the physical 'truths' conceptually involved in their experiments. Among artists we also discover physically based theories of colour and colour combinations such as the aesthetic doctrine of the value of physically complementary colour stimuli.

In contrast to the classical, physically based studies, our *phenomenological* approach primarily begins with colours as *seen* and

how they *appear* to be related to each other; only at a secondary stage does it attempt to specify the stimulus – the cause of the perception in one specific situation. This approach was devised by Ewald Hering who, in 1874, presented what he called the Natural Color System. He named it thus, not because it was supposed to be the most natural method of arranging colour, but because he considered it conveyed a more precise explanation of human colour vision than the Young–Helmholtz Trichromatic theory.

From his phenomenological analysis, Hering postulated that we have six elementary colour experiences: white (w), black (s), yellow (y), red (R), blue (B) and green (G). All other colour perceptions are, characteristically, related to these elementary colours by various degrees of similarity to them. We have demonstrated that these relationships can be represented in a three-dimensional model – the colour space. This can be represented by its two projections, the colour circle and the colour triangle.

At the Swedish Colour Centre Foundation we have been working since 1964 on a research and development project to experiment with Hering's theory and to quantify these similarities. After several years of psychophysical research, we were able to present a colour order and scaling system called the NCS, and the Colour Atlas illustrating the NCS.

The NCS is a systematic method of describing the relationship between colours, purely from their perceptual qualities, which are the only properties that can be seen and evaluated with the help of the natural colour sense. It does not, and should

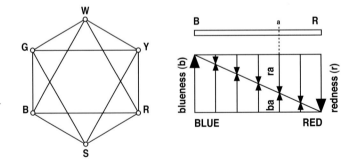

9.1 The relationship between the six elementary colours

not, use any knowledge concerning the attributes of materials (paint, dyes, inks, etc.) nor of physical radiation resulting from, say, colour 'mixing' such as Maxwell's discs. The relationship between these six elementary colour perceptions can be described in a simple model (Figure 9.1). In this model, a line that connects two elementary colours, i.e., B–R describes a series of colours which continually vary from blue to red. From a pure blue, the colours become more and more reddish and end up in the pure red which contains no blue characteristic. This simultaneously increasing similarity with red (redness) and decreasing similarity with blue (blueness) was exemplified by Hering in a bi-polar diagram. In this, a specific proportion of blueness (ba) and redness (ra) is represented by a point (a) on the line from blue to red.

This method is the simplest way of showing how to quantify the similarity between two elementary colours. As we have six elementary colours, we have also to account for six similarities or attributes. The elementary colour attributes are called: whiteness (w), blackness (s), yellowness (y), redness (r), blueness (b), and greenness (g). Thus, the single lines in the simplified model illustrate colours varying only in two attributes related to the elementary colours which form the end points of the scales. Now, one may ask, why is there no line linking green (G) and red (R) or yellow (Y) and blue (B)? The answer is, of course, that as long as the model shows perceptual relationships between the elementary colours and, as long as one *cannot perceive* a greenish-red or a bluish-yellow, such a line would be incorrect.

This should not be confused with the knowledge that one can mix yellow pigment with blue pigment (subtractive mixture). Perceptually, this results in the yellow becoming more greenish and, not until the mix has reached the green, would one perceive some blueness in the green. Nor should the perceptual phenomenon be confused with what happens when one mixes the red and green signal in a colour television (additive mixture), which results in yellow.

For an arbitrary colour perception, the perceptual similarities to the elementary colours can be expressed in a very simple equation. The total similarity to an elementary colour is given the figure 100 – representing the degree of similarity to their elementary colour imagination:

$$s + w + y + r + b + g = 100$$

The sum of the chromatic attributes is called 'chromaticness' (c) and a colour where c = 100 is called a maximal (chromatic) colour = C (all chromatic elementary colours and intermediaries with no traces of whiteness or blackness are maximal colours):

$$y + r + b + g = C$$

From what has been said, it is also clear that no colour perception can simultaneously contain either yellowness and blueness or redness and greenness. From this very fact, these relationships can be graphically illustrated in a three-dimensional colour solid and its two projections, the colour triangle and the colour circle (Figures 9.2, 9.3 and 9.4).

In this way we reached a logical colour notation with figures representing the three NCS parameters: s, c, Ø:

Blackness (s) = degree of similarity to black.
'Chromaticness' (c) = degree of similarity to the maximal colour of a specific hue.
Hue (Ø) = relationship in two chromatic elementary attributes.

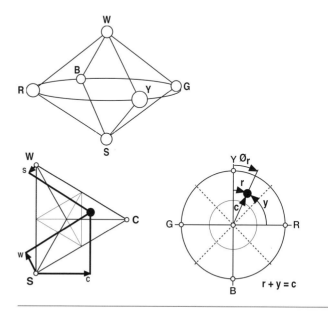

9.2 (top)   The NCS colour space
9.3 (above left) The NCS colour triangle
9.4 (above right) The NCS colour circle

For the colour marked in the model (Figures 9.2–9.4), we can identify,

1 The similarity to black = blackness $s = 10$
2 The similarity to white = whiteness $w = 30$
3 The similarity to yellow = yellowness $y = 45$
4 The similarity to red = redness $r = 15/100$ } $c = 60$
5 Hue $Ør = (15 / (45 + 15)) \times 100 = 25$

Where $y + r$ is perceived as the chromatic component ('chromaticness') i.e., similarity to maximum c which is 100. In our example, $c = 45 + 15 = 60$, which means that the yellowness represents 75 per cent and redness 25 per cent of the 'chromaticness'. The NCS notation for this colour is: *1060 Y25R* in which:

    10 represents 's'
    60 represents 'c'
    Y–R represents the yellow–red quadrant
    25 represents the proportion of 'r' in 'c'.

However, in practical situations, it might be easier first to locate a specific hue 'Ø' in the colour circle in terms of the proportion of chromatic attributes (75 per cent 'y' and 25 per cent 'r') and then to locate its position in the colour triangle in terms of the relationship of 's', 'w' and 'c' (10 per cent 'w' and 60 per cent 'c').

Now let us note that the model is a graphical way of describing perceptual relationships between colours. In our model, the dots stand as symbols for colours and must not be confused with the actual perceptual phenomenon. Let us take an example.

Some colours are often called 'bright'. Colours which are 'dull', 'dirty' or 'shadowed' and are perceptually more or less equal to black will, therefore, be positioned in the colour triangle nearer to black (s). If they are equally blackish, the dots will be marked on a straight line parallel to the W–C line as in S1 and S2 (Figure 9.5). In the same way, Figure 9.6 illustrates the meaning of equal 'chromaticness'. On the w–s line we mark all colours that have no chromaticness. The colours with equal chromaticness will be positioned on lines parallel with the w–s axis as with C1 and C2.

If the descriptive model is good and is a true representation of what is meant to be communicated, it is very practical when considering

9.5 (left)   The meaning of equal blackness
9.6 (right)   The meaning of equal chromaticness

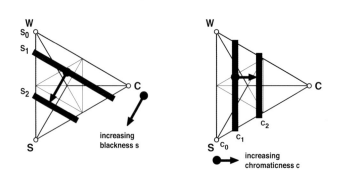

certain relationships. However, one is not meant to use the model as proof of the phenomenon it aims to describe (Figure 9.7).

We, at the Swedish Colour Centre Foundation (Fargcentrum), have been deeply involved in experimental work aimed at discovering the degree to which people are capable of quantifying their colour perceptions in NCS terms. This was a research project to document the Hering theories and to formulate the metric of the NCS colour notation system which would prepare the way for an NCS colour atlas.

The results of more than 20,000 judgements have shown that it is possible to quantitatively determine the degree of similarity to the six elementary colours. A number of subjects, with no knowledge of colour theories, were given the definitions of the six elementary colours. For example we asked participants to tell us 'their imagination of a pure yellow containing no trace of any greenness or redness and also no whiteness or blackness'. Following this instruction, they were then given various colour samples in a controlled viewing situation and asked to determine their similarity to the elementary colours in Figure 9.1, in such a way that the sum of the similarities (elementary colour attributes) added up to 100.

People are capable of making this type of judgement without any available physical references. It is probable that our colour perceptual systems contain some built-in references to which we relate all the colours we perceive. This is supported by more recent

9.7 Another example of illustrating the above concepts is shown graphically in the NCS colour space, colour triangle (nuance) and colour circle (hue) In this case, in the NCS notation, the sample is 1050 Y90R

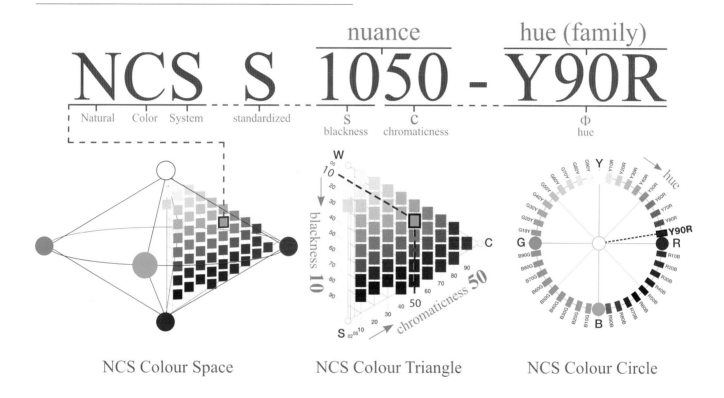

NCS Colour Space　　　NCS Colour Triangle　　　NCS Colour Circle

physiological research findings and can also be verified by Berlin and Kay who have shown that the first 'colour words' in different languages emerged in the following order: white, black, red, yellow, green and blue (words for what here have been called the elementary colours).[1]

Generally, from our experiments, one can conclude that, as we required no physical references for the judgements, it is possible to use the NCS colour descriptive method to specify the colour perception of certain stimuli in *any* situation comprising: (1) the painted surface; (2) the actual light source; (3) the specific viewing conditions (angle, distance, size); (4) the adaptation situation; (5) and possibly the difference in colour sense between observers,

provided the words hold any meaning for them. Thus, the NCS determination method is valuable in all colour analyses of the environment.

There are many names for different colours but often they specifically relate to a meaning or a colour perception peculiar to an individual. 'Sky blue' might, for one individual, represent a whitish blue; for a second person it might represent a strong blue and, for a third, a deep blue. The use of one word for each colour perception is impossible and with the apparent difficulties in colour communication we need a descriptive but numerically based colour notation system. It should be adaptable to different levels of precision and workable without dependence upon colour samples or physical specifications. In other words, it must be based upon the assumption that the human being is the only true colour-measuring instrument. This is true for the NCS and, therefore, it can be said to be a reasonably good solution to the demand for a universal descriptive colour language.

We have stressed the fact that the NCS requires no colour samples or physical specification of colour stimuli to describe colour perceptions. However, in many situations it is practical to have a number of systematically arranged colour samples. The NCS Colour Atlas is essential for colour specification purposes and time-saving, especially for educational purposes or in the study and communication of different colour combinations. The Colour Atlas, comprising almost 2000 colour samples, will cover every tenth step within a range based on today's available pigments. It is possible to identify nearly 15,000 colours by visual interpolation to every fifth step between the systematically arranged samples in the Atlas. Under controlled viewing and illumination conditions, the physical radiation of NCS colours are also specified in the CIE (the Commission Internationale de l'Eclairage system of colorimetry).

In the NCS, one characterizes colours from the point of view of 'quality' and this is possible without any physical colour sample references. This means that we can describe perceived colours in arbitrary situations and, thus, we can study colour and colour combinations in the environment without the need to relate to a specific physical relationship. If we need to establish this relationship then, of course, we have to specify the relevant conditions.

This method has been used to study the loss of visual information in colour television signal, from the studio situation to the consumer's own receiver. Colour situations in landscape and townscape have also been analysed in order to understand more about the role of colour in specific spaces. In these types of environmental colour analyses it was found practical to use the NCS graphical model for notations.

Figure 9.8 is an example of the colour analysis of tree foliage perceived at different distances from near (N), where one could see the colour of the leaves, to very far (F) – when the colour of the forest is only a small part of the total landscape. From a fairly strong yellowish green the colour initially becomes deeper – a more blackish green – and gradually bluish green but with decreasing 'chromaticness'. At a distance of approximately 1 mile, the colour slowly becomes whitish grey and ends up as a reddish blue at about 10 miles distant (in Figure 9.8). In Figure 9.8, only hue is marked in the colour circle; the relationships between whiteness, blackness and chromaticness (nuance) are marked in the colour triangle.

Based on our work in producing the NCS, we have developed a conceptual model for studying colour combinations.[2] This was tested in different examples of colour combinations in nature and man-made environments. We identified three main dimensions (each with three sub-headings) to categorize colour, namely: (1) Colour Interval (distinctness of border, interval kind, interval size); (2) Colour Chord (complexity, chord category, chord type); and (3) Colour Tuning (area relations, colour relations, colour rhythm). Although the model is purely descriptive at the moment and says nothing *per se* whether a composition is beautiful or not, it can be seen as a promising theoretical, empirically based model for future researchers and practitioners.

Over the past 35 years the NCS has been used extensively in several notable and pioneering research projects. These include the research described in the chapters that follow by Grete Smedal, Karin Fridell Anter, and Maud Hårleman. These illustrate clearly how colour perceptions of specified colour surfaces under various viewing conditions, distance, light, surface structure, etc. The aim of these research projects is to fill in the information gaps concerning the behaviour of colour in different situations where practitioners within environmental design obtain their information by a process of trial and error.

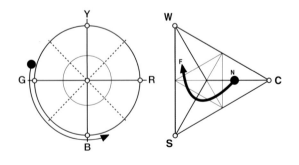

9.8 Variation of tree foliage with distance

If we really want to deal with these types of problem – which are already topical – we must understand more about colour perception and the continuing psychological responses. We must increase our knowledge of the perceptual or subjective colour qualities in order to learn more about the use of architectural colour and, hopefully, a more sustainable future environment. It is not enough to study colour as a physical phenomenon in order to produce coloured materials because first of all we need a colour language which will communicate our experiences, findings and thoughts.

An increasing number of architects are beginning to see and understand the relationship between the elementary attributes of colour – blackness, chromaticness and hue – and the feeling that one wants to attain in practice. These visual attributes of colour have become important tools in actual design. With the help of the NCS notations and an understanding of the phenomenon that perceived colour may differ from the inherent one, it might be possible to handle and predict the final result. Every project then becomes a source of knowledge in itself.

With colour, it is possible to create space, scale, orientation and direction. With colour, it is possible to reinforce or weaken shape. With colour you can conjure up feelings, perceptions and associations. That colour is an attribute of architecture just as much as volume, the plan and the design is becoming increasingly clear for more and more architects and designers. Knowledge of colour, a feeling of colour and an enquiring interaction with the architectural effect of colour have contributed to the development of so many exciting and inspiring projects expounded in the following pages.

Perceived and Inherent Colour: comparing the colour of external façades with colour samples

Karin Fridell Anter

My research stems from my experiences as an architect in Sweden where buildings are often timber-clad or rendered, and in both cases painted. Consequently, their exterior design includes not only a choice of materials – which each carry their own typical colours – but also the choice of colours for numerous painted surfaces. This affords great opportunities to use colour as an important architectural factor – but it can also create problems.

The Swedish façade colour tradition

I begin with a short summary of the Swedish façade colour tradition. First, we have the ubiquitous red house; Sweden is full of them, so much so that they have almost become a national symbol (Figure 10.1). Originally red distemper was used to enhance brick façades and later, to give status, and is found in widespread use on timber buildings. The traditional red pigment is made from a by-product of the Falun copper mine and is used in a distemper paint that gives a range of warm, dark red colours, a totally matte surface together with a special characteristic that, in warm evening light, causes its redness to intensify and almost glow – a particularity which is much loved and appreciated in Sweden. (It is interesting to note that Falun red was especially important to the Swedish economy in the seventeenth century, the copper mine at Falun being located about 250 km north-west of Stockholm. Genuine Falun Red paint is still in production. Its formulation relies upon decomposed red mull extracted from ore with a lower copper content. In addition to copper, red mull contains a rare composition of iron ochre, silicon dioxide and zinc, which together provide a protective coating for timber.)

But not all the traditional houses in Sweden are red; around 300 years ago yellow paint was also used. Essentially, this was an Italian influence originating when Swedish architects travelled to Rome on the Grand Tour and discovered the beautiful baroque palaces with their golden brick or yellowish stone façades. Yellow was first used

in Sweden by the nobility and then gradually by those who could afford it. The reason being that, unlike water based red distemper paint, the formulation for yellow paint required a more expensive linseed oil binder.

The third important traditional façade colour in Sweden is white. Since the Renaissance, the sun-bleached marble ruins of Greek and Roman antiquity have inspired architects to use white. However,

10.1 The traditional Falun red Swedish house

what was not known until much later was that these marble palaces and temples were often originally painted – the shining marble that we see was not the intention of the ancient architects but the result of climatic erosion. White first appeared in Sweden mostly on important buildings such as castles and churches but gradually ordinary town houses and farm houses were also painted white.

In the late nineteenth century, other colours appeared – primarily green. Blue façades, however, do not belong to the Swedish building tradition.

Until the 1950s, it was not too difficult to choose façade colours and to predict the outcome. There was a limited palette of materials and pigments used in construction and the architect or the painter and decorator, using their own or their mentor's experience, would come to know their different qualities. For instance, they would know how yellow ochre or chrome oxide green façades would vary with the weather and the seasons; they would know their appearance when they became old and worn, and they would learn how to combine different façades colours to achieve an aesthetically pleasing outcome.

New selection methods

In the past 50 years we have faced an enormous explosion in the range of new pigments, new paint formulas and new industrially-coated materials. This innovation has opened up new and fantastic opportunities for the creative colour designer – but it also brings new problems. Today no architect or colour designer can fully predict from his or her own experience the perceptual characteristics of all the available pigments and colour materials. Moreover, together with other changes in building production, this has led to a completely new method of colour selection. No longer do we walk on a building site and discuss pigments with the painter; we now choose colour samples from a collection – often before the building is constructed.

And, as previously indicated, the result can often come as a surprise. I suppose most people who have engaged in exterior house design will at one time or another have experienced the same sense of astonishment: 'The painted house does not look as I thought it would!' Indeed, there is a difference between the colour that we see on a colour sample and the colour that we see on a façade

painted according to that sample. There is also another related experience; that the colour we see on a façade is not constant but changes with the viewing situation: the distance, the weather and the season.

Perceived and inherent colour

In order to clarify the situation we have to be clear about the terminology and distinguish between two uses of the word 'colour'. 'Perceived colour' defines the colour that is seen in a specific situation, by a specific observer. This means that the perceived colour of an object varies according to factors such as light and viewing distance. 'Inherent colour', on the other hand, is the constant chromatic quality of the façade. It can be visually measured through comparison with colour samples placed directly against the façade surface. When we use colour charts and colour samples to select the colour of a building, it is the inherent colour that we prescribe.

The problem is that the perceived colour of a building will differ from the inherent colour – and we do not always know how. This problem is well known among colour designers, and each of us, using mainly trial and error, has tried our own techniques to cope with the discrepancy. This has resulted in quite a few buildings where the chromatic outcome did not always comply with anyone's intentions.

Research aims and methodology

Set against the realization that experience alone can no longer provide the solution, I have tried in my research to create systematic knowledge in this field. I have made a broad explorative study of how the colour of painted façades differs due to situation; for example, distance, weather, etc. Most importantly, I have looked for patterns of difference between the colour selected as a colour sample and its perceived colour on a house façade where the colour of the same sample had been applied. The initial challenge was: how does one establish which colour people see on a house? Colorimetric methods are of no use here; this is because they cannot tell what we see in the complex situation where houses are located. Therefore, I had to turn to people's perceptions, and the only way to know what people see is to ask them. With this aim in mind, I have found and tested several different methods which have been combined in my search for understanding. These methods included both naïve and skilled observers, who were asked the question: 'What colour do you see on the façade?' Responses were given in words, by reference to the NCS Colour Atlas or by notations in pre-set scales.

The observational studies cover more than a hundred painted façades of all possible colours, mainly with wooden panels but also rendered façades. About 3,600 observations were made in different seasons and under different weather conditions, usually from a distance of approximately 50 metres.

Results

Using NCS concepts, notations and symbols, I compared the inherent colour of each façade with the variety of perceived colours established by my observers. I found that although perceived colour varied between different viewing conditions, there existed some constant traits in the relationship between inherent and perceived colour. These were:

1 *Nuance shift*: For all the façades in the study, the perceived colour was less blackish than the inherent colour. This nuance shift was accompanied by a compensatory increase in chromaticness or whiteness, or, more often than not, a combination of the two. For example, a dull, brownish yellow colour sample (inherent colour) would appear as a bright, clear yellow façade (perceived colour).
2 *Hue shift*: On many façades, the perceived colour appeared more bluish and/or less yellowish than the inherent colour – this hue shift being stronger for colours with little chromaticness. For example, a rather light, neutral grey colour sample (inherent colour) would give a clearly bluish-grey façade (perceived colour). Also, other colour areas showed a strong tendency for hue shift: green inherent colours often gave bluish-green façades, even when the inherent colour was somewhat yellowish, and yellowish-pink inherent colours often gave perceived façade colours that were bluish-pink (Figure 10.2).

Inherent   Perceived

10.2 (a) When seen over distance the perceived colour of the blue façade used in the test appears much lighter and more chromatic than might be thought when compared with a colour sample of the same hue (inherent colour)

(b) A dramatic change is also seen in the perceived colour of this green façade. Indeed, it turns yellowish toward pure green – or even bluish. Here again, the perceived colour is stronger and a little lighter than its inherent colour counterpart

(c) The inherent brownish-beige is perceived as a greyish lilac over distance. The perceived colour is lighter, often with a strong shift toward a more bluish perceived colour

Possible explanations

My main aim is to provide guidance for colour designers, but as a researcher, I also want to understand the reasons – possibly, involving several interconnected mechanisms – for what I have found. Here are some ideas, although I have not yet been able to test them in a scientific way:

1 One of the likeliest reasons accounting for the difference between the colour appearance of the sample and the perceived colour of the house is the difference between the lighting conditions under which both are viewed. Natural outdoor light is much stronger and embodies a different spectral energy composition than the light in which colour samples are most often viewed.

2 Colour samples are mainly seen against a background of white paper, and in that context, simultaneous contrast makes them appear darker than they would appear against another background. Seen at full scale, our perception of the actual houses is not affected by this simultaneous contrast. Thus, their perceived colour is lighter than that of the sample.

3 Due to the prevailing physical and geological conditions, background colours in nature tend to be a little yellowish. For Sweden, I have shown this in a survey, and it is my educated guess that the same would be true of most parts of the world. In terms of my suggested terminology, I propose that the overall yellowness of the surrounding nature is not 'perceived' although it is 'inherent'. It is simply dismissed by our visual sense, as it exists in all the visual field and therefore adds no specific information. As a consequence of this, objects that lack inherent yellowness, when placed in nature will be perceived somewhat bluish, even if they have no inherent blueness. Similarly, objects that do have inherent blueness will be perceived as even bluer. This could be explained in terms of the complementary nature of colours – blue being the complementary colour of yellow.

4 Finally, I consider our perception of façade colours to be somewhat culturally dependent and, as such, we tend to notice and exaggerate differences between the house we see in front of our eyes and a mental reference to the culturally acquired mind's-eye image of a 'normal' house.

All these hypotheses would require further research, when my results – on Swedish light, nature and tradition – can be compared to similar investigations conducted in other parts of the world.

Further reading

Fridell Anter, K. (1996) *Nature's Colour Palette. Inherent Colours of Vegetation, Stones and Ground*, Stockholm: Scandinavian Colour Institute.

Fridell Anter, K. (2000) *What Colour is the Red House? Perceived Colour of Painted Façades*, Stockholm: Architecture, Royal Institute of Technology. Also available at: http://media.lib.kth.se/dissengrefhit.asp?dissnr=3040

Fridell Anter, K. and Svedmyr, Å. (1996) *Colour Scales of Traditional Pigments for External Painting*, Stockholm: Scandinavian Colour Institute.

Kjellin, M. and Ericson, N. (1999) *Genuine Falun Red*, Stockholm: Prisma & Falun.

Seven Kinds of Colour

Paul Green-Armytage

Different disciplines claim to 'own' the study of colour. In this chapter, I will argue that colour is not one single kind of thing, that the different disciplines are studying different kinds of thing, things which are related, but which are different nevertheless. I propose that there are at least seven different 'kinds of colour'. I further propose that the means used to identify a colour determine what kind of thing it is that is being identified.

Kinds of colour that are 'owned' by different disciplines

Physicists and chemists study physical properties. When dealing with inks and paints they can analyse the chemical composition of the inks and paints and use instruments to measure how a printed or painted surface absorbs and reflects the different wavelengths of radiant energy. Physiologists study the workings of the human eye and nervous system – how the cells in the retina of the human eye respond to stimulation by radiant energy and how those responses are converted into electrical and chemical changes which convey information deeper into the brain. At a certain point the physiologists must yield to the psychologists who are concerned with the experiences of human consciousness. There is a gap in our knowledge which keeps the realms of physiology and psychology apart. As Rolf Kuehni puts it: 'There continues to be a black box into which biologically produced correlates of physical stimuli disappear and out of which color experiences appear.'[1] Physical stimuli are the concern of physicists, biological correlates are the concern of physiologists, and colour experiences are the concern of psychologists. Colour experiences are also the concern of artists and designers. Each group is studying something different, but all would claim to be studying 'colour'. This can lead to misunderstanding and conflict between people who are working in different disciplines and who might otherwise learn from each other and benefit from co-operative research.

Philosophers have been arguing about the nature of colour for more than 2,000 years and still have not reached a consensus. They are divided over whether colours are to be regarded as objective or subjective and over which discipline has the strongest claim to 'ownership' of colour. Rather than argue in favour of one claim or another it is more useful to recognize the validity of all the claims and to accept Barry Maund's idea of a pluralist framework for colour.[2] Such a framework can accommodate the objective and the subjective aspects of colour and the seven different kinds of thing that I now call different kinds of colour.

Seven kinds of colour

To illustrate the relationships between the different kinds of colour, and as an example to show how one kind of colour can be linked to another, I will use a rose – the rose itself and its photographic image as it is displayed on a computer screen, printed on paper and projected on a screen in an auditorium. The photograph of the rose, with a matched colour chip from the Dulux Colour Specifier range of house paints, is shown in Figure 11.1.

A digital photograph is taken of the rose, saved as a JPEG file and displayed on my computer screen. The file is sent to my printer and a print is made. The JPEG file is imported into a PowerPoint file and a data projector is used to show the image of the rose to an

Hot Lips R

11.1 The red rose

audience. Now, are the colours that are coming from the projector and seen by the audience the same colours as those of the rose at the time when the original photograph was taken? There is a chain of connections between the rose and what is coming out of the projector. If the links in the chain have been successfully made, the colours of the image seen by members of the audience should look very much like the colours they would have seen if they had seen the rose itself. That is the main objective of colour technology. Links in the chain which connect the rose to its projected image can be shown to be different kinds of colour. There are various ways in which an individual colour can be identified. The means used to identify a colour determine what kind of thing it is that is being identified. There are at least seven kinds of colour: (1) 'conventional colour'; (2) 'substance colour'; (3) 'formula colour'; (4) 'spectral profile colour'; (5) 'psychophysical colour'; (6) 'inherent colour'; and (7) 'perceived colour'.

Conventional colour

The story begins with the rose itself which most people would describe simply as 'red'. For non-specialists that red is a name for a physical property of the rose as well as being a name for the visual experience they have when they look at the rose. For them, the rose *is* red at the same time as it *appears* red. Although an objective property is not the same kind of thing as a subjective experience, this conflation of physical property with visual experience does not get in the way of people's understanding in general conversation. Since it represents the common viewpoint, I call it 'conventional colour'. The means used to identify conventional colours is observation and the use of everyday language with colour names, like red, that are widely understood.

Substance colour

The rose does embody certain physical properties that can be equated with colour. Flowers get their colours from pigments. Anthocyanin is the pigment responsible for the bluish-reds of red roses.[3] Names for pigments have often come to be used as names for the appearance of those pigments, vermilion being a case in point. Philip Ball refers to vermilion, a synthetic form of mercury sulphide, as 'the finest red pigment' used in the Middle Ages.[4] Vermilion is one of the synonyms for red listed in *The New Penguin Thesaurus*.[5] Names for dyes have also come to be applied to the appearance of dyed fabrics as well as other objects. William Perkin's discovery, in 1856, of a dye derived from coal-tar revolutionized the industry.[6] It was the dye itself that was first called

'mauve' but now the word, like vermilion, can be understood as referring to a visual experience as well as to a physical property. Pigments and dyes are more strictly referred to as 'colourants', but still they are commonly referred to simply as 'colours'. To maintain consistency in the manner of naming the different kinds of colour, I will call pigments and dyes 'substance colours'. Chemical, analysis can be used to identify pigments such as anthocyanin and vermilion as well as dyes such as mauve. If chemical analysis is the means of identification, and if it is the pigment or dye that is being identified, then anthocyanin, vermilion and mauve are names for substance colours. A distinction can be made if needed: substance colour (pigment); substance colour (dye).

Formula colour

Closely related to substance colour is what I call 'formula colour'. Chemical analysis might not be needed; the substances might already be known. The colour chip matched to the colour of the rose shown in Figure 11.1 is a sample from the range of paints manufactured by Dulux Australia. In the Dulux Colour Specifier Atlas, it is identified by the letter/number code P05.H9 and by the name 'Hot Lips'. When you buy a can of Dulux paint, the paint will be mixed according to a formula. The store assistant looks up the formula in a book, takes a can of the specified base, adds tinters to the base according to the formula and mixes the paint. 'Hot Lips' is unusual in that the formula has one ingredient only: true red base. To mix the paint known as 'Red Box' (P04.H9), shown in the Dulux Atlas, the formula is: One litre of true red base plus 1.76 ml of blue tinter and 69.23 ml of magenta tinter. If the colour is identified by its formula, I would call 'Hot Lips' and 'Red Box' 'formula colours'.

Colours reproduced in print can also be identified as formula colours. The chemical composition of the inks is known; more immediately interesting is the relative role played by each ink for each part of a printed image. Photographs are reproduced by using four transparent inks, the so-called 'process colours', which are: cyan (C), magenta (M), yellow (Y) and black (K). This process is commonly referred to as 'CMYK'. Each ink, printed in dots of varying density, can cover any percentage of the paper surface at any given point. Four percentages, one for each ink, constitute a formula for a coloured area in a print. The formula for matching 'Hot Lips' was: C5-M100-Y90-K0.

The concept of formula colours can be extended to the colours seen on a computer screen or television. The relative output of the red, green and blue phosphors, expressed as numbers, constitute a formula which can be used to identify a colour in the display. When the photograph of the rose, with the superimposed colour chip, was displayed on my computer screen, the RGB values for the colour chip were R212-G13-B32. When people refer to RGB or CMYK values, they are identifying formula colours. If necessary, the kind of thing in question can be described more precisely as: formula colour (paint); formula colour (ink); formula colour (CRT display).

Spectral profile colour

A characteristic of materials coloured by pigments or dyes is the way they respond to illumination – the different wavelengths of the spectrum are absorbed and reflected to a greater or lesser extent. This can be measured with a spectrophotometer and plotted as a graph. Such a graph can be used to identify the colour of the material and can be read as a spectral reflectance 'profile'. Instruments can also be used to derive other kinds of spectral profiles: radiation profiles for sources of illumination and transmission profiles for transparent or translucent materials. In each case we are dealing with what I call 'spectral profile colour'. Where clarification is needed, the term can be qualified: spectral profile colour (reflection); spectral profile colour (radiation); spectral profile colour (transmission). The spectral reflectance graph, or profile, of 'Hot Lips' is shown in Figure 11.2.

Connecting physical properties with visual experiences

'Substance colours', 'formula colours' and 'spectral profile colours' all refer to objective physical properties, the concern of physicists and chemists. Most people, however, are more concerned with the consequent subjective visual experiences. If colours are understood to be visual experiences rather than physical properties, their identification must depend on the people who have the experiences. A link can be established between visual experiences and physical properties. People can use a process of colour matching to identify a colour.

Psychophysical colour

Psychophysics is the branch of science which links the physical world with phenomenal experience. Adjusting the output of three lights to achieve a match with a physical sample is the basis of colorimetry. In this way the colour of something can be measured, the measurement being expressed in terms of the relative output of the lights and recorded as 'tristimulus values'. These values establish particular locations in a colour space such as that known as 'CIELAB'. The development of colour measuring instruments – colorimeters and spectrophotometers – depended on a number of human observers having made a number of judgements. These judgements were averaged to create the 'standard observer'. The instruments duplicate the judgements of the standard observer and assign positions in colour space accordingly.

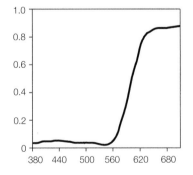

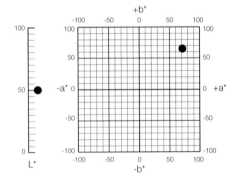

11.2 (above) Spectral reflectance of 'Hot Lips'

11.3 (right)   'Hot Lips' in CIELAB space

The appearance of surfaces depends to some extent on the illumination by which they are seen. Instruments for colour measurement have settings for different 'standard illuminants'. Surfaces that have been measured by an instrument and given the same CIELAB co-ordinates would be judged a match when seen under the specified illumination by the standard observer. Tristimulus values and CIELAB co-ordinates also serve the purpose of identification. If the identity of a colour has been established with a colorimeter or spectrophotometer, the thing being identified I call 'psychophysical colour'. CIELAB co-ordinates for 'Hot Lips' are L*51.06; a*71.23; b*65.48. The black dots in Figure 11.3 indicate the position of 'Hot Lips' in CIELAB space.

Inherent colour

Another way of using colour matching to establish the identity of a colour does not require an expensive measuring instrument. The identification can be done by an individual observer making judgements based on visual experience alone. Instead of an instrument you need a comprehensive set of colour samples, such as those from a colour order system and displayed on a fandeck or in a colour atlas. A match, or close match, can be found between a surface and a colour sample from the system. The name or number used to identify the sample can now be applied to the surface. This process requires that the sample be placed directly against the surface to be identified in such a way that both sample and surface receive the same illumination. This is essentially the means used by Karin Fridell Anter to establish what she calls the 'inherent colour' of something (see Fridell Anter's chapter, pp. 60–63). Fridell Anter specifies the viewing conditions for determining what should be the precise inherent colour of something. Here I am allowing for a degree of latitude in viewing conditions.

When the identity of a colour is established by direct visual comparison between a surface and a sample colour chip, it is the inherent colour of that surface that is identified. The Dulux Colour Specifier system is one of many that can serve the purpose of identifying inherent colours. Colour samples in the fandeck can be placed directly on a surface and an acceptable match can be found. By placing a sample of 'Hot Lips' on a photograph of the rose, and establishing a match (seen in Figure. 11.1), I could now use the name 'Hot Lips' to identify the colour of the rose. It could be expected that two surfaces that have the same psychophysical colour would also have the same inherent colour. The difference between psychophysical colour and inherent colour is that the psychophysical colour of something is identified by using a measuring instrument while the inherent colour is identified by visual comparison of sample and surface when they are placed in direct juxtaposition.

Perceived colour

It is often the case that two surfaces with the same inherent colour can appear quite different from each other when seen in different contexts. A wall that has been painted with 'Hot Lips', when seen from across the road, may not look the same as a 'Hot Lips' paint sample held in the hand. Faced with this fact, Fridell Anter makes a distinction between inherent colour and what she calls 'perceived colour'.[7] The perceived colour of the wall can be established by comparing what you see from across the road with the samples in a colour atlas. The Dulux Colour Specifier could be used but, as Fridell Anter has discovered, the painted wall is likely to appear more chromatic and less blackish than the sample in the atlas and in the Dulux Atlas. As there is no sample more chromatic than 'Hot Lips', it is better to use the atlas of a colour order system, such as the Natural Color System (NCS), which allows for interpolation. As an exercise I laid the 'Hot Lips' sample on the table, held the NCS Atlas in my hand, and made a judgement. The 'Hot Lips' sample looked 'brighter' than any sample in the Atlas but, by interpolation, I identified the colour as 0590-Y90R.

It is a more complex problem to identify the perceived colour of the rose. Judging from the photograph, the petals certainly have the same inherent colour all over but there is great variety in the appearance of different parts of the petals as some parts catch the light while others are in shadow. Monica Billger, who also makes the distinction between inherent colour and perceived colour, deals with this kind of problem by making a further distinction between the overall colour impression and local variations. Billger calls the overall colour impression the 'identity colour' which she defines as 'the main colour impression of surfaces or parts of a room that are perceived to be uniformly coloured.'[8] Local variations can be seen as a result of contrast, reflections, and differences in illumination. If the rose is judged to be the 'same colour all over', we have first to decide, by looking at the rose and referring to the atlas, what sample in the atlas best matches our judgement of that 'all-over' colour. That will be the identity colour. It is then necessary to look at the different parts of the rose and try to forget that they are the 'same colour'. By looking at each part of the rose simply as a coloured shape, and not as part of the rose, it is possible to find colour samples in the atlas that correspond. Different samples in the atlas will be found to match those parts of the petals that catch the light and those parts that are in shadow. These will be the local variations. Where Billger's distinction is important I would use the terms perceived colour (identity) and perceived colour (local variation) as appropriate.

The NCS is unique as a colour order system for perceived colours. While it is true that NCS colour samples can also be used to identify the inherent colours of surfaces the samples themselves are to be understood only as a means of illustrating the system; they are not the system itself.[9] NCS notations for the different parts of the rose that can be seen in the photograph would be different. Strictly speaking, the notations of the samples in the atlas are valid for those samples only when seen against a white background, as they are in the atlas, and under a standard illuminant by someone with normal colour vision. Just as the physical samples from the NCS can be used to establish inherent colours, although the system is essentially a system for perceived colours, so could the atlas of another kind of system be used as a point of reference for judging perceived colours. The distinction lies in the manner of identification: direct juxtaposition for inherent colours, reference to a colour atlas for perceived colours.

Conclusion

Philosophical discussions about the nature of colour have been hampered by the assumption that colour is a single kind of thing. The various positions taken by participants in the debate can be reconciled if it is accepted that there are different kinds of colour, that these are related but different nevertheless. The way to test what kind of colour is under consideration is to note how an individual colour would be identified. 'Colours' can be identified by chemical analysis (substance colour), by reference to a formula guide (formula colour), by use of a spectrophotometer (spectral profile colour, psychophysical colour), by direct juxtaposition with a standard sample (inherent colour) or by referring to a colour atlas (perceived colour). When colours are identified by name in general conversation, it is likely that the speaker will mean both a physical property and a visual experience (conventional colour). The distinctions and terminology proposed here are intended to clarify the relationships between the different kinds of thing that are referred to as 'colours' and to promote better understanding and co-operation between researchers from different disciplines.

Daylight Influence on Indoor Colour Design

Maud Hårleman

In the northern hemisphere, the sun is never fully at its zenith. The situation is the same, yet reversed, in the southern hemisphere, but here I will refer only to circumstances in Sweden. In the period from June to September in Stockholm, the sun rises between 03.34 and 06.34 and sets between 22.05 and 18.45. Yet the highest altitude of the sun is 53, 4° at the summer equinox; in mid-winter it is only 6, 6°. This means huge contrasts in light level between the two seasons. According to Vesa Honkonen: 'The structure of light at the equator is horizontal, with a rhythm of 12 hrs. At the North Pole it is vertical, with a rhythm of six months.'[1]

There are considerable differences between spectral composition as well as light intensity and natural daylight from the compass points. As a function of this, interiors with windows facing north or south are always differently illuminated. Simplified, it can be said that the former are lit by daylight (sky light) and reflected light while the latter are lit by direct sunlight and reflected light. Furthermore, the distribution of light is of importance for the appearance of space and chromaticness, as direct sunlight and diffuse sky light. Daylight reaching south-facing interiors can be said to lack some blueness since bluish-making wavelengths are spread out in the atmosphere and this effect creates differences not only in light colour but also in colour appearance and colour emotion in relation to rooms in different directions.

These circumstances are intriguing when it comes to colour design. South-facing rooms are commonly referred to as warm in opposition to north-facing and cool rooms. Two different theories on best treatment of these rooms circulate, one is a recommendation to neutralize the room light by using opposing colours and the other is a recommendation for a reinforcing effect, using 'warm colours' in 'warm rooms' and vice versa. Lack of knowledge concerning the outcome of a colour design causes problems and probable failures in colouring for professionals and amateurs alike. Though

12.1 The colours used in the experiment

| 1010-G80Y | 1010-Y | 1010-Y20R | 1010-Y80R | 1010-R | 1010-R20B | 1010-R80B | 1010-B | 1010-B30G | 1010-B70G | 1010-G | |
| 1030-G80Y | 1030-Y | 1030-Y20R | 1030-Y80R | 1030-R | 1030-R20B | 1030-R80B | 1030-B | 1030-B30G | 1030-B70G | 1030-G | 1030-G20Y |

many of us know about the daylight influence on the interior colours and spatial atmosphere, how this influence would affect colour appearance has as yet not been scientifically studied. This was the starting point for a doctorate project that was undertaken during summer between June to September in Stockholm.[2] In two empirical investigations, 191 observers made 79 studies on 23 colours in a north-facing room and a south-facing room (Figure 12.1).

The main question to be answered was: how does natural daylight affect north- and south-facing rooms concerning colour appearance? The second question concerned the impact of different daylight on emotions and experiences: do north- and south-facing rooms cause differences in spatial character?

Colour appearance in direct sunlight and reflected daylight (sky light)

Both rooms caused clear patterns of shift in hue and nuance, from the colour used (inherent colour) to the colour appearance (perceived colour). First, differences in nuance were recorded within the room itself. Changes in atmospheric conditions showed as changes in perceived colour. Variations in light were sometimes not seen other than as differences in perceived colour. These variations frequently had a cyclic progression, called colour elasticity, visible in the rooms as transient variations or as persisting somewhat longer periods. Room perceived colour varied in cycles around the inherent colour, as lighter or darker, more or less chromatic and with more or less shift in hue. Normal oscillation was 10–30 NCS steps in whiteness, blackness and chromaticness with inherent colour as base, i.e. it could be darker and more reddish or brighter and less chromatic within seconds. As well as this occasional colour elasticity, each room direction showed distinct significance.

Room perceived colours had in general 10 NCS steps less proportion of whiteness than inherent colours. There was also a clear perceptual difference in chromaticness; reduced whiteness was compensated for by greater chromaticness and sometimes also in blackness. The average increase in chromaticness was 5–10 steps, and the increase in blackness was up to 5 steps. Both series of nuances had their own variations. The whitish nuance 1010 shifted more in hue than the 1030 nuance did. The more chromatic nuance, 1030, became in turn more chromatic. The various hues had individual patterns for chromaticness.

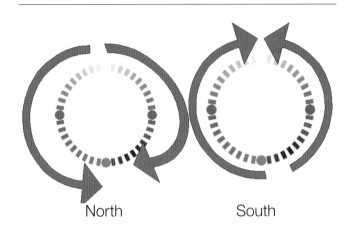

12.2 Hue shift tendencies towards blue in north-facing rooms and yellow in south-facing rooms

North   South

Second, the pattern differed between the compass directions, in both hue and nuance. Chromatic shifts were heavily influenced by compass direction. Sunlight and diffuse daylight in the south- and north-facing rooms respectively caused opposing hue shift tendencies; all colours shifted towards bluish hues in the north facing and towards yellowish hues in the south-facing room (Figure 12.2).

The north-facing room

The diffuse skylight in the north-facing room caused a great chromatic increase in bluish, greenish and pinkish colours. It was an unexpected yet an indisputable result that pinkish rooms increased most in chromaticness in this direction. Greenish and pinkish rooms shifted towards bluish hues. Bluish rooms, on the other hand, showed another tendency. In some cases, reddish-blue decreased its bluish content and turned blue as greenish-blue did. Summing up, it can be stated that the north-facing direction causes most reddish-blue rooms to shift towards increased reddish content. There is a breaking point in the reddish blue area where the hue shift is often, but not always, replaced by a hue shift going in the other direction. This uncertainty may be a function of the 'purple' and 'red' wavelengths at the ends of the spectrum, and due to small divergences in the spectral composition shown as huge hue shifts.

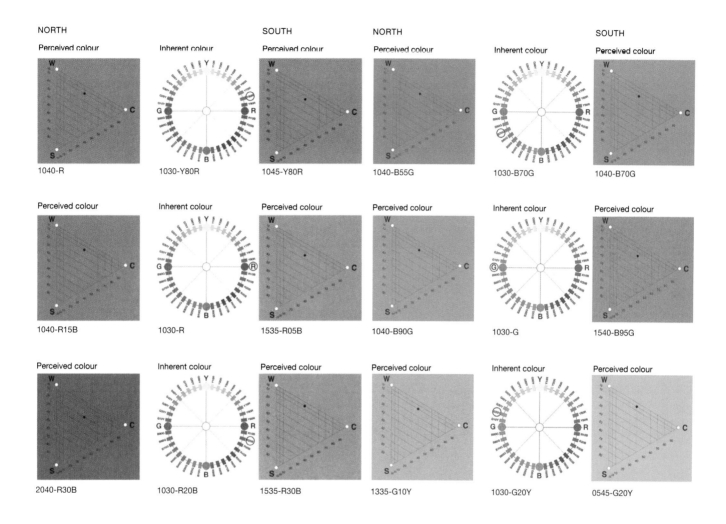

NORTH		SOUTH	NORTH		SOUTH
Perceived colour	Inherent colour	Perceived colour	Perceived colour	Inherent colour	Perceived colour
1040-R	1030-Y80R	1045-Y80R	1040-B55G	1030-B70G	1040-B70G
Perceived colour	Inherent colour	Perceived colour	Perceived colour	Inherent colour	Perceived colour
1040-R15B	1030-R	1535-R05B	1040-B90G	1030-G	1540-B95G
Perceived colour	Inherent colour	Perceived colour	Perceived colour	Inherent colour	Perceived colour
2040-R30B	1030-R20B	1535-R30B	1335-G10Y	1030-G20Y	0545-G20Y

12.3 Shift in hue and nuance for reddish and greenish colours

Yellowish rooms decreased in chromaticness and shifted from yellowish towards a greater amount of green or red attribute. Greenish-yellow rooms shifted towards greenish, and yellow rooms shifted the same way in decreasing light. Reddish-yellow rooms, on the other hand, shifted towards a greater amount of reddish attribute as did yellow rooms in an increased light level (Figure 12.3).

The south-facing room

Direct sunlight made all colours increase in chromaticness. Yellowish rooms increased most in chromaticness and yellowish hues shifted towards yellow. Yellowish-green and yellowish-pink rooms shifted towards more yellowish hues. Greenish and pinkish rooms (green and bluish-green, pink and bluish-pink) tended towards bluish hues but with only a few steps. Bluish rooms in sunlight shifted towards green, and reddish blue most often shifted towards blue. In the south-facing room, hue shifts tend from breaking point area towards yellow.

Influence of the compass
directions in room experience

As subjects reacted to situations and different perceived colours according to the direction of illumination, this showed up as variations in room psychological experience. In the strongly illuminated south-facing room, inherent colours with a yellowish content, G20Y, Y20R, and Y80R, appeared with surprising chromatic intensity. Thus connotations linked to these colours were experienced and expressed in terms of stronger verbal nuances. Inherent Y20R and Y80R were considered as soft and fluffy in the south-facing room, while in the north-facing room, having little or no yellowish attribute, the room was considered as bare or empty, hard and cold in comparison. Inherent R appeared as yellowish-pink in sunlight and was portrayed as childish, pure and innocent while in skylight it appeared as bluish pink and thus represented impurity and sophistication.

North-facing rooms were significantly less *elevating* in yellowish-pinks and bluish-greens. Differences in direction of illumination caused weakening or strengthening of associations linked to the colours by colour connotations. Nature and quiescence or slowness and tranquillity were common descriptions for greenish rooms facing both directions, along with clean and fresh. The greenish room G, appeared in daylight as bluish-green and made observers describe it as difficult to grasp, and depending on weather, it was alive or plastic, disgusting or restful, pushy or relaxing. In sunlight, perceived colour from the same inherent colour provoked descriptions such as warm, calm, soothing and gloomy.

In conclusion, it was shown that daylight from the different compass points caused a clear shift in hue and nuance. The perceived colour was consistently more chromatic and less whitish than the inherent colour used. Nuance 1010 shifted more in hue, while instead 1030 increased in chromaticness. Even minor colour differences resulted in major differences in colour experience. The north-facing room in yellowish colours shifted towards reduced yellowness in both hue and chromaticness. Indications were that north-facing rooms in reddish-blue become more reddish than south-facing rooms.

The Longyearbyen Project: approach and method

Grete Smedal

Each colour design project will involve certain issues and its own various stages of development. Indeed, each environment studied, independent of its size and complexity, will comprise varied emphases through the following stages:

1 Registration of the existing colours
2 Analysis of possibilities and limitations
3 Development of an overall colour concept
4 Presentation to client or public
5 Detailed description of the colour plan
6 Implementation

In this chapter, I describe how I worked through these stages in a very complex and lengthy project in Longyearbyen, Spitsbergen, Norway. I was commissioned in 1981 by my client to devise a full colour plan for all its buildings and installations – which at the time meant every building in the town except for some government-owned buildings. Initially, the colour plan was intended to cover the next ten years but, due to the changing function of the town, the town grew and extended. Thus, the project has been ongoing for more than 25 years and, with new façades continuing to appear, is still under development. My approach to environmental colour together with the tools I needed to take this project through all the different stages will illustrate the process and the result as it appears today.

Registration of existing colours

Known in Old Norse as 'Svalbard' and lying between the 76th and 80th parallel, close to the North Pole, the Spitsbergen Archipelago is part of Norway. At the start of the project, Longyearbyen was a 'company town' that, except for the above-mentioned government buildings, was completely owned by the coal mining company Store Norske Spitsbergen Kulkompagni. Thanks to the Gulf Stream, the climate makes it possible to establish a settlement here with reasonable conditions for human life. However, the situation must be considered extreme in several ways:

1 *Light* – Three months of total darkness and three months of full midnight sun cause very different lighting conditions – an applied colour can appear quite different throughout the year. In the remaining six months of more or less 'normal' light, the angle of the sun, snowstorms and fog, etc., will increase the variation of how colours are perceived.

2 *Vegetation* – In a setting where no trees or shrubbery alleviate the contrast of the built environment, man-made structures are exposed directly in the terrain, that is, seen against snow for six or seven months or, in complete contrast, against a dark, gravel terrain for some months. During a hectic summer period in July and August, the yellowish autumnal-type colours of grass plus small groups of low creeping Arctic flowers, introduce a short-lived and sparse chromatic scale.

3 *Architecture* – Having been completely razed in the bombing of the Second World War, all the existing buildings had been rebuilt, mostly in timber, since the 1950s. However, as more recently new industries have developed in the 1960s and 1970s, such as tourism and scientific study, various architects have brought new thinking to the earlier design of rough, simple and functional miners' accommodation and family houses.

4 *Existing façade colours* – Being extremely aware of the above-mentioned colour variation, a colour-matched documentation of the inherent colours seen on the existing façades was achieved using NCS colour samples, while perceived colours were annotated using the NCS diagrams. When the project began, most of the façades were brownish, with a few houses in dark red or ochre.

Analysis of possibilities and limitations

What is special about this project is that my client, the Company Board, presented a single body with whom to discuss ideas, and one decision-maker for the whole town! When the project began, I briefly explained to the Board how, unlike other systems of notation, the NCS worked and was based upon perception – and they immediately grasped the idea. From the outset, the NCS proved to be an extremely good tool for understanding and communicating colour. Indeed, with its scales and 'areas' based upon perceived similarities, the NCS provides an excellent platform for such work and for the illustration of visual colour groups. Groups of colour nuances will appear differently in changing light and

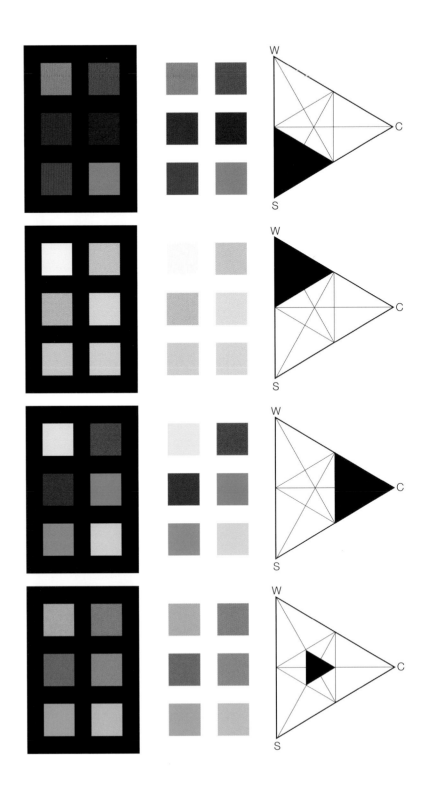

13.1 Group nuances will appear different in changing light and background

background situations. For example, with regard to the annually shifting colour of surroundings, Figure 13.1 demonstrates these variations in principle. Blackish colours would merge into the gravel terrain in summertime and, conversely, would provide strong contrast to the snow. In contrast, whitish colours would function in a diametrically opposed way, that is, seen in high contrast to the exposed black-brown terrain but less distinct under snow.

Excessively strong chromatic colours would, in most situations, introduce a brutal contrast to the subtlety and less chromatic quality of indigenous natural colours.

However, colours approaching similarity to white, black and maximum chroma can have the potential to make a sufficient contrast, while not being too strong, at most parts of the year.

A question recurrent in environmental colour design – similarity or contrast – became crucial, and demanded a clear decision: should one attempt to hide the man-made structures in this setting, or was a distinct contrast appropriate? As can be seen from the analysis, it would not be possible to merge imported colours into the natural setting in all its shifting situations. For instance, what would 'disappear' in one part of the year would stand out in strong contrast in other parts of the year. Consequently, the decision was made to enter into a dialogue with nature. In other words, to let the man-made structures define themselves with their own characteristic colour scale – inspired from, but not imitating, the colours of nature.

The overall colour plan

The possibility of grouping colours led me to the notion of identifying different zones of the town with the same nuances in different hues. In this way it became possible to achieve an overall colour idea while allowing a separate description for each of the different functional areas (Figure 13.2).

I decided that the one-family houses in the Lia district should embody a slightly different nuance than the larger residential rowhouses further south. All the hues used in this area were designated in the green and yellow-red region of the colour circle – which meant no proximity to blue, except for a very few houses designated in a slightly bluish-green.

13.2 Map of different areas in NCS circles and triangles

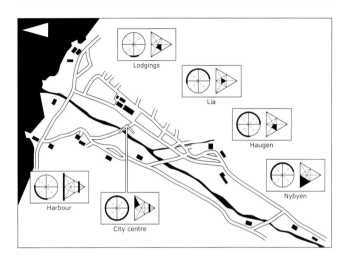

For the more formal activities and larger volumes associated with the buildings in the Haugen area, a more blackish nuance colour group was chosen, with hues drawn from all around the colour circle.

The rough barrack buildings closest to the glacier in the inner part of the Nybyen valley were planned in an even more blackish nuance.

The town centre, which comprises a main street with public utilities such as offices, restaurants, hospital and shops, was conceived in very whitish colours representing many different hues. This decision aimed to distinctly separate this part from the rest of the town and also to reflect light into the street during darker periods of the year. To establish a distinct contrast, details, such as doors and window frames, etc., are designated in very strong chromatic colours.

At that time, the newly built Lodging Houses established a contour line towards the fjord on one side and the mountains on the other. This was planned in different dark blue hues, almost equal in blackness and chromaticness.

With its many non-permanent structures, the Harbour area was planned in greys with bluish and greenish smaller installations and details.

Presentation

As the basis for the clients' decision to continue the process, I illustrated the overall idea in different ways, that is, collages of the selected colour groups together with their NCS notation communicated a visual as well as intellectual understanding of the concept. As a consequence of this presentation, the Board accepted the proposal and gave the go-ahead!

It was then that I could turn to the colouration of each individual building and illustrate the reality of the proposal in more detail. While the process I undertook was a time-consuming task, together with all its advantages and problems, it would be easy today to accomplish this using digital media with PowerPoint slides, etc. Again, in order to prepare the Board and townspeople, I coloured different parts of the town plan in mixed techniques including gouache and aquarelle to exhibit many examples of the colourful town of the future.

Colour plan

It was of immense help for me at this stage to be able to describe the use of colour using NCS notation. For instance, in that they do not refer to any specific colour manufacturer or colour charts, they remain neutral; moreover, they will remain as standards and will last a long time. However, before the implementation of the colour proposal could begin, every existing house at the time was described in terms of its façade colours and in its detailing.

Implementation

It was a rather lively period in Longyearbyen when the first seven buildings in Lia were painted during the first summer! Their colour contrast to existing buildings was enormous. Even though the townspeople had been prepared for such change, this initial installation of colour plan aroused strong emotions – especially when the reality appeared at full scale. However, as time went by, and as the concept of the colour plan increasingly became visible, opinion changed. It gradually became obvious that the colour of each individual house was less important than the totality of the colours registered in the different groups. The similarity of nuances began to connect to the colours in a way that were considered familiar – and the level of acceptance and satisfaction grew.

The situation today and in the future

Over the ensuing years, the identification and establishment of a colourful townscape profile have become a natural if not required part of the inhabitants' daily life. We have all learned quite a lot about the perception of shifting colour under changing light and climatic conditions – and the importance of colour as a means of identification. Colour has become a part of the experience and a lively topic of discussion. Indeed, it has added an impulse to the quality of life under these extreme conditions (Figures 13.3, 13.4).

Of course, demands on physical sustainability are very important and must be afforded a high priority, but it was considered not to give them monopoly in the planning process of the growing town. The basis of this project was an understanding by the Board that quality of life depends on more than physical factors. Aesthetic values were also considered important – which is quite remarkable considering the circumstances. Indeed, the decision by the Board to commission a colour plan for all the façades of the town is remarkable because wood does not rot this far north. In this extremely cold dry climate so close to the North Pole, paint is unnecessary for maintenance; its function here would not be to preserve but to decorate and beautify.

As Longyearbyen continues to grow – from 1,200 inhabitants at the onset of the project – to around 2,000 presently, the demand for additional official and residential buildings has made it necessary to continue and extend the colour plan. However, still as its foundation is the first overall sketch of the grouping of colour nuances. Although new ideas, new forms and a different architecture will demand new solutions, the town planners have decided to continue with the central colour plan idea. Indeed, building regulations at Longyearbyen include colour as part of the approval for new buildings at the planning stage.

Furthermore, from the standpoint of continuity and for 'archaeological' reasons, the building authorities have commissioned an archive for the future. In this, the façade colour of each and every building in the town is now described in NCS notation on a database. The notations of inherent colours, related to the NCS standard as illustrated in the Colour Atlas, will provide valuable information about how different colours appear when first applied, and also monitor what happens to them over the years (just imagine if we had such information from the past from other cities around the world!).

13.3 (left) It was here on the small houses in the Lia district that the colour plan first was implemented and, with it, reactions to the proposal appeared

13.4 (below) The colours of autumnal hillsides in Longyearbyen, plus those found on surviving miners' houses, inspired the colouration of houses in the district of Nybyen

Will Longyearbyen's colour plan survive or will it become gradually eroded over time? It might be interesting one day in the distant future, and armed with its archival colour registration, to revisit and witness the fate of this Arctic town – a town historically and totally colour planned from 1983–2010.

4

PART 4 ARCHITECTS AND COLOUR AT THE BUILDING SCALE

In 1976, Victory Vasarely proposed that the universal characteristics of the colour systems employed in the 'form-colour' units as seen in his Op Art paintings of the period provide us with a glimpse of the polychrome city. The concept of the 'polychrome city' had already been the dream of his fellow painter Fernand Léger, and even earlier in Germany of Gottfried Semper. However, eager to break free from the limitations of the picture frame, and in order to explain why this was, in the reality of that time, a pipe dream, Vasarely describes the schism that occurred during the Renaissance between the artist and the architect. He suggests that, hitherto, painters and sculptors worked in integrated construction teams who, from the cities of antiquity to the ancient Greek temples and through to the cathedrals in the Middle Ages, had produced an architecture as a 'total work of art'. But it was the birth of humanism and its accompanying creative outburst and thirst for knowledge in the *Quattrocento* that caused architecture and art to bifurcate into discrete disciplines and separate avenues of investigation. The Renaissance had caused the artist to abandon the ancient use of a symbolic architectural colour and turn, instead, to an investigation of the visual appearance of objects in space. Indeed, while the painter employed colour to record perceptual phenomena experienced in the real world, the sculptor rejected polychromy in the investigation of the interaction and contrast between a colourless solid form and the space surrounding it. Not only did the identity of artists gradually become detached but, encouraged by commissions from wealthy Renaissance patrons and the developing notion of a 'work of art', their work became portable – either framed to be hung on a wall, or placed on a plinth – and thus became divorced from their original architectural context. This, for the first time, saw a 'painting' or a 'sculpture' as an entity – to be valued and viewed not as part of a building but as *art for its own sake*.

Our legacy is a contemporary notion of volume and form as defined by the visual elements: form, shape, line, texture and colour. This principle was expounded at the Bauhaus by teachers such as Johannes Itten, Paul Klee and Wassily Kandinsky, etc., and although they had much to say, write and teach about colour, the isolation and 'otherness' associated with architectural polychromy, despite flickers of colour from Bruno Taut in Germany and Gerrit Reitveld in Holland, continued well into the twentieth century. However, in post-war France, Fernand Léger accepted a commission to work with architects Nelson, Gilbert and Sebillotte on the exterior of the Memorial Hospital at St. Lo. It is this collaboration that perhaps provides the seed for what is happening today because what marks our present period from its immediate past is the plethora of partnerships between artists and architects. A notable collaboration occurred in the 1970s in the multi-disciplinary practice of Ricardo Boffil and his Taller de Arquitectura in Barcelona, and more recently, artists working in the design teams at Herzog & de Meuron in Basel, often experimenting with new technologies, have helped pioneer inventive techniques in the elaboration of the building envelope. Several such examples of architect–artist collaborations are included here, such as Jaap Drupsteen's glass panels for Neuterlings Riedijk Architecten's Media Centre in Holland, Martin Richman's dichroic film installation on Niall McLaughlin's Peabody Housing in London and the work of Alain Bony – an artist whose Studio Bastille works closely with Jean Nouvel. Even Will Alsop, whose architectural design process tends to begin in the colour and liquidity of his huge studio paintings, is known to conduct a close and well-known relationship with the artist Bruce McLean. What is so exciting about this development is that the artist is gradually beginning to return to play a role in issues concerning the built environment – and that such a union, albeit tentative at this stage, tends to bring a greater and more exciting sense of colour to architecture.

However, while a positive and committed engagement in architectural colour provides the common denominator in the following chapters, what is demonstrated in Part 4 is a plethora of approaches to architectural polychromy: from the intuitive to the methodological; from an adherence to historical colour traditions to the determined eradication of any cultural and aesthetic baggage.

Part 4 opens with a second chapter by Lois Swirnoff in which she elaborates on the marriage of function and aesthetics. This is followed by a chapter by Jean-Philippe Lenclos that, from a French perspective, monitors a sea-change in which he detects a crucial turning point in the story of colour for architecture.

Color Structure: a perceptual techtonic

Lois Swirnoff

The term 'techtonic' refers to building: a structure or construction, considered as essential to architectural function. It embodies, also, the idea of engineering, referencing the success of the part, giving support to the whole. Where a techtonic really functions, it is evident in the appearance of the building, as well: the marriage of function and aesthetics. Think of Saarinen's TWA terminal building at John F. Kennedy airport, or Pier Luigi Nervi's railroad station in Rome, or the scheme projected by Calatrava for the PATH station at Ground Zero in New York. These are examples of architectural expressiveness, as well as brilliant architectural engineering.

To assert that color can be a techtonic we assume that it is a potent perceptual tool; color can both *build* form and *trans*form. Its paradoxical nature, its ambiguity, can serve visual roles that are semantically opposed. Perhaps for this reason its use has been avoided, until recently, in architectural praxis. In both instances, forming or transforming, structure is implicit.

To combine function and aesthetics, how they are utilized is as essential to architecture as how buildings are perceived. Spatial organization of part to whole, the experience of solidity or transparency, of openness or closure, of stability or flight; formal expressions of basic architectural design depend upon material choices. Renaissance palazzi and Gothic cathedrals expressed grounded solidity in the former, or soaring elevation in the latter – through the treatment of stone.

Contemporary architecture is served by new materials, the titanium used by Frank Gehry is a kind of skin which reflects sunlight off his sculptural forms. This byplay of light and volume actively engages the eye, and connects his buildings to the physical and geographic environment. Materials sensitive to light are currently being developed for architectural use, as surfaces, which have the potential to reflect hues. But the byplay of spectral hues *per se*, indiscriminately, does not necessarily enhance architectonic form.

Enter color. Defined as a dimension, color interacts with form, i.e., volume; it is the essential component in three-dimensional grouping, and is a major influence on the perception of space. Color's dimensions, classically defined as three – hue, brightness and saturation (chroma) – behave in the context of three dimensions as physically related to assessments of distance, attributes of focus or localization, delineation by contrasts, of shapes and areas. As a non-linear dimension, it is intrinsically related, in perception, with form and space.

For architects and urban designers these characteristics offered by color are potential, not yet fully utilized. Because color can articulate, as well as conceal formal elements, it can render support or counterpoint to architectonic features. In vernacular expression, for example, a domestic façade uses contrast of juxtaposed colors to emphasize architectural features – windows and doors. Such contrast devices have been observed universally, across cultures, using distinctively differing palettes. Attention to areas of entry, the doorway, or window apertures are areas of significance; hence they are articulated. While the materials, surfaces or colors differ in treatment-expressive of their respective cultures – this architectural code is universal. Without limiting color usage to these traditional and ubiquitous examples – color contrasts as focal or localizing apertures in façades – the use of color to contrast areas or emphasize building masses can enhance or clarify their orientation, and differentiate the part from the whole. Subtle shifts in hue or brightness as well as bolder color contrasts can achieve these perceptual results.

In the urban scheme, color groupings are used as assimilating elements, connecting rows of buildings which define neighborhoods. Eighteenth- and nineteenth-century districts in Boston are still distinguished by their red brick façades. In Manhattan, brownstone town houses remain in place on streets unchanged or challenged by contemporary development. Thus, on the urban scale, time and place are marked; history made visible. In Stockholm, contemporary city districts are differentiated by color zoning, to comply with the existing architectural surrounds. Color is signified within ranges of basically warm color palettes. Stockholm's neighborhoods, therefore, are readily distinguishable, resulting in variety within unity, and conferring clarity and beauty to the urban scale. In Oslo, Norway, contemporary color designers comply with strictures which integrate their color schemes in new neighborhoods with the old.

In nature, color plays an essential role. All visible forms in nature are colored. The very identity of species – the zebra's stripes, the iridescence of birds and bugs, the depths of seas – are literally defined by their color. Chromatic display is not limited to the issue of survival, solely as attraction or camouflage. Articulation of tropical birds in flight occurs when brilliant primary colours are contrasted with saturated blue skies. Variations within species are expressed, not only by the shapes of birds and animals, but by their colouration. Color also builds natural forms. Geological canyons are virtually constructed by chemical components laid down over time, subjected to the physical forces of weather and light, which can be identified and read by juxtapositions of color. Temporal delineations to the human eye, these are perceptual signs or signatures of time. Trapped by semantic distinctions, we tend to separate delectation from seriousness, but nature seems to have it both ways.

How does color form? There are strategies of design, basic to three-dimensional contexts, which we have identified and expressed. Challenging the ingrained habit of totally separating the formal constituents, form and color – even form contra color – inculcated in Design education, I developed the theory that color is a dimension, by addressing both simultaneously. Over decades, with my students, I constructed models and studied three-dimensional geometric forms, with relation to their *appearance*. Inclusive and fundamental is light and shadow. The discovery of perceptual ratios of lightness/darkness reflected from angles, and volumetric surfaces provided a basis for the understanding of trans*form*ation. A visual grammar resulted. The variety and depth of these experiments cannot be recounted here.

We studied the effects of color on spatial depth and distance at tabletop and architectural scales, concluding that color (hue) is inherently spatial, and that each spectral hue differs in its spatial nature, a fundamental point that as yet is not explicable in existing color systems. When juxtaposed, hues exert tensions which can radically affect the perception of space. As Josef Albers asserted, colors are never experienced individually, but always in context. When this context is spatial, color perceived in space behaves *as* space; vividly visual, and nearly tangible.

In combination, hues work together in grouping as patterns. Mathematical symmetries can be played as radically diverse patterns, in both two and three dimensions when color is combined with the rational structures. By assessing these models visually, we have learned that the human visual system, the eye and brain, are extraordinarily adaptive to color/formal stimuli. As Design Science,

while eschewing calculated measurement, our experiments have been rigorous. The eye, in all cases, has been the final arbiter.[1]

Color in contemporary architecture remains a new challenge. While color is highly expressive, and by association connotes affective states of feeling and meaning, to correlate its use solely with 'expression' leads to the incoherent, largely arbitrary use in the contemporary environment. Relegated now to advertising and relentless marketing, the commercial use of color is overly dominant. Seen everywhere, in electronic media, in print and in the environment; aggressively stimulating, it actually de-sensitizes us.

In architecture and urban design, color decisions should not depend upon the tastes or preferences of the client or builder, but is the job of the highly sensitive human eye of a gifted designer. Cast as 'decoration', inferring a non-essential addition to the built environment, if color dimension is used instead as an intrinsic part of the process of structuring the building or the urban place – as a techtonic – it becomes a humanizing connection of the individual to the place. Paradoxical as it may seem, identity and meaning are conferred by color, when in use, it is consciously related to its context, as part of the perceptual process of building. More than mere embellishment, color adds vividness and the richness of visual metaphor to the built environment. Perhaps the logic of poetics is relevant here. Verbal metaphors depend upon the precision of expression to convey meaning. Poetry is based in the economic and poignant *articulation* of language.

Color structures may add complexity to architecture, but as they can articulate architectonic properties – surfaces, volumes and spaces – and their relationship to the site, color can clarify an architect's visual intentions, and greatly enhance the built environment.

15

The Globalization of Colour

Jean-Philippe Lenclos

When Gerrit Rietveld designed and built the Schröder House in 1924 using the architectural principles of de Stijl, he invented a new chromatic space for architecture. The raw material for his colour was provided by industrial paints deployed to structure and compose his architectonic space. Later, when Le Corbusier built la Cité Radieuse (1947–52), it was also coloured with the aid of pigments – used to infuse a more intense life into the volumes of his buildings. Le Corbusier declared that 'architecture is a play of volumes under light'. He added that the presence of colour is the true sign of life and, when it appears, everything is sparkling new.

The planning of new cities in the 1960s saw the beginnings of experiments in urban colour – as exemplified in the Markisches Viertel, a new quarter in Berlin – that seemed to echo Fernand Léger's theory of the polychrome city (Figure 15.1). But with the availability of extensive colour notation systems, such as Pantone and the NCS (Natural Color System), and the newfound ability of paint manufacturers to produce vast colour ranges – further increased by the

15.1 Markisches Viertel in Berlin

paint mixing machine – the 1970s witnessed a new phase of colour in the marketplace. Also, with the onset of computer technology and its ability to 'see' over a million hues, our experience of colour became further extended – even beyond the capabilities of human vision. By the 1980s we were to experience a veritable explosion of interest in colour, especially urban polychromy.

This architectural colour resurgence began mainly in Europe but particularly in France where new towns, such as Cergy Pontoise, Le Vaudreuil and Evry, came to be planned and executed in a painted colour (Figure 15.2). Together with street furniture, streetscape, lighting, strategies for urban colour were also imported to economically revitalize the heart of old cities such as Saint-Germain-en-Laye, Lyons and Nîmes, and also to bring chromatic personality to the new industrial and residential areas which later began to spring up around them. The influence of this colour movement quickly spread to Japan, soon afterwards to Korea and later to China. Consequently, through invited workshops, media interviews, publications and exhibitions I was busy proliferating my geography of colour methodology in Tokyo during the latter part of the 1970s, and in Seoul during the second part of the 1980s. Meanwhile, in order to develop their expertise, representatives from colour agencies, such as the Tokyo Colour Planning Centre, together with government-sponsored students from Korean and Chinese universities were regularly visiting my Atelier 3D Couleur in Paris. Architectural colour had now assumed a political dimension and was viewed as a value-added factor in the experience of the built environment. A calculated if not competitive approach to colour had also reached South America, Russia, Eastern Europe and the Middle East. By the 1990s, the methodological colouration of cities was, indeed, becoming a global phenomenon.

However, the 1990s also saw something different happening in the world of architecture. Hitherto, paint had offered a cheap and easy means of applying colour to buildings, deployed especially on a poor architecture to transform and enrich its experience. But paint was less used on high quality architecture. Instead, the building envelope relied more on the subtlety and inherent chromatic sophistication of traditional materials and on an adventurous experimentation with new materials used to provoke, shock, catch media attention and also to challenge manufacturers to produce even more technologically advanced construction materials and finishes. Compounded by the growth of the international design competition, we had arrived at a completely new expression of

15.2 Jean-Philippe Lenclos' colour installation at Les Linandes, a housing development designed by Jean Paul Viguier and Jean François Jodry in Cergy Pontoise

architecture involving not merely the function of the building, but an important new role which also involves a marketing strategy. I call this the 'image function' – image being the 'autograph' of both the architecture and, indeed, the designer who created it. A generation of internationally celebrated architects had emerged who developed instantly recognizable styles as witnessed in the work of, for example, Renzo Piano, Jean Nouvel, Herzog & de Meuron and Frank Gehry. In their hands, architecture becomes an art object – a well-publicized sculptural event on the world stage. For instance, Gehry's flowing use of titanium on the Guggenheim Museum in Bilbao is perhaps the best-known archetype of one landmark building transforming a poor industrial Spanish port into a popular international destination.

As we moved into the new millennium, this transformation brought about a new approach to architectural polychromy – one involving a tactile dimension as well as a focus on visual effect. No longer considered only as value-added, colour is now seen as an architecturally integrated value on the computer-modelled building alongside form, space, volume, shape and light, etc. I call this the 'new *expression* of architecture' in which architecture today cannot be created without colour. However, I do not refer here to colour exclusively in terms of pigment for, in a real sense, the concept of the painted surface is passé. Instead, I refer to the colours of the new materials, to the use of coloured light and to the dramatically changing hues now made possible by the surface finishes generated by the new computer technologies. This new architectural expression is not only concerned with the chromatic nuances caused by texture, relief, reflectivity, gloss and the patina of natural materials, but it also exploits state-of-the-art finishes, often involving microscopically induced and chromatically ambiguous surface effects that imitate the fragmentation of luminous waves seen in fish scales and butterfly wings. We now celebrate the unexpected and the mysterious – found in nacreous effects such as colour shift, optical interference, iridescence and pearlescence, etc. This transformation was already evident in our daily lives, in cosmetics, in domestic appliances and in fashion and accessories. However, the delicate, precious and often enigmatic colour effects often derived from a particulate technology developed by the chemical industry and initially found on, for example, household industrial design products, had become transposed to the monumental scale of buildings.

Yet another colour phenomenon is commonly seen in today's cities across the world where buildings are no longer designed to function as an architectural event to be experienced during the light of day. Using a programmed choreography of coloured light, they can transform into a dynamic after-dark spectacle which can either complement or contrast with their daytime appearance. Well-known examples of this dual existence are found in Jean Nouvel's Agbar Tower in Barcelona which, after nightfall, assumes a new and vibrant persona (see Figure 16.6).

I am convinced that we are now experiencing a very important period in which architectural colour, now expressed in material and illumination rather than paint, is creating a new chromatic dialectic between form, space, structure and light.

16

Evoking a Response

Alain Bony

My fascination with the potential of the illusory nature of the coloured surface – especially the transparency of the glazed surface – began as an art student when I studied painting at the Van de Kelen School in Brussels. However, this fascination soon became transferred to the scale of buildings – a transition that coincided with my close and ongoing collaboration with Jean Nouvel which began over twenty years ago.

My environmental colour approach concerns the sensation of light – the transformation of the architectural surface essentially using texture, brilliance, reflection and transparency. As part of this surface transformation, colour for me must generate meaning. It is quite reductionist to speak of colour *per se*; I would rather speak of vibration. I believe that colour is inseparable from the surfaces of the global environment and it is at this interface where one must exploit all the possibilities. Indeed, it is the nature of the interface, i.e., the architectural support, which dictates the parameters in which one must compose and create. Each space and its context are unique and must be treated in a specific way – playing with shadow and with light. I rarely work with flat colour, seeking instead to provoke reactions through the illusion of an unstable colour – the aim being to elicit emotions of a pictorial nature. Indeed, the main intention is to create a sensation, a feeling; the goal is to provoke a response, whether positive or not. This is extremely important for me (Figure 16.1).

One must avoid disconnected colour – usually resulting from working exclusively with mock-ups, scale models or drawings to be later applied to specific elements of a building. This approach is one associated with a colourist, and it is completely different from mine. Colour must be at one with the building; working directly on the building's surface or the intended building material is the only way; it implies a different contemplation that allows one to avoid an isolated or decorative intervention. Consequently, it is important to work at full scale from the outset; it is also important that the architect is aware of this so that he or she can play their part in the experimental research stage. The difficulty lies then in reproducing at the actual scale of a building what has been achieved,

albeit at full scale but in detail, in the studio. For example, passing from a one-to-one sample surface treatment to a building surface of several hundred, or even several thousand square metres, is a challenge which requires that we have to be in permanent attendance either throughout the fabrication process or during the building construction process itself. For example, when realizing the façades of the Kultur und Kongresszentrum for Jean Nouvel in Lucerne, the panel fabrication company charged with recreating the façade colour effects we had created in the studio didn't want to take the risk of reproducing them at full scale. This meant that we had to personally intervene and work on the panels in the

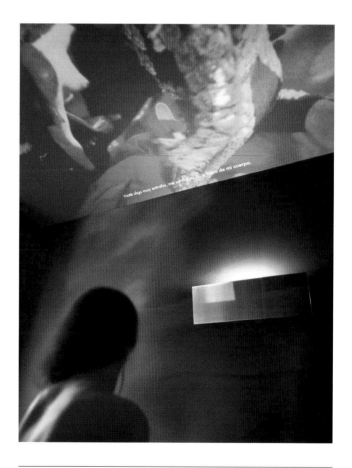

16.1 Jean Nouvel's concept of ceiling projections in the bedrooms of 'The Hotel' in Lucerne is complemented by Bony's modulated wall colours that simulate the play of light, shade and shadow

16.2 Using two colours of textured pigment directly applied to the metal cladding of Jean Nouvel's CLM/BBDO ad agency in Issy-les-Moulineaux, Bony's intention is to create the impression of an encrusted ship's hull as a foil to the slickness of its interior offices

16.3 'Camouflage' installation screening an open market area at Expo 02 in Morat, Switzerland

factory within the industrial manufacturing process. In another Jean Nouvel project, the CLM/BBDO advertising agency in Issy-les-Moulineaux, the fabrication company didn't know exactly how to translate the image we wanted to achieve, so we ourselves had to work directly on the building façades (Figure 16.2).

Architecture is above all a story of confrontations, and my long association with Jean Nouvel has been a defining one for me. I also collaborate with a number of other architects with different sensibilities but the best results are achieved when I am allowed great freedom. The orientation of a project generally results from a direction communicated by the architect, usually through the medium of sketches. The architect will also express objectives in terms of chromatic ambience: base colour, matt or gloss, reflectivity, transparency, etc., and in terms of tactile impression: flatness, relief, roughness. The cumulative experience of such projects in the past two decades means that I now have a palette of possibilities and

opportunities with which to play. While experimentation remains critical to the creative process, each project allows me to expand the scope of this palette (Figure 16.3).

Today, a vast array of industrial paints, lacquers, varnishes and colourants is available. My collaboration with the artists Isabelle Clerte and Henri Labiole seeks to transpose these products from their traditional frame of reference and apply them in new contexts in order to realize specific effects in relation to a particular project. For instance, one can use a steel paint on concrete to obtain new effects, and a surface can be textured to create a different relief – which again can be modified by a particular chromatic treatment. I have also worked on steel panels with varnishes and pigments habitually used for car bodywork – experimenting with combinations of varnishes and pigments to achieve a precise transparent colour relationship with the surface of the building.

The starting point for a project usually involves the familiarization with the physical context of the building in question and the nature of prevailing daytime and night-time light conditions. In our search for the poetry of a wall, we also make reference to contemporary art and draw inspiration from twentieth-century abstract artists, such as Pablo Picasso, Jackson Pollock, Sam Francis, and especially Yves Klein and Marcel Duchamp. During the experimental phase we constantly explore new and innovative surface effects using traditional techniques in a novel way or by researching the potential of new technologies. The resulting architectural interventions can be envisaged in terms of three standpoints. The first refers to the application of a medium or a material to the wall, such as copper, fabric, paper, paint, etc. If paper is used, on interiors, this will often carry a print or an airbrushed rendition to 'create shadows'; if paint is used, this can sometimes be thrown in the manner of the Tachists or directly poured down a surface directly from the can, such as on the Lycée Duhoda in Nîmes (Figure 16.4). The second approach is to literally attack the surface of the wall – with

16.4 Architecture meets Tachism as a result of Bony's pouring diluted mixtures of acrylic paint over Jean Nouvel's sports facility for the Lycée Duhoda in Nîmes

tools that scratch, score, scrape, gouge or chisel. Once a surface has been thus abraded, colour, for example, may be rubbed into the lesions. Burning represents another dimension of our surface attack, when blowtorches are used to scorch, char and blister the wall (Figure 16.5). The third category is an 'industrial' approach; for instance, when lacquers and enamels are applied to bring colour to elements of a building, such as when we transformed the metallic louvres on the Agbar Tower in Barcelona (Figure 16.6).

These approaches aim to tap into the poetics of a building, the ultimate installation and perceptual effect completely transforming the architectural surface. In this manner, we attempt unashamedly to create a work of art on the scale of a building to be spatially experienced under varying daylight and electric light conditions. Each project we undertake is different and, guided by the architect's particular desire, seeks specific solutions. The work is complete only when its static depiction – such as in a photograph – no longer succeeds in translating the reality of the emotion experienced in the actual space.

16.5 (top)   Scorched interior classroom in the Lycée Duhoda, Nîmes

16.6 (above) Jean Nouvel's Agbar Tower, Barcelona

On Colour and Space

Matthias Sauerbruch and Louisa Hutton

Prejudice for the white body over the decorated surface

The preference for the white volume over the decorated surface can be traced all the way back to Plato's Ideal. There are also the analogously dialectic pairings of Apollonian versus Dionysian, classic versus romantic, and that of the line drawing versus the use of coloured areas. Through all cultures, whiteness has been associated with perfection, cleanliness and innocence. The use of colour therefore detracts from the Ideal and leads one to the lesser regions of (dirty) reality.

Whiteness appeals to the intellect and is a mark of education, whereas colour has a direct – and therefore untrustworthy – effect upon the instincts. And there is the presumed superiority of the intellectual recognition of space as opposed to the direct sensual experience of a corporeally perceived space: this prejudice plays into the subject of colour in architecture.

What's more, there is prejudice against the literal superficiality of the application of colour onto a surface. This is coupled with colour's physical instability, so that the ensuing ephemerality of the surface is seen to undermine the serious and enduring solidity – both literal and metaphorical – of the volume. So the coloured surface was – and is – perceived as subordinate to the white body (there being the assumption that if the form is not coloured, it can only be white). To quote David Batchelor,

> Figuratively, colour has always meant the less-than-true and the not-quite-real. In Latin, *colorem* is related to *celare* – to hide or conceal. In Middle English to *colour* is to embellish or adorn, to disguise, to render specious or plausible, to misrepresent.[1]

And for Batchelor, colour represents

> [The] disobedient, the eccentric, the irregular and the subversive … To be called colourful is to be flattered and insulted at the same time. To be colourful is to be distinctive, and, equally, to be dismissed … Colour is uncertainty, doubt and change … Colour is other.[2]

The same author writes on the resulting *chromophobia* – as he terms it – that 'manifests itself in the many and varied attempts to purge colour from culture, to devalue colour, to diminish its significance, to deny its complexity.'[3] This happens in two ways. In the first:

> Colour is made out to be the property of some 'foreign' body – usually the feminine, the oriental, the primitive, the infantile, the vulgar or the pathological. In the second, colour is relegated to the realm of the superficial, the supplementary, the inessential or the cosmetic. In one, colour is regarded as alien and therefore dangerous; and in the other, it is perceived merely as a secondary quality of experience, and thus unworthy of serious consideration. Colour is dangerous, or it is trivial, or it is both.[4]

Related, of course, is the question of taste. As Goethe commented,

> It is also worthy of remark, that savage nations, uneducated people, and children have a great predilection for vivid colours; that animals are excited to rage by certain colours; that people of refinement avoid vivid colours in their dress and the objects that are about them, and seem inclined to banish them altogether from their presence.[5]

Ruskin, when writing that if colour were employed in architecture, then at least the colours of natural stone should be used, was echoing the sentiments of not only many of his contemporaries, but also most of ours. Muted colours are universally judged as tasteful: today the prejudice is as strong as ever.

Semper and polychromy

There have been many shifts in the debate for and against polychromy in architecture. The penultimate conflict was Neoclassicism's strong hold on whiteness in opposition to the polychromy discovered in the new archaeological sites around the 1830s, when the supporters of the latter maintained that the use of colour was not accidental but essential. Semper, of course, belonged to this group, and for him colour was the most sublime form of dressing – and not, as for other architects, merely the decorative enrichment of architecture. Semper defined architecture through its covering layer rather than through its material structure. He traced his understanding of the beginnings of civic architecture back to the first structures erected for temporary use during gatherings for religious or civic purposes. These would have been temporary scaffolds covered with fabric, the scaffold being there in a purely supporting role. The material was woven and, carrying the symbolic and architectural function of decoration and celebration, created atmosphere. Thus, for Semper, the origin of civic architecture – that is, of spatial enclosure for symbolic as well as functional purposes – lies with woven fabric.

Semper developed a theory he called *Stoffwechsel* (literally: material transfer – the same word being used in German for metabolism), to explain the transfer of formal characteristics from one material to another, or 'succeeding' one (his terms being analogous to the developing theory of evolution). For example, he described the layer of paint that was added to buildings in an age of solid construction – that is, following the earliest constructions of the temporary scaffold kind – as maintaining the original textile tradition of a coloured layer on the surface. For him the space was formed by this coloured layer of paint, 'the subtlest, most bodiless dressing … It is the most perfect way to do away with reality, for while it dresses the material, it is itself immaterial.'[6]

In the discussion of the opposition between form and surface, it is thus not surprising that Semper favoured the surface. He privileged it over form because he was interested in the seduction of the surface, or, as Mark Wigley puts it, in a 'visuality entangled with sensuality'. Semper commented on colour: 'It ranks among the earliest of all inventions, because the instinct for pleasure, as it were, inspired man. Delight in colour was developed earlier than delight in form.'[7]

Four decades later, in 1907, Adolf Loos, basing his writings on those of Semper (particularly the *Principle of Dressing*), published his *Ornament and Crime*. There followed among architects a general distrust of the sensuality of decoration. Ornament was removed to purge the decorative excesses of previous periods, and pure abstraction of form became the goal.

Colour and architecture in the 1920s

The impetus for using colour in modern architecture came from painting. In the first decade of the twentieth century, colour had been freed from form in this discipline (as in the work of Fernand Léger), and it was precisely this liberated use of colour that was of interest to architects. They needed to discover ways of combining colour and space without regressing to associations with the decorative and the ornamental – which had been so firmly jettisoned in modernism's radical new departure.

Three architects who used colour in the 1920s were Theo van Doesburg (in collaboration with the painter van Eesteren), Le Corbusier and Bruno Taut. Each of them had different aims, methods and results. They all surmounted the association of colour with decoration, and worked with large expanses of colour that were directly combined with architectural space. It is interesting that these architects all had a direct relationship with painting – in that they had either associates who worked as painters, or previous or concurrent careers as painters themselves.

Theo van Doesburg created spaces that were articulated through hovering planes of colour. Form and colour were seen as two complementary and independent systems that created spaces full of tension that barely held together. The overall intention was one of abstraction, in which the physical volumes were optically destroyed and the coloured planes, were, to quote Gideon, 'brought into floating relationship with one another'.[8]

The de Stijl palette was very restricted, and their forms were limited to the purely rectilinear. Le Corbusier, however, called the de Stijl application of colour as practised by van Doesburg '*camouflage architectural*', not approving of colour being used to undermine physical space. Having preached 'whitewash' in the 1920s (and not mentioning colour at all in *Vers une Architecture*), Le Corbusier ultimately allowed the ideas of layered space that he had been following in his Purist paintings influence the real space of his architecture. Indeed, Arthur Rüegg has argued that in Villa la Roche the architect and the painter are united – the villa in effect becoming a still life with the layered space of Le Corbusier's – and Ozenfant's – Purist paintings.

According to Le Corbusier, colour should not be used to conceal actual spatial proportions. He coloured entire wall surfaces so that the walls as individual elements became carriers of colour but would not disturb the overall spatial effect of his architecture. The planes of colour, in a palette of mostly earth and natural tones selected for associative purposes – such as pale blue for sky – were used for their perceptual capacity to affect space (pale walls recede, dark walls stabilize). They would then serve as anchors for the overall spatial composition (as three-dimensional versions of the two-dimensional Purist paintings). The overall space was nevertheless predominantly painted white, so the coloured areas were seen as interventions played off against a neutral background. Batchelor comments that Le Corbusier's use of colour thus was to make his architecture 'even more white'. So here colour is being used not to generate or manipulate, but to control space. But, in our view, Le Corbusier did employ, if not *camouflage architectural* then *camouflage urbain* in his housing scheme in Pessac, near Bordeaux (1924):

> The Pessac site is very enclosed. The grey concrete houses gave rise to an unbearable compressed mass, lacking in air. Colour was the solution to generating space … Some wall surfaces are painted in burnt sienna, while clear ultramarine makes entire rows of houses recede. Elsewhere, pale green façades fuse with the foliage of the gardens and trees.[9]

At times, even a dissolution of form is achieved – when corner planes meet – in differing colours – and the solidity of the architecture begins to be challenged. In addition there is an intention to camouflage when Le Corbusier merges architecture and nature.

But for whatever ends Le Corbusier was using colour, he understood that polychromy extends the architect's range of tools: 'With polychromy the skilful architect has before him an endless bounty of resources … Polychromy is as powerful an architectural tool as the plan and section.'[10] In contrast to van Doesburg and Le Corbusier, who followed their artistic sensibilities in employing colour, Bruno Taut's intention went beyond the purely artistic in that he too employed colour as an agent of social reform. His use of large coloured areas on the walls (and even variations of colour within the single window frames) of his housing estates in Berlin stood for a new freedom and the alleviation of monotony. His mission was to create various identities within large housing estates – keeping in mind that the people who would be relocating to his estates were coming from overcrowded flats in the oppressive (and monochromatic) backyards of Berlin's expanded-to-bursting nineteenth-century urban structure.

Taut's words on polychromy are similar to those of Le Corbusier, however:

> As colour has the capacity to increase or reduce the distances between buildings, to affect the scale of the buildings so that they appear smaller or larger, to bring buildings into harmony with nature or to appear as contrast, and for other reasons … so one should use colour just as logically and consistently as one works with any other material.[11]

But Taut in turn accused Le Corbusier of using colour purely aesthetically: 'His architecture is concerned with purely salon-aesthetics. The architect builds as the painter paints – that is, he builds images.'[12]

Notwithstanding the work of these three individuals and their supporters, what followed was the myth of whiteness as propagated by Le Corbusier in the late 1920s (apparently after a change of heart, having seen the 'white' Acropolis on his trip to Greece). The architect promoted whiteness not only as an aesthetic stance, but also as a moral one (noting Wigley's observation that the buildings were *painted* white, they were not naked, which would have been too sensual). Colour was seen as an unnecessary addition to the formal and constructive idea of architecture, and by 1927 the white-painted Cubist boxes of the aptly named *Weissenhof Siedlung* in Stuttgart set the definitive trend. The irrationality of colour was seen as a threat to the rational logic of functionalism. In fact, the monopoly of whiteness was supported by the suppression of colour and materials through predominantly black and white photography, and by journalists' rather selective coverage.

Colour as a resource

Now, of course, with over a century of technological developments, the nature of and the possibilities inherent in the surface have undergone enormous changes since the time of Semper and Loos, and since that of van Doesburg, Le Corbusier and Taut as well – but nevertheless the work of these architects is still relevant today. Although critical of certain aspects of the modernist legacy, in general, we see our work as located in its wake. For us, this includes the potential to use colour as a resource in creating space, believing that the modernists' credo of 'material truth' can be reconciled with a broadened view of the potential of colour.

From the start of our practice in the late 1980s we have devoted a lot of time to the preparation of drawings for various competitions and presentations. In doing so, we noticed – as others had before us – that one can take advantage of the ability of colour to create space through the juxtaposition of darker and lighter tones, or of cooler with warmer hues. This phenomenon was well documented by Josef Albers in his book *Interaction of Color*.[13] It is illustrated with equal conviction in his series of paintings *Homage to the Square,* where the painter investigates the creation of different spaces within the constant of a square format. The painter calls the space that appears *actual fact*, whereas he designates the physical space of the canvas *factual fact*. To quote Albers,

> In visual perception a color is almost never seen as it really is – as it physically is. In order to use color effectively it is necessary to recognise that color deceives continually … What counts here is not so-called knowledge of so-called facts, but vision – seeing.[14]

Albers emphasizes the experiential side of perception – not the rational – and reminds us of the deception of appearance.

While our entries for the urban competitions remained theoretical projects, we had the chance to experiment with colour more directly on various commissions for domestic environments. We realized that colour could also be employed quite pragmatically to overcome the tight confines of English Victorian houses that are generally only 5 metres wide. In fact, the London house projects became a literal exploration of that territory between *actual* and *factual* as described by Albers – that is, between the space as visually perceived and the physical space as bounded by the historical side walls. The simple device of using large blocks of colour to form compositions independent of the original structure allowed the spatial limitations of these narrow buildings to be transcended. Working in this way, a co-existence of the visual, the haptic and the corporeal can be achieved. This is enabled and indeed intensified by the intimate scale of the projects that insist on bodily engagement, and the roaming eye seems to be able to touch the surfaces, the spaces. Just as importantly, the use of colour can help give identity to the domestic spaces and can contribute to creating places with sensual and atmospheric qualities.

We are inspired by the moods created by certain works of art, as well as by their transcendent qualities. Of course, the experience of an inhabited space is extremely different from that of the primarily visual space of a painting or an installation. The lived space will be not only seen, but also touched, felt, smelt, heard – all this in the course of going about the routines and rituals of everyday life. Thus it will mostly be experienced as the mere background to one's everyday activities; whereas the space of Art – even if it engages one's corporeal perception, is generally experienced in the detached context of a gallery or museum. But despite, or perhaps because of, architecture's inevitable solidity and its provision of spaces for even the most mundane of activities, we are tempted to try to escape both its substance and its permanence in search of the immaterial and the ephemeral.

The spaces we design are, of course, not made of colour alone – or even coloured light, as in some works of art such as the installations of James Turrell; rather, we enjoy using colour in combination with natural materials. In fact, we deliberately contrast areas of colour with those of natural materials – timber, stainless steel, glass (with varying degrees of transparency and reflectivity), concrete (polished and rough), the honed surface of smooth plaster, the shine of a chromed finish, the various textures of different stones. In addition to the richness of such juxtaposition, the coloured area itself also has its own kind of materiality: its surface texture, its characteristics of lustre or absorption. This means that the coloured surface is never purely abstract: there are the various textures and reflective qualities of coats of paint, ranging from a fine depth in the surface, to a dull flatness, to the reflective depths which appear within the flatness of a lacquered finish. And there are, of course, varying degrees of transparency, translucency, and reflectivity that can be explored in combinations of colour with glass.

The one obvious instance of the spaces of art and architecture literally coming together is to be found in works of *trompe l'œil*. Here the space of the painting is integrated with that of its setting so that the ambiguity in perception between two and three dimensions is simultaneously revealed and enjoyed. The illusion of a unified space may prevail, or instead an oscillation between Albers' *actual* and *factual* once the rational side of the brain has understood the deceit.

A similar kind of deception – creating the illusion of the extension or contraction of physical space – is achieved through the use of mirrors – most famously in Versailles' Hall of Mirrors, or more recently in the installations of Dan Graham (or indeed in virtually any corporate lift or hotel bathroom the world over).

Illustration through four projects

With the following four examples of our realized projects we will illustrate our use of colour – looking at how it can support and enrich the main intention of the work on an urban scale, as well as how it can contribute to creating places of sensuous quality and strong identity. There is no single theory or set of rules that guides our work with colour. Just as in our architecture, the emphasis is on the physical experience of the projects themselves rather than any preconceptions, so our work with colour follows no dogma. Although themes naturally develop from one project to another, we aim to develop new ideas for each project. Each building offers a particular reading of surface, and the use of colour ranges from a literal application of colour on the surface to an exploration of the thickness of the surface layer itself. Our approach is essentially intuitive, but it acquires a kind of scientific nature through its serial quality and the iterative processes employed. We usually investigate a large amount of varying colour combinations – through the various stages of design – before we settle for the final one. In the process we try to rationalize our perceptions, but the final decision is, however, always made by the eye.

In the GSW Headquarters, the application of colour strengthens the urban idea – that of forming a new ensemble of various building elements that accepts Berlin's formal heterogeneity as a principle for development. Each of these elements is given a different material or colour treatment. The identity of the new grouping is given mostly by the high-rise's west façade, which, seen as a layer in itself, addresses aspects of sustainability (it is in fact a 1-m-thick thermal flue) while shaping the image of the whole complex through the use of its various reds on its sun-shading panels. The latter are controlled by the inhabitants of the offices, so the façade becomes a city-scale dynamic painting that combines aspects of occupancy with those of sustainability: at the same time the new slab as a whole acknowledges the fact of the Cold War in its alignment with the Springer high-rise and the group of high-rises along Leipziger Strasse that were built in response (Figure 17.1).

In the extended Highbay Warehouse for Sedus, we use colour to deliberately manipulate the solidity of the form, resulting in a kind of camouflage that supports the overall idea of reducing the visual mass of the building by blending it in with its landscape setting. The warehouse lies in the foothills of the Black Forest near the small town of Dogern, and is by far the largest element in the area, being quite visible from the main road. At the same time, its great scale presents an impressive elevation towards the Rhine and the hills beyond. From far away, the coloured surface seems to dissolve this large mass into its landscape context. The optical mix of the skin blends with the warm brick reds of the neighbouring façade while at the same time harmonizing with the immediate tones of the village, the agricultural landscape and the hues of the distant hills.

The selection of the actual colours followed a design process in which many colour combinations were tested – both as large-scale elevations and small-scale photographic collages. Before the final decision, a one-to-one mock-up on the façade was tested. It is a

17.1 Gridded units of colour are a hallmark of the Sauerbruch and Hutton practice on their conversion of the GSW Headquarters building – an office building in Berlin

17.2 (below) A further example of comparatively small units of colour that, over distance, perceptually disrupt the scale and dematerialize the mass of Sauerbruch and Hutton's Highbay Warehouse for Sedus in the Black Forest

17.3 (right) A fragmentation of form through a matrix of symbolic colour, in this case screen-printed glass panels on the external skin of Sauerbruch and Hutton's Fire and Police Station in Berlin

shiny glass body of the extension. It supports the overall intention of making a clear distinction between old and new, and demonstrates the new uses given to this former goods yard fragment. It was a deliberate decision to use the two colour families of red and green, as – apart from the Post service – the Fire Brigade and the Police Force are the only German institutions that can clearly be identified and represented by their colour (Figure 17.3). The various hues are combined so that from a distance there is a unified appearance, while as one approaches, the colour treatment becomes differentiated. The merging of the two colour families achieves an optical depth on the surface; the real depth of the façade becomes apparent when the glass louvres are opened.

The building of the Pharmacological Laboratories in Biberach looks like an inhabited painting. It consists of a simple volume with an outer glass skin, onto which a polychromatic pattern has been printed. This treatment gives the building its own scale and a surprising sculptural quality, as well as a striking and lively contemporary image that sets the institute apart from its peers. The pattern was generated by enlarging a microscopic image of one of the drugs produced by this pharmacological company. It thus becomes symbolic of the nano-world of biological research into which one seems to plunge upon entering the building. As an architectural element, the patterned skin unites the building's diverse parts into a unified whole. It is seen as a diaphanous veil that allows insight into the depth between the solid building and the ephemeral layer, and at the same time can be read as the building's

building that is pictorial in two ways: on the one hand, it presents the structure as a large-format painting; on the other, it lends Sedus a new identity (Figure 17.2).

In the Fire and Police Station in Berlin, our application of colour makes a clear differentiation between the dull, absorbent surfaces of the existing stone and brick neoclassical building and the new

extremity. On a pragmatic level the glass skin works as a layer of adjustable sun shades as well as a climate modifier that creates a buffer zone around the insulated body of the building. There is an enjoyable degree of subversion in this use of colour in association with such 'serious' buildings as these (Figure 17.4).

In our use of colour, we follow neither a didactic nor an academic approach. Rather, in our search for an architecture of intelligence and integrity, we continue the Modernist legacy of treating colour as a resource in the creation of space, and in addition we use colour to imbue places with sensual character and memorable qualities. Although one could argue that such qualities could be achieved solely through the judicious use of materials (as, for example, in Mies van der Rohe's Barcelona Pavilion), we think that the possibilities of colour, both to manipulate space and to work directly on our senses, make it far more effective – and enjoyable. In fact, the use of polychromy in our architecture is so intrinsic that each building is not imaginable without its colour.

We are interested in an architecture that engages the user and the passer-by, and that, in addition to performing excellently on a functional level, captures their imaginations. We believe that this can be reached through the handling of the surface to achieve a visual richness, a kind of optical layering. The optical dissolution or manipulation of form introduces uncertainty, doubt, ambiguity. It engages you. It makes you look again – as in Jacques Lacan's reference to an empty sardine tin that, bobbing about on the ocean, contained something like the ambiguity of jewels as it twinkled in the sun. This is similar to the deception in *trompe l'œil*, where one's imagination is caught, teased. We don't want to prioritize vision over our other senses of spatial perception – corporeal, kinetic, haptic, aural, olfactory – but, to quote Albers, 'seeing is coupled with fantasy, with imagination'.[15] We are looking to create an architecture that engages its user actively – perhaps this is analogous to T.S. Eliot's description of reading as a creative act, in which, actively reading, one can share in the act of creation with the author.

Acknowledgements

This is a modified version of a lecture given at the Gottfried Semper (1803–1879): Greece and Contemporary Architecture Symposium, Athens, in October 2003.

17.4 Screen-printed enamel on mechanically operated glass louvres provides an ever-changing architectural colour persona on Sauerbruch and Hutton's Boehringer Ingleheim Pharmacological Research Laboratories, Biberach

Iconic Engineering:
reflections on the subject of colour in architecture, ornament and city planning

John Outram

When the time comes, in any of my projects, to decide on colour, a sort of quadrille takes place. The girls step forward and the boys step back.

The male incapacity with colour must derive from their gender stereotype. Boys stop playing with crayons around the age of five. Girls never stop playing with clothes, make-up, hair and then interiors. Women have an intuitive grasp of colour. It is nothing but a skill born of experience. Practice makes perfect. The only men who are capable are those who use colour in their work – such as graphic artists. Twentieth-century architects tended not to include colour in their design vocabulary. They abandoned it when they made the 'Corbusian Turn' towards 'le plastique pur', and avoided employing early twentieth-century abstract art to re-build the conceptual motor of architectural decoration.

In 1993, the concrete industry spent £200,000 on creating a teaching pack for architecture schools. They launched it in the city in which the pack had been created – Cambridge. Professors who taught this subject were invited from all over Britain. I was building the Judge Institute at the time and was asked to show the delegates over the site and give a short resumé. I saw that the latest form of surface treatment described in the pack was the bush-hammered concrete of the Barbican Centre. The technique involved casting deep vertical grooves whose tips were then smashed off with a mechanical hammer. On drawings the effect looked 'distressed' – like faked antiquing. In reality, it was perfectly vile. The Barbican feels like a prison whose walls could only be breached by explosives rather than by merely removing a few modest bricks. Its surfaces seem as if clawed by some huge beast with broken fingernails.

There was nothing in the professors' pack about a concrete that was cast into legible shapes invested by a dense chromatic solidity. I called it 'Photolithic' so as to manifest the paradox of a 'light' that is as heavy as matter. I did this by fractioning my aggregate

sizes down to a 'pepper and salt' of calcined flint and twice-burnt coal. These made it clear even to the eye, let alone the hand, that my colour-casts were grittily solid and not merely paint. Nor did the teaching-pack describe 'Doodlecrete' – a coloured concrete inlaid with a scripted pattern in a different colour. Nor was there any of the 'Blitzcrete' I had built, in 1985, in Wadhurst Park, a widely illustrated building judged by *The Sunday Times* as the 'best country house built since the war'. Its columns were surfaced with a concrete made from coloured cement. This was inlaid with big chips of multi-coloured broken brick in precisely specified sizes, fractions and hues (Figure 18.1).

18.1 One of the columns on the Millennium Verandah of John Outram's design for a private house at Wadhurst Park

During the design of the Judge Institute, I wrote that my purpose was to invest decoration with a significance that fed on its physical support until the inscribed member was consumed by a fabric of meanings which knit about it like the coils of a digesting serpent (Figure 18.2). It was my way of changing the mere matter of our urban prisons into intelligences by which we could escape from them. It was entirely futile to merely attempt the literal substitution of solidity by glass. Not only was glass a solid, and one that merely revealed the quotidian banality of typists' knees and wastebaskets, but no energy-efficient wall should be more than one-third glass. Nothing is more dolorous to me than the view from some high modern tower across the newborn termite mounds of its neighbours, still glistening from births quite innocent of architectural insemination.

Colour and pattern serve to de-materialize a solid, predictable and orderly architecture. But this works both ways. It frees us from the prison of a merely urban domesticity. But, by effecting this 'escape', it also allows the physical body of the urban lifespace to remain as predictably domestic as it has been for nine millennia. An effective surface-scripting culture removes the need to tug, warp, and fold, like some necrophiliac Doctor Frankenstein, on the lumpen corpus of construction in the way that it is tortured, today, by an iconically illiterate 'design profession'. An architecture which is conceptually cultivated has no problem with allowing its physical body to be as archaic as our own … An urbanity with a conceptual vitality encourages physical health in ourselves.

It has to be considered remarkable, and perhaps even incredible, that a medium of such antiquity should have never been worthy of a text that adequately explained 'how it works' with its human subjects, or how it is 'worked' by its inventors. The lack of this text, either subtle or simple, must be the reason why the medium has always been found to be only partially useful, because it is always inadequate to its purposes.

How else does one explain the peculiar 'cult of Antiquity' that found it necessary, for example, to remove every trace of colour, in the 1930s, from the Elgin Marbles? It had been known, since the excavation of Pompeii in the eighteenth century, that the Pentelic marble architectures of historical Antiquity had been waxed, stained and otherwise painted with symbolic patterns – 'texts' older (as can be seen at the 9,000-year-old Catal Huyuk) than writing itself. Yet, ever since the fifteenth-century Italian Renaissance, the chromatic surfaces of the 'Classic' could not be admitted for fear that it would destroy the bleached bones of the 'ancient' authority of Classicism – an authority which sought to overbear the Christian architecture of French Gothic by appealing to a prior genesis – even though that lay behind the mythic veil of the 'Age of Gold'! Why has no theorist even come close to analyzing how these peculiar formal rites function within the imagination? To have done so would enable the architectural medium to be used directly and without the confusion of specious ideologies – like that of 'Modernism'. To have achieved such an explanation would avoid the contemporary elaboration of

18.2 Colour and pattern in Outram's extraordinary interior for the Judge Institute in Cambridge

'design philosophies' that are not only incredible but useless to practice. Why is it impossible to imagine that it is this extraordinary failure of architectural philosophy that has led, in the greatest measure, to the contemporary abandonment of the medium itself?

The invention of Cubism and the liberation of construction from all 'pseudo-tectonic' formal constraints, have allowed practitioners such as Libeskind, Gehry and Hadid to widen the boundaries of building. Yet these expand with neither the sense of an orthodox syntactic orthography, or a flowering into a semantic conceptuality. The algorithmic agitation spreads like some punctured reservoir whose contents seem as unlimited as they appear incapable of fertilizing the lifespace deserts of contemporary 'land-use planning'. What are the buildings of these 'designers' (who can call them 'architects'?) but the final curtain upon the tectonic theatre of Architecture-as-Platonic-carpentry?

An ordering around the phenomena of colour and pattern, key media in what I call 'iconic engineering', is a way of channelling these aimless floods into usefulness. But these are insubstantial media unsuitable to bridling by the ideology of physical mechanism inherited by Modernism from the Purists and Rigorists of the eighteenth century. The generically 'haptic' tribe of Architects will either have to rise to the challenge of mounting these slippery steeds or give way to being led by those who can ride such media – even if they become a new profession of iconic engineers.

It would not be surprising if Architects resisted any such usurpation of their dominance of 'building design'. There is no-one more hated by the contemporary architect (and especially those of the first degree), than the interior designer. There is nothing the architect dislikes more than that he should labour through all of the (often self-imposed) technical elaborations of construction, only to find everyone's attention focused upon a veil of patterns and colours drawn over all of his technical competences by a mere 'decorator'. The ego of the architect is bruised, if not fatally wounded, by being displaced from the attention of the world by a professional whose main skill is the retailing of histories and narratives woven into a beguiling 'surface-scripting' that can, and indeed usually does, bear no relation to the haptic enthusiasms of the 'constructor'.

But why, one may ask, does the Architect not learn a few of these tricks? All architects were, and one must hope still are, taught the powers of 'abstract design'. All architects are expert in rhetoric. It is a requirement of our trade that we be proficient in persuading our clients to part happily with very large sums of money. All architects can read a contract and a specification. While it is true that it is not easy to become iconically literate, our used-to-be-learned profession could organize itself better to make such a literacy quicker to obtain. Why not compile an online library of texts from which their readers could browse with a view to becoming literate in iconic engineering for architects? It might make a welcome change from computational geometries that treat the human lifespace as a thought-free zone.

When I wish to compose an iconic array I 'switch off' (well, take a nap, actually) so as to wake more attuned to a verbally and iconically fertile mental mode. One must leave to one side the spatio-physical mode of constructional design. It is not that of 'iconic engineering'.

But these are only two among the many modes of being of which humans are capable. We drive with our hands and feet. But this is not how we eat, or sing. Why can architects not master the surface-scripting of the buildings that they, and they alone, know how to entirely design?

When I completed Duncan Hall, back in 1996, to house the Faculty of Computational Engineering in Rice University, Houston, a diversity of persons, none of whom I previously knew, offered their informal approval – even extending to gratitude (in Houston there are glass office-buildings whose sole communicative essay is a four-figure cadastral number stamped onto their foreheads). There were students and professors of Engineering. There were professors of the Humanities. There were their partners, sparky as only Texan girls can be. It seemed to me that the professors of Engineering enjoyed the fact that their building had a more arcane textuality than their Humanistic colleagues. Duncan Hall found itself a 'destination' on the Art-bus tour of Houston. Even a curator of the Menil, a museum dedicated to a fairly rigorous 'modernity', felt that she could admire it. It was later said that undergraduates who left its interior to pursue their studies in other of the campus buildings, suffered the pangs of a novel agony that we christened 'chromatic deprivation'! All of this made me as pleased as giving pleasure to others must do, although as everyone knows, this can never be the motive for intellectual work of any consequence.

What did surprise me, however, was the report that the professors of the architectural faculty had banned their freshmen from entering my interior. Yet building security reported that some of these professors had been detected roaming, very late at night, in the brilliantly lit, but empty, interior of my nearly completed building. It seemed that, although they feared for the souls of their tender charges, they themselves would not be denied the terrifying experience of my polychromatic patternings! (Figure 18.3).

Far from 'corrupting' their de-instructed undergraduates, I began to understand that what these professors feared most about Duncan Hall was the possibility that their freshmen might ask them how to bring the ancient medium of architecture forward to the point at which it could be used directly, in all of its dimensions, to perform in the here-and-now. Perhaps their professorial colleagues from the other Humanities, or even the Engineering Faculty, might ask them to explain my colours and patterns. My guess was that the

18.3 Outram's mediation of the ideal city in the painted steel, sheetrock and printed fabric of his interior of Duncan Hall, Rice University, Houston, Texas

professors of Architecture knew neither how to explain the workings of their ancient medium nor how to work it themselves. Worse than this was the fact that they not only refused to learn how architecture worked, but would expel any student of the medium who showed too close an attention to 'architecture' as it is commonly understood. What better proof was needed than that they dared not allow me into the faculty, and dared not grille me to find out what I was up to? Not that Rice was entirely alone in this. To be discouraged, to the point of expulsion, is the not-uncommon fate of the architecturally-gifted in the average school of architecture today.

The ultimate purpose of architecture is to mediate the 'ideal city'. This is not to blueprint a perfect community. The ideal city is, rather, a city that knows how to inscribe ideas into the human lifespace. If such ideas treat with reality, or realities in all of the many ways they can be understood, then the citizens of such a place have the opportunity to exist with a certain nobility. For it is always more noble to act in the light of the real – *sub specie aeternatis* – in the mirror of eternity.

It is here that the notion of community emerges. Every individual is the creature of his culture. Reality, while it should never exclude matters of a general nature, matters of concern to anyone, must always be of a time and place. Thus it is that if a city manages to 'publish', in the way that architecture can, its political, economic and ethical constitutions, then life in it can be lived in the light of these, whether subtle, brutal or both. Such a life cannot but be more noble than the one that is lived on a stage without any such self-knowledge – a stage of the merely 'positive' materiality created everywhere during the twentieth century. The century past was a theatre unfit for human occupation.

Its 'truths', of naked wood and bare cement, were banal to the point of idiocy. But behind the condescension of this 'Welfare Ethic' of the 'Existenzminimum' there lay the more evil ethos of silence, the imperative to say nothing, to be mute, lest the New Chapter find its voice. Karl Kraus, of the 1910 Vienna Circle, said: 'If anyone has something to say, please come forward and remain silent.' He should have spoken. One must always speak – or others will. Practice makes perfect.

So I am pleased to report that the interior of Duncan Hall was made of painted steel, sheetrock and printed fabric. Not even the wood was brown. Its materials were irrelevant. Its 'structures' were conceptual, not physical. The ideas superseded, digested and replaced the 'thingyness of things' that last stand of the haptics. My giant columnar modules sidelined the last remnants of the puerile numeromancies of 'Classicism', the 'regulating lines' that even Wittkower had admitted were so dull, and easy to perform, that they would never interest a mathematician.

It was reported to me, three years into the life of Duncan Hall, that more people sat with their backs to the windows in Meeting Room No. 1 than sat looking out over the second-floor luxuriance of Rice's evergreen live-oak trees. My reporter, Professor Keith Cooper, put this down to the fact that people could see the polychrome vault of the Shaper Ceiling through the glazed upper half of the wall to the Martell Hall. I gave this phenomenon the name of the 'Trial by Gluteus Maximus' (Figure 18.4).

Find a room overlooking a beautiful park. Place a meeting table parallel to the 'window wall' and count people as they file in to sit (on the gluteus maximus muscle of the posterior). Do this for three years. If more continue to sit with their backs to the park, looking in at the room, you have a decorative culture capable of supporting ideas. If they could discourse a reality, one could achieve nobility. If not, then not.

I had even managed to inscribe the mammalian phylogeny, and the human ontogeny, on the external columns which bracketed the entrances to the five wings. This I had done using iconographies native to the Mayan, Vedic, Hellenic and Renaissance periods. I wished to reflect on such a 'crossing', a miscellaneous miscegenation, down on the Gulf of Mexico. But more important than any of these epiphanies, for such discourses never cease, was the fact that it had all been properly commissioned and built according to all of the vast diversity of necessary technicities of contemporary construction. This was no surly, stubble-chinned, manifestation of 'protest'.

It was Victory.

The professors of Architecture could not accept any of this. Lacking intellectual authority over their own medium, they preferred to lower themselves to the emotional level of the adolescents they supposedly led towards understanding and promote a 'politique du pire' in the hope that the shattered lifespace of the USA, by being made

18.4 Outram's design for the ceiling in Duncan Hall, Rice University

much worse by the deliberate acts of its disaffected architectural intelligentsia (still dreaming, like Peter Eisenmann, of Italian hill villages), would somehow right itself by popular demand. It was a futile ambition. It consistently destroyed cohort after cohort of young minds.

I recalled the plaintive question of one of the professors at the launch of the Cambridge concrete teaching pack. 'But, John,' he asked, 'how do you choose your colours?' What could I reply? They were all embedded in an iconically illiterate design culture – a culture which they were condemned to teach. And they were Men – without even a woman's intuitive capability for colour. We talked 'techne' for a bit and then broke up.

The 1930s Moderne was a short-lived attempt at post-Cubistic surface scripting. It proved intellectually barren. Perhaps this was not surprising considering its brief, two decade, lifespan bracketed by the World Wars. But it was at least capable of a few, too few, graphical felicities. I recall a brasserie in Paris, and the work of Ely Jacques Kahn in New York. Le Corbusier, a failed interior-decorator until his forties, could not even manage these slight effects. Loos neither. He retreated from a sense of the failure of his attempts at decoration (rather ferocious ones) into a chaos of spaces papered with rich veneers – always a sign of iconic decadence. Mies did not even try. He spent a quarter of his budget for the Barcelona Pavilion on slicing a boulder of Anatolian onyx. And that was for a room that did not even have walls – very useful. Only Wright could compose colours and patterns. The demolished Tokyo Imperial Hotel would have been interesting to examine. Not that Wright ever made verbal sense.

Le Corbusier proposed, at the beginning of the twentieth century, to close the academies of decorative art. I have often wondered, after my experiences with our academies of architectural instruction, if things would be improved if they too were shut. But I prefer to believe that all that is needed is for them to procure, even for 'ready money', but certainly with all speed, some credible architectural theory. The first to do so will attract huge funds from a public entirely exhausted by the stupidities of a profession that is today building structures which are a monument to a vast tide of hidden technical defects, consistently 'in denial' of energy efficiency, and absolutely incapable of inscribing a lifespace fit for occupation by a species that can think.

Code, Space and Light

Michiel Riedijk

Take a good look round and you'll see that everything is coloured.

K. Schippers

Code

Architecture is colourless. The designing of architecture is a mental process that finds visual expression in drawings. Played out in the mind of the designer, this process is only made visible in ballpoint doodlings on napkins and cigarette packets or muscular diagrams in fat felt pen strokes on sketching paper. An architectural design is wrested from the mind in clumsy sketches and grimy scale models.

Layout, proportions and measures are established in a bland world of black lines on white paper with no regard for colour, material or cultural significance. In the architectural project, colour is a code. There are codes for unambiguous communication through drawings, codes for distinguishing on site and in all weathers between concrete and plasterboard, magenta for party walls, blue for structure, yellow for services. Colour codes are like an aura of the building to come, voluptuous red for intimacy, cobalt blue for a sublime detachment. These codes can be phoned through from musty airport lounges to the building site.

Thicknesses in microns followed by a number and letter combination define a building's ambience and spatial quality. A watery paste of pigments on an indifferent and preferably homogeneous ground makes a difference between attractive and ugly. Colour is a code in a world of thoughts and evocations which may at some time have to become a reality of brick, concrete, steel, wood and glass.

19.1 Screens of coloured relief glass composed by graphic artist Jaap Drupsteen for Neuterlings & Riedijk's Netherlands Institute for Sound and Vision in Hilversum show famous images from Dutch television

19.2 Inside the Institute for Sound and Vision, the foyer divides the upper auditorium from the subterranean archives

How colour is used and expressed in a building is decided by that building's material form. The distinction between structure and finish made by uncoupling the physical properties of interior and exterior allows colour to be regarded as a separate design layer in the elevations, distinct from the material used. This is both the beauty and the tragedy of using paint to colour buildings. It can be painted over at any time. Thus, expressing the building and its cultural significance is left to the whims of the janitor. Paint as a colour medium would appear to run counter to the architectural desire to express a design in enduring, permanent terms.

Ultimately, the colour of a building and its interior are defined in its most elementary form by brick, wood or concrete and hardly at all by the cocktail of pigments splashed over it. It seems, therefore, that the colour of the material itself is the only true means of expressing the architect's obsessions and desires.

Space

In El Lissitzky's 'Proun Room', spatial form and colour application have been disengaged. Colour planes wrap round corners like gaudy butterflies, drift like coloured ghosts across the transitions between walls and floors or ceilings. The tectonics of the elevation, the anchoring of space in material, grooves, widenings and ridges, has been denied. Lissitzky and later Theo van Doesburg sought in vain to challenge the architectural dictatorship of the spatial form and its materiality by using colour to deny or alter the basic form of interior spaces and volume. Here colour seems to have become an ideological signboard, a doomed painted revolt against the primacy of material and spatial form.

Light

There is the colour of thin translucent slices of lapis lazuli; the brownish yellows of touchy-feely travertine given the kiss of life by the play of natural light; bluish-grey twilight shot through with the red of rear lights on an autumnal November day in Rotterdam. Smudges of red and mesmerizing green out in the mass of coloured glass wash over interiors and frontages. Colour appropriates material when daylight picks out wrinkles in the surface, rudely etched shadow lines or satin-soft bluish-grey concrete. Light invests colour with meaning; whether pale and natural or shrill and artificial, light lends significance to material as the purest of architectural means.

Architecture is space crystallized in material. Material is coloured. Colour is architecture (Figures 19.1, 19.2).

The Illusive Façade

Niall McLaughlin

In December 2002, we won a design competition entitled *Fresh Ideas for Low Cost Housing* organized by the Peabody Trust. The site was in Silvertown in East London, between Royal Victoria Dock and the River Thames. We concentrated on the following design issues:

1 A rational layout of the interior, with a large flexible living space which has unusually high ceilings for low cost housing.
2 The view from the building over the strange post-industrial landscape of the London Docklands.
3 The strange chemical history of the site that in its past had included factories making sugar, coloured dyes, jam, golden syrup, gutta percha, soda, TNT, soap and matches. The glister in the name Silvertown came from Stephen Winkworth Silver who built a rubber factory on the site in 1852 manufacturing wet-weather clothing.
4 The nature of modern industrialized construction, in which a timber frame is wrapped in a decorative outer layer.

We imagined our building as being like a row of packing crates stacked up near the water. However, once you make the timber carcass, you have to wrap it in something, usually a layer of brick, wood, or tiles which returns the industrial product to a reassuringly traditional appearance. For our project we looked at the kinds of industrial wrapping that might be used as the final layer of the building but, given the site history, we wanted something bright and sweet and chemical, and it also had to be inexpensive.

On this project we collaborated with the light artist Martin Richman. He suggested a material called Radiant Light Film – a product by 3M who make everything from dental adhesive to Post-it notes. The film has dichroic properties, that is, colourless metal oxides on the surface of the film that disrupt the reflection of light, producing interference patterns that appear as iridescent colour. As the angle of incidence changes so, too, the colour changes – causing an ever-shifting chromatic relationship between the surface, the light source and the viewer. This effect, which occurs on the surface of petrol and peacock's wings, was discovered by the eighteenth-century

20.1 The installation of dichroic film to the exterior of Niall McLaughlin's Peabody Housing in East London creates an ambiguous architecture – one that dramatically shifts in colour depending upon the angle of view

20.2 Now you see it, now you don't. Seen from a different angle, the Peabody Housing façade chromatics subtly change

French physicist and civil engineer, Augustin Fresnal. He made a study of polarized light and postulated that light moves in a wave-like motion. This had already been suggested by Thomas Young, but while Young had assumed the waves to be longitudinal, Fresnal was convinced that they vibrated at right angles to the direction of their transmission. Consequently, Fresnal explained the phenomenon of double refraction and went on to invent a lens used in lighthouses, searchlights and camera viewfinders that bears his name.

The south façade of the building is wrapped in a cladding of dichroic material held in glass frames. These façade units have a 200mm depth and contain two groups of offset louvres set behind an exterior face of roughcast glass: the first centred within the depth of the case; the second on the back wall. The louvres are fabricated from sheet acrylic, each covered in dichroic film which, being offset from the one in front, cause the filtered range of colour to multiply. Light hitting the façade is reflected back from the different layers – the escaping light captured on the cast-glass front layer to create a

shimmering effect that varies in response to time of day or weather condition (Figures 20.1 and 20.2).

In time, a stand of silver birch trees will add an extra layer to the façade. They will cast shadows on to the surface and in turn catch reflected coloured light. At times the light effect is robustly geometric; at others it is evanescent and fugitive. Our aim is to create a dreamlike quality, as though the image of the façade will not fix completely in the mind. In other words, we wanted to connect our building with the shifting, uncertain and fugitive properties of this place.

Colour

Legorreta + Legorreta Architects

God gave us everything: life, earth, wind and sun.
And all of them have a common value, a marvellous value:
Everything was given with colour!
Without it the world wouldn't exist,
our life would be an unbearable monotony.
Colour is the basis of our life,
Of our happiness and sorrows,
it is the symbol of our emotions.
Colour is … life!
It is not a complement, it is a fundamental element.
Therefore I shout and shout again:
'Viva el color!'

Ricardo Legorreta

Driving to my father's ranch in Texcoco, I found a house with the walls painted in opposite chromatic colours. While I was taking pictures of this intriguing exhibit, the owner appeared and I asked him, 'Why did you paint it this way?' He was surprised by the question, because there wasn't any particular reason. He said: 'Simply because I wanted to paint it that way.'

Ricardo Legorreta

We believe that's what happens with colour all over Mexico. When we go to the markets, when we see the things that the people weave, everywhere colour appears intuitive.

The colours of the Mexican markets are a constant source of inspiration for architecture. The variety is extraordinary, from natural tones to brilliant colours, even extremely strong colours. Colour is an integral part of people's lives.

Chucho Reyes, the naïve Mexican painter, was an inspiration in the use of colour and its incorporation into popular art. Muralists,

21.1 Legorreta + Legorreta's distinctive use of colour on their San Antonio Library, New Mexico, extends the Mexican tradition reaffirmed earlier by the polychromatic exuberance of Luis Barragan

sculptors, painters and architects, we all feel and accept his influence. His use of colour was intuitive, free and happy. If it were not for his talent, it could be said that his use of colour was irresponsible.

We love popular art. It's ingenuous, fresh, intelligent and deep. In popular art, we can see all aspects of life. We like to be surrounded by dolls. We don't like to collect them, but we buy them, we live with them and they disappear.

Through popular art we learn continuously about the freedom of colour. There are no rules, only emotion and true liberty. The results are fantastic.

With respect to colour, we believe that we are self-taught. Of course, we learn from everything we see, but nobody can tell us how to formulate it and what theory we should adopt.

There are moments when we are designing when, instead of saying, 'I am going to do a red wall', we say, 'I'm going to do a red colour that will be a wall.' This is typically Mexican. Sometimes we are more interested in the colour than in the object that has it.

In the office, while working, we talk about colour. Sometimes we make mistakes and we have to change it. What was our mistake? Usually it is simply due to the fact that we didn't achieve the emotional quality that we were seeking.

As in love, each day we love colour more. We cannot live without colour (Figure 21.1).

The Colour of Money (It Doesn't Matter)

Will Alsop

For me, the role of colour in my work is not fundamental; it's merely an aspect of something bigger that I am part of. Form is also incidental. Nonetheless, both colour and form in my work have prompted numerous journalists and critics to ask the question: 'What does it all mean?' I always have to disappoint by not knowing.

I have spent a lifetime eradicating these questions from my soul in a reductive process, diminishing philosophy and theory to the notion (maybe, further). I am making progress.

The cultural baggage that we carry is being off-loaded, slowly; but to start a work we need a noise ... but where does it come from?

I work with people to broaden my own responses and vision. I use painting and its openness to suggest possibilities. Both these democratising practices have led me to the understanding that it does not matter. Choice of colour can be random or indeed left to

22.1 Will Alsop's elevated Sharp Centre building at the Ontario College of Art and Design as photographed by an on-site neighbour who takes shots of the building from his apartment each day

the vagaries of other decisions. In this way it is possible to avoid the tyranny of taste, and open up the world of ideas to a less predict-able and more diverse environment (Figures 22.1, 22.2, 22.3).

I have noticed, and enjoyed, fabric stores where rolls are randomly placed alongside one another. There is no aesthetic judgement made as to the arrangement, and yet the resultant experience is always good.

Boredom is a greater danger to society than any threat. Colour makes a contribution towards the alleviation of ennui, but only if the designer has the intelligence to think the intelligent.

Best practice is worst practice – it is dangerous.

22.2 Will Alsop's project for a 19-floor condominium on Ontario's West Side. The coloured stripes are achieved through the use of powder-coated aluminium and screen-printed glass

22.3 Wintergarden with three restaurant pods above
the main entrance to Will Alsop's Gao Yang project in Shanghai

5

PART 5 COLOUR PSYCHOLOGY AND COLOUR AESTHETICS

Colour is life, we should not scorn this means of instilling life into our works.

Anton Gaudí, 23 January 1915

However, whether an approach to architectural colour is integrated into the design process or supplemental to it, whether haptic and intuitive or academic in intent, the outcome will always embody a colour response. Findings from experiments exploring the way we respond to colour in the architectural setting are dealt with in detail in the colour research and architectural psychology chapters that follow.

It is not surprising to know that the great Catalan architect was inspired by colour; after all, when a new baby is born in Spain, it is greeted with the phrase 'dor a luz' – a new life and light comes into this world! The importance we attach to our perception of light and colour and its emotional effects upon us is not only celebrated by artists, poets and architects, but arouses lifelong passions among different scientists trying to understand and measure its effects upon human beings and life itself.

We need light to see the world around us and colour to add beauty to our aesthetic sensibility. The effects of light and colour on man, however, go beyond our common-sense assumptions and expectations; writers from poets to evolutionary biologists alike have praised man's good fortune. Indeed, Nicholas Humphrey in the first chapter of this book puts forward the proposition that our ability to see colour could have evolved only because it contributes to our biological survival. Rikard Küller's (1981) mammoth *Annotated Bibliography* of 1,700 references, commissioned by the Commission Internationale de l'Eclairage (CIE) summarized the psycho-physiological literature on activation, and firmly established the importance of three systems, mediating the non-visual effects of light and colour: (1) on the cutaneous system. This is activated when ultraviolet and infrared radiation reaches the skin. Skin pigmentation, and the development of vitamin D are some of the main effects; (2) on the pineal-hypothalamic-pituitary system. Light affects the pineal gland where it blocks the sleep hormone melatonin, which in turn influences the hypothalamus which is involved in our emotions, and the pituitary gland which regulates other hormones; (3) on the reticular activation system. Visual stimulation passing through the reticular formation activates the central nervous system as a whole. Both external stimulation through the ARAS and internal activation through the DRAS affect our state of arousal. These effects, and in particular Seasonal Affective Disorder (SAD), are discussed by Professor Rikard Küller in Chapter 27.

The question of whether red is a more activating colour than blue is discussed by reference to two opposing schools of thought. One is based on colour light and measured by physiological changes in the central and autonomic nervous system and the other is based on colour pigment applied in interior and exterior spaces while varying the dimensions of hue, chromatic strength and lightness. Two experiments are discussed where subjects experience realistic full-scale red and blue spaces (and rooms) and where both physiological and affective measures are taken. This is followed by an investigation as to whether differences in hue affect our perception and feeling of warmth at the cognitive as well as the physiological level. The third area considers the hypothesis that red accelerates the subjective experience of time. These experiments are discussed in the context of others conducted over the past 80 years (1926–2008).

Other chapters consider the ongoing debate of colour aesthetics and colour preferences on a longitudinal basis (Mikellides, Chapters 23 and 25) and in relation to the context of colour applied to buildings (Janssens and Küller, Chapter 24). Colour synaesthesia is integral in the music of Bliss's Color Symphony, 'metamorphic variations' and Scriabin's Symphony No. 2, Fourth Movement Tempestuoso, but also in the thoughts of artists and architects. In Chapter 26, a synaesthete student of architecture writes about the subject in relation to his own experience.

Colour psychology is an area increasingly of interest and involving interdisciplinary research of our better understanding of the influence of light and colour on our emotions. It is not surprising to observe that at the latest AIC conference on the subject in Stockholm in 2008, 173 papers were submitted on the subject.

Sir Hugh Casson (1976), writing in the preface of the first edition of this book, said that 'there is no truer colour responsive instrument to be found than man in all his variety, and that the best way to study colour is to use it'.[1] If we keep on using colour, and at the same time observe, measure and study its effects on people, we might be able to answer which chromatic effects belong to the domain of fairy tales and which to the domain of knowledge.

Colour Preference: the longitudinal perspective

Byron Mikellides

Colour preference is a topic which has attracted the 'attention' of nearly every researcher or writer on colour and light psychology, over the past 100 years or so, from Cohn's first empirical study in 1894 to the latest reports on the subject in colour conferences and books. Nicholas Humphrey, in the early 1970s, suggested that rhesus monkeys found blue light more pleasant than red light.[1] In later experiments, however, he suggested that this interpretation of the behavioural results in terms 'pleasantness' as improbable; instead he proposed that monkeys 'do things faster in red than blue light'.[2] Hans Eysenck, 30 years earlier, gained his PhD on the subject and proposed a 'universal order' of preference possibly rooted in biology and related to our aesthetic appreciation. Acking and Küller in their classic 'Interior Space and Colour' study in the 1970s found differences in preference within hues far greater than between hues when they controlled for lightness and chromatic strength. At the AIC Conference on Colour Psychology in 1996, five papers dealt with different aspects of colour preference. The first examined the relationship between colour chips and colour objects (Taft and Sivik); the second examined different theories of colour preference in relation to urban places (R. Küller); the third examined the validity of colour preference as a measure of Personality (L. Oberascher); the fourth examined colour preferences in architectural studios (A. Kiran), and the fifth was on cross-cultural differences in Japan, China and Indonesia (M. Sato). At the AIC conference in Stockholm in 2008, a total of eight papers on colour preference were presented.[3]

Why such interest? What is the practical use of these studies for the design professional? Do they raise any theoretical issues for the psychologist? What can we learn from the various measuring techniques, ranging across observational, qualitative and quantitative methods? Are these techniques valid? Some of these questions will be examined in the light of the findings of a longitudinal study of colour preferences (1970–2007) among architectural students at the Oxford School of Architecture. When lightness and chromatic strength are controlled within a homogenous population, in terms of age, aspirations and interests, do colour preferences change as a result of fashion, marketing and time, or are they stable over time and between the genders?

The findings of this study provide evidence of the strong popularity of and dislike for specific colours, of the general order of preference proposed by Eysenck, and of the influence of fashion, politics and attitudes over time. When Eysenck collected all the published research he could find on the subject in 1941,[4] and calculated the average ranking of colour preference in 21,060 subjects of different cultures, the general order of preference was found to be: 1. Blue, 2. Red, 3. Green, 4. Violet, 5. Orange, 6. Yellow. The order was highly significant and was the same for both genders. However, the actual colours were not specified other than as 'saturated colours'. In the Oxford longitudinal study, the colours used were matched to the same lightness and chromatic strength (2070 R90B, 2070 Y90R, 2070 B90G, 2070 R50B, 2070 Y50R, 2070 G90Y). Students took the rank-ordering preference tests during the first week of their architectural studies, before reading anything on the subject other than their interest in design. The size of the sample was 1,340. The main results are briefly summarized below, followed by a discussion related to previous studies on the subject.

1   The order of preference for the six colours among architectural students remains the same as that identified by Eysenck in 1941. However, as can be seen from Table 23.1, while the order is the same, the strength of the most popular and least popular colours is not.
2   Blue is by far the most popular colour chosen by both genders, while yellow is the least popular colour.
3   Red and green compete in popularity for second place. For male subjects, red is their overall second preference, compared to green for females.
4   Orange is the second least popular colour by both genders.
5   Violet is middling and more popular with the females.
6   Females dislike orange and yellow more than males.
7   With regard to colour preference changes due to fashion, marketing, political attitudes and symbolism, the results of this longitudinal study provide interesting and contrasting changes in colour popularity over the four decades. For example, while orange is the overall second least popular colour over the whole period, it was the most popular colour in 1970 and the second most popular colour in the 1970s, after blue (Figure 23.1).
8   Violet, on the other hand, was most popular in the 1990s, though it did not reach the popularity of orange in the 1970s.

Table 23.1 Mean (average) rankings of colour preferences
(best liked – 1, least liked – 6)

Colour	Overall ranking Oxford	Overall ranking Eysenck	Male Oxford	Female Oxford	Male Eysenck	Female Eysenck
Blue	2.63	1.42	2.64	2.64	1.4	1.6
Red	3.12	2.20	3.08	3.15	2.4	2.5
Green	3.19	3.18	3.25	3.04	2.5	2.52
Violet	3.63	3.92	3.70	3.45	4.3	4.14
Orange	3.97	5.07	3.93	4.14	4.9	5.13
Yellow	4.45	5.21	4.40	4.58	5.5	5.03

9   Another interesting case was the increasing popularity of green since the 1970s. However, it took 20 years to displace blue as the most preferred colour especially in the early 1990s. This can be related to the increasing popularity of green politics, the Green Party at the time, and ecological awareness, particularly among the younger generation.

23.1 Mean ranking preferences over four decades

It is interesting to note in this context that cultural background and age have an influence on colour preference, as the same green sample (B90G 2070), while unpopular with architectural students in the 1970s, was the most popular colour in Botswana and Kenya.[5] Tom Porter also remarked that the same green was also the most liked colour among 60–90-year-olds in Oxford.

It is clear therefore that while age, culture and other factors influence colour preference, there are certain stable relationships regarding the popularity of some colours over time. Support for some of the above findings comes from an unexpected area of study where colour preference tests are used as personality tests aiming to provide a more unconscious personality profile of a person. While this analysis is beyond the scope of this chapter, architecture students during the same period ranked the set of eight colours used by Dr Max Lüscher – each colour being specifically chosen for its emotional value. The overall order of preference based on 960 students over the years 1970–2007 was: 1. blue, 2. green, 3. yellow, 4. red, 5. violet, 6. grey, 7. black and 8. brown. Although these colours were not controlled in terms of the chromatic strength and lightness dimension, blue was still the most preferred colour though it was a much darker colour (R90B 6070). Another interesting result was that Lüscher's vibrant yellow was the third most popular colour chosen.

While colour researcher Dr Leon Oberascher considers that 'a meaningful interpretation of colour preference seems to be more promising within the framework of research on everyday life-styles than personality diagnosis',[6] one must consider studies on experiments which attempted to relate abstract preferences based on aesthetic judgements to preferences related to colour in context. Every researcher is aware of the influence of age, gender, culture and fashion in generalizing from colour preferences, but there are very few contextual studies that can help the designer in practice. The early experiments reported in the first edition of *Colour for Architecture* (1976) by Carl-Axel Acking and Rikard Küller on interior colour and Lars Sivik on exterior colour, where colour was systematically varied in its three dimensions of hue, chromaticness and lightness (whiteness and blackness) found a lack of general results from the evaluation of the 'pleasantness factor'.[7] They found no simple dependence either upon chromatic strength, lightness or hue. The differences found within each hue were much greater than between different hues. These studies were based on simulated colour designs of perspective interior drawings and exterior façades.

Another important issue is whether the preferred colour in abstract colour preference studies involving small colour chips is the same as when colour is an aspect of an object. Very few studies have been published on the subject. Whitfield and Slatten (1979) consider 'prototypicality' – where certain products are identified with certain colours as a key factor, i.e. blue potatoes or blue cheese – will not be preferred as they signify something different.[8]

Lars Sivik and Charles Taft (1996) challenged this view of the reported poor correspondence between colour chips and colour objects.[9] Subjects rated 10 colour chips and 6 digital photos of objects in the same colours as the chips on semantic differential scales. The results show a good correspondence between ratings of colour chips and objects. Out of a total of 390 comparisons between ratings of chips, in only 16 cases (4 per cent) was the colour of the chip judged qualitatively different from the colour of the object. These related to antique chairs and computers and involved red, green and purple where the inappropriateness of colour was important. So prototypicality is important for certain objects which are strongly associated with certain colours. In the same way, lime green and lilac chromatic colours were not as popular in urban restoration work in Lund.[10]

In another study by Sivik (1976) where deep blue and pale lilac – both unusual colours in Sweden – were used in Gothenburg,

people disliked them when evaluating them in a simulation study.[11] However, when people were asked to rate them in the real environment, while their evaluation of the lilac remained unchanged, their evaluation of the blue building became significantly more positive. Occupants of the building liked it even more. In another study in the old part of Stockholm involving the colour restoration of the eighteenth-century building of Maria Ostra, colours of medium chromaticness in the yellow-red sector of the colour circle were rated highly in both the simulated laboratory study as well as in the real environment.

Küller suggests that the key factor for increased pleasantness in the built environment may lie in the balance between complexity and unity.[12] In a restoration experiment, where two-storey buildings of concrete and wood were repainted in dark red with a black cornice, and the doors a strong green and red, when the scheme was evaluated *in situ*, there was an increase in both pleasantness evaluation as well as perceived complexity. In Chapter 24, Jan Janssens and Rikard Küller discuss the latest project of the most recent studies on preferences for the colour of façades, first, in reality and later in the laboratory.

As far as theories explaining the various colour preference studies go, the picture is less promising other than speculative postulates put forward from the results of a single experiment. In the latest published study in *Current Biology* in 2007 by neuroscientist Dr Anya Hulbert, using flash cards of colours of various nuances, concluded that the difference between the genders – indicating a strong preference for red and pinks for females – is so robust that 'they appear to give biological and not simply cultural substance to the old saying: "pink for the girl and blue for the boy"'.[13] The speculative explanation offered was that the fruit-hunting matriarchs have certainly benefited from the ability to home in on ripe red fruits. The same argument was also applied for the most preferred colour blue, that is 'a clear blue sky signalled good weather' and 'clear blue also signals a good water source'. However, if one considers the longitudinal data shown in Figure 23.2, one can see that despite cyclical variations due to fashion and taste, in the past four decades, the second most preferred colour is a competition between green and red, and it is males who like red more than females. Also, in the Lüscher data discussed earlier, the female preference for red is significantly lower than that of males!

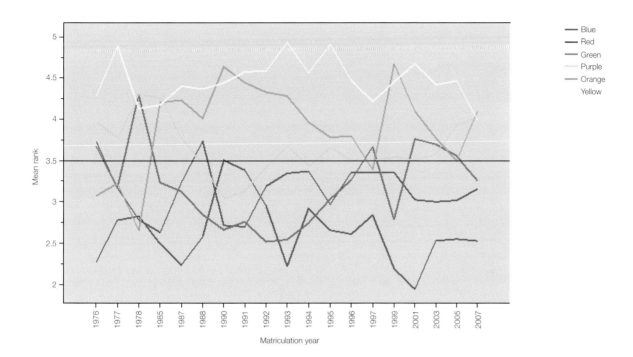

Blue
Red
Green
Purple
Orange
Yellow

Mean rank

Matriculation year

23.2 Mean ranking preferences by year (the lower the mean, the higher the preference)

Colour preference studies, both experimental as well as contextual, will no doubt continue to interest researchers in the field of colour psychology and experimental aesthetics. Theories ranging from biological and wavelength profiles, to 'prototypicality' or 'arousal' will be put forward to explain the colour preference and aesthetic judgements on our ever increasing exposure to colour and light. However, we are not yet in a position to put forward a simple theory which will account for all the empirical studies reported above.

Preferences for Colours on Buildings

Jan Janssens and Rikard Küller

A brief history

It is said that one of the greatest painters of the last century was once asked what his favourite colour was. 'Blue', he stated, but when asked to justify his choice, he promptly changed his answer: 'Well, red, then.' True or not, this story illustrates the dilemma of colour preferences among professionals. The layperson, on the other hand, does not seem to be afflicted by the same doubts. This is amply demonstrated in numerous studies on colour preferences carried out since the end of the nineteenth century, for instance: 'The color preferences of 559 full blood Indians' (Garth, 1922); 'Color preferences in the insane' (Katz and Breed, 1922); 'Color preferences of extroverted and introverted individuals' (Rakshit, 1946); 'Colour preferences of criminals and noncriminals' (Akhtar and Swigh, 1974). That not even our close relatives were spared can be exemplified by a study of the 'Color preferences in the Gibbon' (Wilson and Danco, 1976) – see Küller, for a review.[1]

At the height of this research, the German psychologist, Hans Eysenck, compiled over 20,000 preference ratings carried out in previous experiments in what we would today call a meta-analysis. In his famous paper of 1941, Eysenck concluded that colours were preferred in the following order: blue, red, green, violet, orange and yellow (see Figure 23.1).[2] Eysenck's study had an enormous influence on all those who engage in colour design. However, one objection that can be raised against most of the older studies is that the colours were presented on slips of paper. This lack of context means that we cannot know whether Eysenck's general order of preferences will be valid when colours are applied to real objects, for instance, on a building. Another objection is that in many of the early studies the colours were poorly specified. To talk about red and green colours is rather vague, and without further details there is no way of knowing whether the 'red' in one study matched the 'red' in another study.

The Swedish psychologist, Lars Sivik, was probably the first to carry out a scientific study of the perception of building exteriors in different colours. He applied more than 60 colours to two types of buildings – 'high-rise house' and 'low-rise house' – by means of a photographic simulation technique.[3] The colours were carefully described by means of the Swedish Natural Color System, and the results were presented as isosemantic maps of the colour space. One main conclusion of this laborious work was that colour preferences for buildings differ considerably from colour preferences in general.

Today, science is much better equipped to tackle the complicated questions of colour preference in the real world. Since the 1960s, our research group at the School of Architecture and Built Environment, Lund University in Sweden, has been developing methods to assess people's attitudes and reactions to the built and natural environment – a scientific field now known as Environmental Psychology. One of our main areas of interest has been the study of colours in indoor spaces and in urban architecture. Such studies have been carried out both in the field and in the laboratory. One aim has been to study the possible effects of indoor colours on the well-being and comfort of those who are exposed to the colours for some time. Another aim of our research has been to find out how the appearance of a building can be changed by means of colours, and how this in its turn might influence the perception of and preference for the building. This will be described below in some detail.

Computer simulation of buildings in different colours

In one of our more recent studies, preferences for the colours of building façades were investigated, first, in reality and later on in the laboratory.[4] After a considerable search, we settled for four buildings in Malmö, a medium-sized town in the south of Sweden not far from Lund. Each building had a distinct character, and the choice represented everything from housing and office buildings to industrial premises. Each of the buildings was photographed, taking great care to include also the closest surroundings to the left and right of the building. The next step was to load the pictures into a computer and change the colour of the predominant building in a systematic way. In addition to white, two varieties each of yellow, red, blue and green were employed. Finally, the outcome was converted into colour slides.

Some 150 people of both genders varying in age between 17 and 60 took part in the actual experiment. The participants consisted of students at a university in southern Sweden, none of whom were specializing in architecture or aesthetic design. Their task was to express their preferences for the four buildings, presented in the nine colours mentioned above, on a response form by means of four-grade scales. Effects of learning and fatigue were controlled for by showing the 36 images in two different orders of presentation (this is known as a balanced experimental design). The participants were also shown a picture, which contained the nine colour samples but no buildings, and were asked to rank their preferences for the colours themselves.

The results showed that several different things had an influence on the participants' preferences. Irrespective of colour, some of the buildings were better liked than others. Best liked was a little, old one-family house, followed by a modern office building and an apartment house, whereas the industrial building was the least liked. However, the preferences were also influenced by the colours, and the soft yellow and white were generally most appreciated, whereas the two green, and the soft red variety, were the least liked. The rank order between the buildings mostly remained the same, irrespective of which colour they had, but there was one marked exception. The strong yellow colour was fairly well liked, but not when it appeared on the industrial building. As concerns the participants, there was a slight difference between genders, males sometimes preferring the stronger variety, whereas females preferred the softer variety, of the same colour (Figure 24.1).

Based on these results, it is now possible to compare the preferences for coloured buildings with the preferences of colours as such. We will first compare the participants' preferences among themselves. In the first row of Table 24.1, the overall preferences of the coloured buildings have been rank-ordered from 1 to 9, where 1 represents the most preferred colour and 9 represents the least preferred colour on all the buildings taken together. The second row shows the ranks of the colours as such. Obviously, there are some similarities, for instance, for the reds, and for the soft green, but also considerable differences. The strong blue is first ranked by itself but ranked sixth on the buildings. The white shows the opposite pattern and ranks much higher on buildings than by itself. When we compare our participants' preferences for colours only with the results from Eysenck's study, there is considerable consistency except for the yellow, which seems to be much more

24.1 The preferences for a building are strongly influenced by its colours. Soft yellow and white colourations are generally most appreciated, whereas green and soft red colours are least liked. Illustrations shows order of preference for one of the buildings from best liked (top left) to least liked (bottom right)

Table 24.1 Rank order of colours of buildings and of colour samples. The bottom row is an approximation of Eysenck's results

Colour	Y +	Y -	R +	R -	B +	B -	G +	G -	W
Buildings	4	1	3	7	6	5	9	8	2
Colours only	2	4	3	8	1	7	5	9	6
Eysenck 1941*	7.5	–	3.5	–	1.5	–	5.5	–	–

*Ranks from Eysencks' study have been adjusted to be comparable to ours.

appreciated today than it was 65 years ago. Is this an effect of the manner in which the colours were presented, or is it an effect of time itself? Of this we cannot be certain.

Why are some colours preferred to others?

At least in Sweden, people seem to prefer more subdued and traditional façade colours on most buildings, with the natural earthy hues as the most predominant. To understand the reasons behind this we will have to consider three different kinds of circumstances: the biological, the cultural, and the individual. Evolution has endowed humans with one of the most advanced colour visions in the animal world. Without going into physiological details, we can conclude that the ability to perceive thousands of different colours must have had, over the millennia, a great survival value. To our ancestors it must have been of vital importance to be able to judge the ripeness of a fruit, or the angry warning of a flushed face. The human brain is pre-programmed, through its DNA, to respond to some colours with increased interest and attention.

We also have to reckon with the continuous impact of the traditions and artefacts of human society. Each culture, and subculture, has its own colour tradition. By using the same colours over again in specific settings, every member of the group will learn to value some of them and dislike others. Political parties and religious communities excel in the symbolic use of colour. Red, black, brown, purple – do they not mean something to every one of us? In the Islamic religion, a certain green colour, Munsell 7.5G 8/4,

holds a specific significance. According to the index of paint sales in Turkey, this colour is highly preferred in religious parts of the country, and this tradition has been taken with them by country people when they move to the big cities. However, in contrast to our biological heritage, the cultural meaning of colour can gradually change. In Sweden, the combination of blue and yellow (the colours of the Swedish flag) is used to signify national pride. Today, the same colours will make some people feel highly embarrassed.

In addition to the general biological and specific cultural factors, preference for a certain colour may be uniquely individual. Childhood experiences are especially important in establishing such a preference, for instance, the colour of a favourite toy. By means of the new techniques of brain imaging, we are beginning to understand the mechanisms behind such imprinting. It involves links between the sensory parts of the cortex and specific nuclei for reward and aversion, among others located in the limbic system of the brain. Such preferences are highly resistant to extinction and have a lasting effect on the individual's behaviour later in life. However, the highly flexible human brain is constantly prepared for revisions and additions even later in life.

Returning to which colours are preferred on buildings, the results of our own, until now unpublished, research support the conclusion that both biological and cultural factors are at work.[5] The relationship between the colour of the building itself and its surroundings seems highly relevant. The building in question must not stand out too much but, on the other hand, it should not be completely inconspicuous. To deviate a little, but not too much, from the

surroundings will attract the attention of the onlooker and, generally, create a positive evaluation (Figure 24.2). Furthermore, the colour of the building should, within certain limits, meet the expectations of the beholder. In traditional environments with small-scale dwellings, any deviation from the original colour scheme might remain unpopular for a long time. In modern, large-scale settings, on the other hand, new and surprising colorations might be quickly accepted. Thus, colours are not only a matter of personal taste and, even if a colour is inherently beautiful, in the context of the built environment other factors might be much more important.

Colour, Arousal, Hue-Heat and Time Estimation

Byron Mikellides

In both scientific and introspective accounts, colours have been classified and grouped in various ways depending upon the hypothesized influence or effects of such groupings.[1] One of the most widely held groupings is that of 'warm' and 'cool' colours. Hues such as red, orange, and yellow are seen in addition to their warmth, as exciting and stimulating, whereas hues such as blue, turquoise and green are seen, in addition to their induced coolness, as calming and relaxing (this has been referred to in the scientific literature as the 'hue-heat hypothesis'). Applications based on these properties of colours are not confined to the work of architects and artists but also to clinicians in an attempt to pacify or calm down aggressive and anxious patients by using blue and green colours. They are also used to stimulate depressed patients by using red and orange colours.[2]

Some researchers have criticized these studies and suggested that the effect of hue on warmth and excitement is an intellectual one, involving cognitive processes, and not based on physiological processes which affect the whole organism. In an attempt to answer this type of criticism, namely, that the effects of these colours are not only based on stereotyped verbal associations, but also that different colours actually evoke different feeling and emotions affecting the entire organism, Robert Gerard, in his classic study in 1958,[3] concluded that the two wavebands of radiant energy at the opposite ends of the visible spectrum, i.e., blue and red, exert a differential biological influence on the organism as measured by general activation in the central and autonomic nervous system: EEG (electroencephalogram), blood pressure, palmar conductance level, respiration, EKG (electrocardiogram) and heart rate.

Further support is given to Gerard's work by an experiment carried out by Ali in 1972.[4] Coloured lights (blue and red) were projected directly on the eyes of 10 normal subjects for 6 minutes and EEG were recorded throughout the period. The results of this study showed greater cortical arousal following the presentation of Red light and lower cortical arousal following a Blue light.

Parallel to these attempts to validate the reported effects of the warm and cold colours through physiological measures, there has been a different approach to establish the meanings people associate with different colours. This approach differs significantly for the above in that: (1) the three dimensions of colours (hue, chromatic strength, and lightness) were systematically manipulated in an attempt to ascertain their relationship to the dimensions of colour meaning; and (2) the data thus obtained were treated by more powerful methods of statistical analysis such as factor and cluster analysis which were not available to the early researchers.

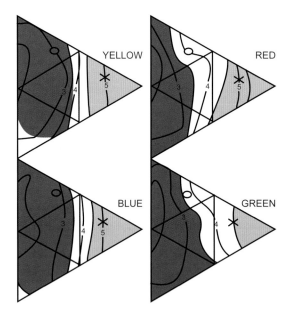

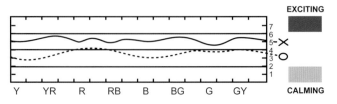

25.1 Compare the O and X in each of the four triangles Y, R, B, G. The perception of excitement increases as chromatic strength increases. Source: After Sivik (1976)

Lars Sivik was the first to demonstrate, using the technique of photo simulation, that it was not hue which affects how exciting or calming a colour is but the chromatic strength of each hue (Figure 25.1).[5] Acking and Küller also showed with the use of perspective drawings of interior spaces, and later on in full-scale spaces, that weak colours give a room an impression of calm while strong colours give an impression of excitement.[6]

The four studies referred to above were well designed by serious researchers in the field of colour psychology. Within their own parameters, they show systematic relationships between colour and 'arousal' through physiological measures (Ali, Gerard) and through semantic differential analysis (Sivik and Küller).

There are, however, some fundamental differences between the two sets of studies. In the first two studies, the content of colour stimulation was coloured light while in the last two studies the content was colour pigment. Furthermore, in the first two studies, subjects experienced the colour light stimulation in an abstract form in the laboratory, while the last two studies were carried out in the context of simulated interior and exterior spaces.

The two experiments described below were intended to bridge the gap between these sets of experimental approaches. Why not measure both physiological as well as affective reactions of people? Why use patches of coloured light projected on the retina, colour slides, or even small drawings and simulated spaces when we can use surface pigments in real-life places – the sort of spaces we actually experience? Test not only exposure of 60-seconds intervals but longer periods when subjects could be experiencing real environments. The main technique used in this experiment to measure activation is through EEG and EKG.

When a person is awake but relaxed, alpha rhythm abounds. This rather slow, high amplitude rhythm has a tendency to disappear when the person is stimulated, but returns when the person is relaxed. Too much stimulation results in continuous blocking of alpha, involving the whole nervous system, a state generally referred to as stress. Thus, by measuring the proportion of alpha in EEG, it is possible to find out whether an environment is under-stimulating or over-stimulating. Changes in pulse rate can also be used as an indicator of activation and stress, though this is more difficult to interpret.

At the Environmental Psychology Unit, School of Architecture of the Lund Institute of Technology, a room measuring 3.5 x 4.5m, with an adjoining control room where the monitoring equipment was placed, was used for the experiment (Figure 25.2). One half of the room was painted red (NCS 1674-Y9OR), the other half was painted blue (NCS 1859-BO4G). Paint covered the walls, floor, ceiling, and fittings.

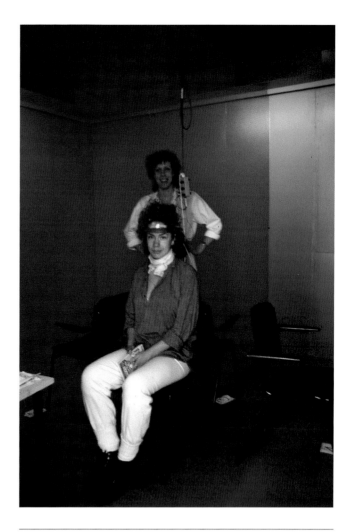

25.2 Participant after the attachment of electrodes in the experimental room (Experiment 1)

Blue was chosen instead of green because the spectral sensitivity of the eye is about the same in the blue and the red regions, while the sensitivity is different in the green region. The general lighting of the room was provided by Luma Colorette, a fluorescent tube which has an even spectral emission and good colour rendering (5400 Kelvin, CRI-91). It was important in this study to use colour samples which would satisfy not only the NCS parameters and colorimetric measurements, but also the correct subjective evaluation of colour appearance. This test was satisfactory and the two colour samples conformed to the mapping of colour names in Sweden.[7] Temperature was maintained at a constant level through the automatic sensor at 22°C. The participants wore lightweight garments throughout the experiment. In order to measure the EEG, electrodes were placed centrally and parientally, over the left and right hemispheres. A pair of electrodes was also used to record the pulse. The frequencies for the EEG analyses were in accordance with clinical classification.

Twenty-four subjects took part in this study. Each subject spent 20 minutes in each colour. Each condition was divided into three parts: 'reading', 'fixating', and 'closing eyes'. After the experiment, electrodes were removed and the subjects' introspection was taken. Time estimation and galvanic skin response measures were taken during this period. It was hypothesized that the red visual field should be more activating, which should be indicated by attenuation of the alpha rhythm, and possibly the delta and theta rhythms.

The data were treated by means of several analyses of variance for both EEG and EKG recordings. The most important result of this study was, paradoxically, that there were no statistically significant differences in the experience of a red or blue space on the central nervous system. Arousal at the cortical level was the same for both red and blue. Arousal as measured by reduced alpha was, in fact, in the opposite direction from the predicted one: there was more alpha and theta in the red visual field than in the blue one. There was also more delta activity (a brain activity indicative of a sleepy condition) in the red visual field than in the blue one.[8]

At the autonomic nervous system level there were no differences in EKG (pulse rate, arrhythmia) and galvanic skin response. Although autonomic measures are not accurate indicators of arousal and are often more susceptible to individual variation, they produced almost identical mean scores for the two conditions. There were

differences in all EEG frequencies between the male and female groups, but these were not the differences we were looking for. There were no differences between either the male subjects or the female subjects with regard to the red and blue spaces.

The results of this experiment support Sivik and Küller's findings: provided we control chromatic strength and lightness, there are no differences between the two hues as far as excitement is concerned.

In another study involving two seminar spaces, one painted red (BSI O4E53) and the other turquoise (BSI 16E53) at the Oxford School of Architecture, both high in chromatic strength, two groups of subjects (architecture students and laymen), evaluated the two spaces as equally stimulating.[9]

In this experiment, the strongest red paint on the market was tested. Its actual specified strength was 15 per cent more than the blue sample under standardized conditions. The two colours used were judged to be subjectively equal in chromatic strength and lightness. Yet no differences were found. The implications of this research for design is clear. For colour exposure of up to 20 minutes, this supports Sivik's affective-connotative studies that chromatic strength (saturation) is the key dimension affecting how exciting or calming a colour is perceived and not the dimension of hue as was previously thought by colour design manuals.

In the second experiment, two identical spaces, measuring 2.8 x 2.9m were painted Red and Blue respectively (NCS 1958 Y90R and NCS 2158 B09G) in the Lighting Laboratory at Lund University (Figure 25.3). Appointments were individually made with 24 male and female subjects for two three-hour sessions per subject on two different occasions within a two-week period. During the two periods, EEG and EKG recordings were taken and the subjects completed various forms measuring a variety of subjective reactions, including temperature and time estimation as well as environmental description by means of semantic differential scales and story writing.

Special attention was given to the design of the interior spaces. The aim was to make each room feel as normal as possible without losing the distinct feeling of immersion in blueness or redness. Two special abstract oil paintings were commissioned by the Swedish artist Gunnar Sandin, to add some character to each room. The floor was covered with matt grey linoleum. The curtains were drawn so that the subject was not tempted to watch the outside world, yet offering an unmistakable feeling of a homely window. The curtains were white with a faint floral pattern of either red or blue of low chromatic strength (NCS, C = 20%). The entrance to each experimental room was covered with a full drape instead of a door to add a little more interest to the space. Temperature was maintained at around 22°C by means of thermostats.

The most important result of this study is that as far as cortical arousal is concerned, there is positive support for the hypothesis that red is a more activating colour than blue as indicated by difference in delta frequency ($p = 0.018$) and the strong tendency in alpha ($p = 0.161$). Delta rhythm is indicative of a drowsy state and characterized by high amplitude, low frequency waves; the difference between the two colours in delta was observed in both hemispheres and in both stage when measurements were made, that is, during the first and second hour of colour exposure. During the second period of exposure, subjects were more relaxed (as indicated by an increase in delta activity) for both colours. As far as alpha activity is concerned, there was a strong trend in support of the main hypothesis. This tendency, however, did not reach statistical significance. This suggests that when the subjects have been in a room for nearly two hours, the effect of colour is even stronger than during the first hour. There were no differences in the theta and beta frequencies between the colours. All the analyses reported here were also carried out with room illumination as a covariate; this did not alter the results presented here.

As far as cortical activity is concerned, the results of this experiment support, in a qualified way the previous results of Ali (1972) and Gerard (1958) with coloured light.

In the autonomic nervous system, however, the picture is very different. In this experiment pulse rate was higher in the Blue room at 71.5 beats per minute and lower in the Red room at 68.4 beats per minute ($p = 0.03$). These results are the opposite of the hypothesis stated by Gerard (1958). Whether light or pigment, they are also the

25.3 The Red and Blue experimental rooms (Experiment 2)

opposite of the hypothesis formulated by all other researchers.[10] The only other colour study which offered an alternative hypothesis to heart rate was that of Küller (1976).[11] In observing that the heart rate was slower in a colourful room than the grey one at one-hour, two-hour and three-hour intervals, he put forward the hypothesis that cortical arousal is accompanied by cardiac deceleration. This line of theorizing is also in accordance with work by Lacy and Lacy.[12]

Another interesting finding is in the case of arrhythmia (variability of heart rate) which was higher in response to red than blue. Is this negative relationship between heart rate and variability of heart rhythms another case where a compensatory homeostatic mechanism is working within the autonomic nervous system? The combined use of variability and level of heart rhythms is certainly a novel way to evaluate the autonomic balance, which merits further investigation.

There are several theoretical implications and practical applications of this research. At the theoretical level, the validity and reliability of the various cortical and autonomic measures are brought into question. The link between EEG and EKG as well as their relationship to affective measures is also of theoretical interest. The hypothesis regarding cortical arousal and cardiac deceleration also deserves more experimental work. At the practical level chromatic strength was shown to be important at the cognitive-affective level through a variety of subjective studies. First impressions could be important to the designer and there appears to be no differences in the most saturated red and blue colours available commercially in affecting visual excitement. However, longer periods of up to two hours show differences in hue affecting our organism at the physiological level, provided the colours used are not so overpowering and when colour constancy is controlled by leaving enough reference points unpainted.

The hue-heat and the blue-flame hypotheses

Just as in the review of the psychological literature on colour and emotional arousal there are conflicting directives between colour connotation studies and laboratory experiments with regard to the importance of the hue dimension on the subjective feeling of warmth and heat. Furthermore, there is the observation by artists and scientists that although Blue is considered cold and

25.4 Mean heart rate in Blue room and Red room after 1 – 40 min and 2 – 110 min

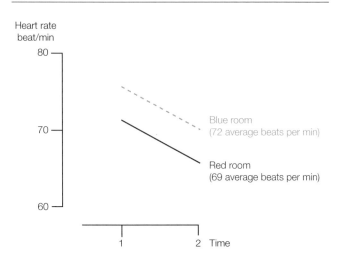

cool, the blue of a gas flame is hotter than that of an orange or red flame! Indeed, when James Turrell, the renowned artist and psychologist, gave the keynote address to the AIC International Conference in Oslo prior to the new millennium, he made the impassionate plea to 'stop teaching the colour wheel unless you are going to teach the spectrum'. He went on to say: 'Stop teaching colour symbology. Red is not warm and cool is not blue, it is just the opposite.'

The problem is that all the anecdotal reports that Red is considered a warm colour and Blue a cold colour is strongly supported by the vast majority of the published perceptual and cognitive studies.[13] These studies used colour samples, simulated colour spaces in the form of colour slides and drawings, coloured light in a variety of contexts on a longitudinal basis. This shows that time, taste, culture or other intervening variables could not have been responsible for the consistency of their findings.

However, none of the five or so laboratory studies to date,[14] which have attempted to measure the difference by means of behavioural, physiological and temperature estimation techniques, have succeeded in finding a measurable difference of any practical importance.

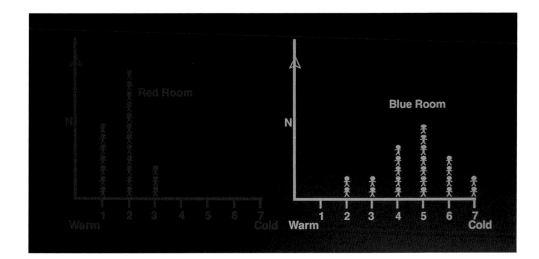

What are the implications of these studies for the designer? There is no doubt that the inducement of visual warmth by exposure to Red light or Red paint is elicited in a variety of contexts. Men and women from various cultures and various ages report this apparent warmth consistently, and as such it has direct design implications for the professional. Architects are involved not only in designing buildings but in creating spaces with certain perceived qualities and atmosphere. By manipulating the hue dimension, they can create a space which people will perceive as warm or cold at the cognitive level. Whether designers want to provide an immediate impression of warmth or coldness as people pass through a space or spend some time in it, the impression of apparent warmth is real in the sense of being consistently reported as such.

The hue-heat hypothesis has in fact been given support by Fanger, Breum and Jerking (1977) though the difference in perceived temperature associated with colour was small at 0.4°C, and was argued by the three experimenters to be of no practical significance.[15] This study, however, supports the notion that the direction of apparent warmth along the line of the perceptual studies may have some basis at the physiological level, which could be detected by the development of more refined techniques in the future. However, the implication of the hue-heat hypothesis for the practising engineer, as compared to the architect, who is interested in direct measurable difference in comfort rating, is missing. As such, it cannot be used for energy conservation in any serious way, and the scepticism

of heating engineers is understandable. In fact, regarding the only study where participants spent long periods of time,[16] there were statistically significant difference between the first and second-hour temperature evaluations; that is, the perceived temperature was estimated colder in the second period (after 90 minutes) or the magnitude of 0.8°C in a Red Room and 0.7°C in a Blue Room – while the real temperature went up by 0.5°C. At the same time, no statistically significant differences between the two rooms were found as far as colour was concerned. This experiment epitomizes the existing state of knowledge as far as the conflicting conclusions between the perceptual and laboratory studies are concerned; for while the same subjects reported no differences between the two rooms in temperature estimation, highly significant differences ($p < 0.001$) were obtained in the subjective evaluation of apparent warmth based on the semantic scale of warmth = (1), cold = (7), mean score for Red = 1.8 and mean score for Blue = 4.7 (Figure 25.5). This observation was also supported by the participants' comments in the open-ended question regarding the atmosphere of the room, as well as their story writing. Clearly the validity of the hue-heat hypothesis depends upon whether the design implications concerned are considered at the cognitive level or at the physiological level.

James Turrell's passionate plea to stop teaching the colour wheel and colour symbology adds another dimension to the debate. Perhaps the lack of support of the laboratory experiments to date is a testimony of his support of the blue flame hypothesis. Perhaps Richard Gregory's conclusion is appropriate here in that 'there is a conflict between designing experiments simple enough for analysis and sufficiently complex to reveal the full richness of phenomena'.[17]

Colour and time estimation

The review of the literature on colour and time estimation does not resolve the conflicting reports regarding the hypothesis that Red accelerates the subjective passage of time.[18] The experimental evidence from all published studies to date using both coloured light and colour pigment at various exposure times have shown no consistent differences in the estimation of time intervals. Nor is the hypothesis that greater physiological arousal causes the acceleration of subjective time supported by Caldwell and Jones (1985)[19] using 30- and 45-second intervals (coloured light) or Mikellides [20] using 25- and 95-minute intervals (surface pigment). The various direct implications of this work reported in books and design manuals is not therefore borne out by our knowledge of the subject based on perceptual and laboratory studies. Whereas there are consistent differences between perceptual and laboratory studies in hue-heat, for time estimation there are conflicting reports within the perceptual studies, as well as within laboratory studies. The likelihood is that other variables, such as individual differences, arousal, preferences and context mediate in these findings. The interaction between and interdependence among these variables may prove a formidable task for future research. This is illustrated in the experiment by Humphrey and Keeble[21] who found that background noise decreases the time monkeys spent in Red compared to white lights but only to those monkeys who find the noise aversive in the first place!

All that may be tentatively said at this stage is that if exposure to red accelerates the subjective passage of time for short intervals,[22] then the observation cited in Mikellides and Porter (1976)[23] that factory workers spent less time in toilets painted red than blue may be explained by the faster subjective time clock hypotheses and may be said to have some repercussions for spaces involving short stay intervals! However, the studies involving longer time intervals at Lund and Oxford do not lend themselves to this hypothesis. The case therefore of the direct effects of colour on time estimation cannot be made.

Colour Synaesthesia:
seeing sound and hearing colour

Andrew Jones

Synaesthesia is a neurological condition, a cross-sensory experience in which one sensory stimulus is accompanied by another, different sensory stimulus. For instance, to synaesthetes, numbers, letters and musical notes or chords may appear to be coloured. Even words can also evoke a particular personality. While it may appear to be an over-developed tendency for sensory metaphor, e.g. 'gloomy day', as a sensation, it embodies qualities that set it apart and suggest that it is a genuine perceptual phenomenon. For example, the sensation is always vivid; it is an automatic or involuntary response to a stimulus. Furthermore, the same experience occurs consistently over time, is highly memorable and is one that synaesthetes have experienced since childhood.

Recent studies suggest that the synaesthetic condition is moderately prevalent, that is, one in 23 people experience the phenomenon. Although tending to be clustered within families, possibly as an inherited trait of the X chromosome, synaesthesia is not necessarily always congenital. It can also occur, at least temporarily, as a result of external influence, such as from psychoactive drugs like LSD, or be triggered by eye disease, migraines or brain damage. This condition is known as 'adventitious synaesthesia'. Non-synaesthetes can often experience a form of 'pseudo-synaesthesia', that is, when they find themselves considering one sensory experience to embody aspects of another, such as when a piece of music is described as 'bright'. While this suggests that the mind considers the senses, at least, to conceptually share experiences, it is, nevertheless, set apart from genuine synaesthesia. This is because it is not a consistent or involuntary reaction, nor is it innate – one that can be said to have been experienced since childhood.

Not to be considered as a dysfunctional or debilitating condition, synaesthesia does not interfere with a person's quality of life nor with their ability to function normally. Indeed, most synaesthetes would view their condition as a gift, and would find it difficult to consider their perception of the world as anything but 'normal'.

However, the condition is capable of providing insight into the human condition. Scientifically speaking, the study of this phenomenon should be able to tell us a great deal about the processes of the brain.

The synaesthetic experience can vary from person to person; in particular there is an experiential difference between 'projective' and 'associative' synaesthesia. For example, when graphemes (symbols such as letters and numbers) produce a colour sensation, some synaesthetes experience this as being 'projected' on to the written symbol while others, the majority, will tend to experience the colour by association, that is, in the mind's eye. When a stimulus produces a synaesthetic effect, it is known as an 'inducer', with the resulting synaesthetic experience being the 'concurrent' effect.

There are other forms of synaesthesia. For example, days of the week, dates, numbers, etc., can embody personalities or, in some cases, genders. In another type of synaesthesia, numbers may appear in spatial 'mental maps', known as 'number forms', when a digit will occupy its own fixed position in space. However, there are two basic forms of colour synaesthesia: music–colour and grapheme–colour.

(1) Music–colour synaesthesia

In this form of synaesthesia, colour is experienced as a result of a musical sound such as a tone, key or timbre. The particular inducer can vary between synaesthetes, including any one or a combination of stimuli. Some people, like Beethoven, Scriabin and Sir Arthur Bliss, may experience only musical keys to be coloured, while others may experience both chords and individual notes as embodying colours. However, there is some consistency between individual synaesthetes as most report that as pitch becomes higher, colour becomes brighter.

Music is often experienced in terms of much more than simple hues. There is often great variation in the chromaticness and/or whiteness of the colour – a consensus that depends upon factors such as in what key or octave the tone is played. Musical passages can also induce the sensation of coloured shapes; often colours move about, metamorphose into shapes or, as the music progresses, stream in and out of the mental field of view.

(2) Grapheme–colour synaesthesia

This type of synaesthesia is the most common, when each individual grapheme (letters, numbers, etc.) appears to have its own colour with which it is shaded or tinted. Typically, there is no consensus between synaesthetes as to which letters are imbued with which colours. However, when the condition is examined among large groups of subjects, it has been shown that there are some consistencies, such as the letter 'A' frequently being said to be 'red'.

Synaesthetic colour is a fascinating phenomenon. Scientific studies of its vivid, often dramatic experiences show that a synaesthetic perception is one similar to that of 'real' colour. Indeed, to a synaesthete, the colour experience of, for example, a musical chord, is as real and normal an experience as a non-synaesthete seeing printed colour on a sheet of paper.

A personal account

This writer is a synaesthete; I experience both music–colour and grapheme–colour synaesthesia, although the latter is not as strong as the former. I have had synaesthesia as long as I can remember, but I wasn't fully aware of it until I was 17. The reason for this early lack of awareness was possibly because, when I perceived colours in certain situations, it was so innate to my perception that I didn't realise I was seeing colours; it was simply how these events were perceived and I didn't know that they could be perceived any differently. Nevertheless, when I think back, I am able to recall memories of, say, a particular letter or musical chord, as having its own hue. These tend to appear in my mind's eye as sensations or shapes of colour set against a black background, and occasionally occupying their own positions in space.

My most vivid synaesthetic experiences arise from music. While tones have their own hues, chords produce much stronger colour sensations. For example, the chord 'A' is a pale, greyish green, 'B' is a purplish red and 'C' is a light lemon yellow. Minor chords tend to trigger the same hues as their major counterparts, but in darker, more sombre nuances.

As with other synaesthetes, the higher the pitch, these hues become brighter. However, sometimes heightened pitch can also make hue more or less saturated; at other times, for example, with distorted guitar music, the colour can appear more 'fuzzy' or less defined. Often, complete pieces or passages of music will have their own colour – independent of any colours of tones or chords within the piece. I suspect that this over-riding colour experience is related to the key as, for example, music in the key of 'G' tends to induce an overall orange sensation. Sometimes, as a melody progresses, it will describe shifting coloured shapes against a black background. Furthermore, when listening to orchestral pieces featuring multiple instruments, they become 'separated'; as differently coloured and differentially shifting and changing shapes. The shapes appear either one on top of another or spatially closer or further away. In these experiences, there is always the strong sensation of the instruments being 'layered' one upon another. For instance, when listening to Johann Pachelbel's 'Canon in D', I always perceive this as an overlay of a series of shifting pink lines. As more instruments are added, more lines appear until, when the harmony becomes richer, they increasingly intermingle until a final culmination in a total suffusion of pink in the final chord.

As well as music, I also perceive numbers and letters as having their own hues. Experienced in the mind's eye, this is associative rather than projective – numbers or letters appearing in their 'appropriate' colours against a black background (Figure 26.1). For instance, the number 3 appears as a bright orange, while the number 4 is a deep

26.1 Andrew Jones' letter and number synaesthetic colour associations

blue. In my synaesthesia, the letter 'S' is bluish-green, the letter 'B' a dark crimson hue – much darker and more chromatic than the similar hue experienced from the sound of a B chord or note. For me, reading is not an especially colourful experience because, rather than project the colours onto the letters, I experience them internally. However, if I focus on a letter, it is immediately recognised as possessing its own hue personality. Words are also often imbued with colour, a sensation often triggered by the first letter of the word but occasionally by another letter. Words can also change colour as they are read, a transformation caused by a prominent change in the letters that form it.

The various studies of the phenomenon demonstrate that synaesthesia is a genuine perceptual reality. They also help us understand the neurological differences that occur in the synaesthetic brain. Explanations point to the existence of connections between form-processing and colour-processing centres that do not occur in normal brains. There are also a number of models of neurological pathways that potentially explain synaesthesia. For instance, one suggests that outputs from the form-recognition and colour-recognition pathways in the brain are associated. As this association occurs after each stimulus recognition, this model implies that the condition is more conceptual than perceptual. A second possibility involves feedback down each sensory pathway. In the synaesthetic brain, feedback from the convergence of the two pathways may be disinhibited, allowing information from the colour-recognition pathway to travel back down through the form-recognition pathway, or vice versa. A third model proposes patterns of horizontal cross-wiring between the form-processing and colour-processing pathways, allowing information to move between pathways at one or more points. Since a certain degree of cross-wiring already exists in normal brains, this idea carries a certain amount of weight and would suggest that these crossed wires are simply more prevalent in people with synaesthesia.

It is, of course, entirely possible that the truth reflects a combination of some of these models, or even all of them. Given the many varieties of synaesthetic experience, it is possible that different synaesthetic pathways occur in different individuals.

Further reading

Baron-Cohen, S. and Harrison, J. (eds) (1997) *Synaesthesia: Classic and Contemporary Readings*, Oxford: Blackwell Publishers.

Harrison, J. (2001) *Synaesthesia: The Strangest Thing*, Oxford: Oxford University Press.

Robertson, L. and Savig, N. (eds) (2005) *Synaesthesia: Perspectives from Cognitive Neuroscience*, Oxford: Oxford University Press.

Sagiv, N., Simner, J. and Collins, J. (2006) 'What Is the Relationship Between Synaesthesia and Visuo-Spatial Number Forms?', *Cognition*, 101(1): 114–28.

Simner, J., Mulvenna, C. and Sagiv, N. (2006) 'Synaesthesia: The Prevalence of Atypical Cross-Modal Experiences', *Perception* 8(35): 1024–33.

Light, Mood and Seasonal Disorders

Rikard Küller

The clock

If you have ever owned a cat, you will know that these loveable animals can go to sleep at any time of the day – or night – and then get up fully awake to go hunting. We are different. Our brains contain several pacemakers that tell us to go to sleep at night and wake up in the morning. The most important of these are the suprachiasmatic nuclei (SCN) and the pineal gland. These pacemakers are commonly called 'the biological clock'. One would think that this clock, after millions of years of evolution, would be set to the astronomical day-and-night cycle of exactly 24 hours, but this is not so. Instead the human clock is approximate, and its pace differs somewhat between people. Some people are early birds who wake up by themselves in the morning, but get sleepy early in the evening. Their clock is running fast. Others have slow clocks. They are night owls, who like to stay up late but find it difficult to get up in the morning (Figure 27.1).[1]

27.1 The average person sleeps eight hours each night, whereas a cat spends 16 hours asleep. However, in contrast with humans, Moggy has no circadian rhythm

This genetically determined variation is known as the circadian rhythm. Lower a person into a cave, where there is no difference between day and night, and after a few days this person will become circadian, that is, begin to follow his or her internal pace. Then, some will fall asleep every 23rd hour, others every 24th, 25th or even 26th hour. This is a natural variation, and there must be some reason for it, evolutionary speaking, that we do not fully understand. For the world's population at large the average length of the circadian rhythm is around 24–25 hours, and many more are night owls than early birds. Suppose that you were on a 23-hour rhythm and your wife on a 26-hour rhythm, then you would see her wide awake only a few times every month. Fortunately, in our daily life we are not circadian, but get up and go to sleep at approximately the same time as everybody else. It is here that light comes in.

Light

When it gets light in the morning, our eyes are stimulated, and by means of different nerves this stimulation is transmitted to the suprachiasmatic nuclei and to the pineal gland. These formations are extremely important since they have the ability to regulate the circadian rhythm. The activity of the suprachiasmatic nuclei exhibits an intrinsic circadian rhythm, which functions as a clock and also dictates the changes in rhythm in the pineal gland. Situated at the centre of the brain, this gland produces a hormone called melatonin that dominates the brain during sleep. Among others it is antagonistic to various activity hormones, such as adrenaline and cortisol, which are useful when we need to perform at our best.[2]

When the eyes are stimulated by light, the production of melatonin is blocked more or less completely, and the other hormones are set free. Melatonin peaks between 2 and 5 o'clock during the night. It is a precondition for sleep, especially deep sleep, which is extremely important for health and well-being. During deep sleep the body is recuperating, and it is also now that the immuno-defence system, which protects us from disease, is most active. Cortisol and the other activity hormones instead peak during the morning and afternoon, preparing the body and mind for full action. Melatonin, cortisol and all the other hormones regulate the internal state of our bodies and minds in a number of ways. Some are so intricate that science has hardly begun to understand them, whereas others are at least partly understood.[3]

In order to become fully synchronized with the astronomical 24-hour clock, ideally we should expose ourselves to daylight during daytime and complete darkness during night. As everybody will have observed, these conditions are scarce in modern life. Most of us live in a world, where light can be switched on at any time, by ourselves or by others, and where complete darkness is a rare thing. Many are hardly exposed to any daylight at all. An increasing number of people are travelling, working or living underground. For instance, in Shanghai during the 1980s, two million square metres of subterranean space were built, including supermarkets, hospitals, hotels, restaurants, entertainment centres and factories.[4] Add to this all the installations above ground, where there are almost no windows. It is lucky for all those, who work there, that the biological clock is not affected by daylight only.

The human eye contains two types of receptors that have been known to science for a long time. These are the rods and cones. The rods are extremely sensitive to light and are therefore used during the night when it is very dark, but they only provide us with a black-and-white picture of the world. The cones, on the other hand, need much more light in order to function, but then give us a world full of colours. People with normal colour vision possess three kinds of cones, with peak sensitivity in different regions of the spectrum. Until a few years ago it was believed that the rods and cones also constituted the link between the light out there and the clock inside us. Recently, however, a third kind of receptor has been identified, namely a photosensitive retinal ganglion cell with a vitamin A-based photo-pigment called melanopsin. It is a scientific mystery that this type of cell was not discovered a long time ago, and it is now believed to be one likely candidate for regulating human chronobiology.[5]

Whatever the truth may turn out to be, the fact is that all the different types of light that exist around us have the potential of resetting our biological clock.[6] As will be expected, natural daylight works very well in this respect, but also the common light bulb, the fluorescent tube and the more recent halogen lamp are capable of resetting our clock. One issue among scientists has been to find the minimum lighting level required, and another has been to identify the most powerful wavelengths in this respect.[7] Although some answers have been obtained, serious arguments are still being raised. One hypothesis that is relevant is that the sensitivity of the eyes might be different at different times of the day and night. The discovery of the photosensitive retinal ganglion cell has added new wood to the fire.

Seasonal Affective Disorder (SAD)

Light influences human health in several different ways. Natural daylight contains a certain amount of ultraviolet (UV) radiation, which is important for the growth and maintenance of the skeleton. When the skin is exposed to UV radiation, it responds by producing vitamin D, which promotes the metabolism of calcium and phosphorus in the body. Deficiency of this vitamin might lead to the serious deformities in children known as rickets and in elderly people in brittle or easily broken bones. Extreme exposition to UV radiation, on the other hand, might cause severe damage to the skin, including allergies and skin cancers. Interesting from our point of view is the fact that UV radiation might also have effects of a more general nature, including improved working capacity and resistance to certain kinds of infection.

Daylight also contains infrared (IR) radiation that influences the metabolic state of the body and regulates its temperature. IR radiation penetrates deeply into the skin and muscles resulting in an increased circulation of the blood. When the surrounding temperature is higher than that of the body, heat will be taken up by radiation. This in turn gives rise to a host of other reactions. Actually we spend much time orienting ourselves towards or away from sunlight, preferring shady places during the summer and looking for a glimpse of the sun during the winter. It is well known that body temperature will influence physical as well as mental performance.

Since these effects are reasonably well known and understood, I will not deal with them further. Instead, I will focus on disturbances of the circadian rhythm. These may occur for any one of three reasons; namely: air travel over several time zones, night shift work, and seasonal differences in day length. In the former case the symptoms are known as jet lag, and in the latter case as seasonal affective disorders. These symptoms partly overlap, and I will confine myself to discussing seasonal affective disorders, because they are more severe and generally last longer. And they are related to light in a very direct way.

As is now well known, the human species emanated from Africa hundreds of thousands of years ago. It was here, close to the equator, that we inherited our biological clock from our ancestors. On these latitudes the external conditions for adjustment of the clock are ideal, since day and night are of about equal length throughout the year. Furthermore, dawn and dusk are distinct events, turning bright daylight into pitch darkness in less than an hour. When humankind migrated north and south, the conditions became less ideal. For instance, in Lund, where I live, there is about 18 hours of daylight in the summer, but only 6 hours in the winter, and in the far north of Sweden there is hardly any daylight at all during midwinter. These seasonal variations put great strain on the biological clock.

Seasonal affective disorders (commonly known as SAD) are very common in Sweden and in other countries located far to the north or south of the equator. Several major seasonal patterns have been identified. By far the largest subgroup reports sadness during the winter, in the northern hemisphere usually from November through February. The second largest subgroup reports sadness during the autumn only, generally in October and November, and another quite small group reports sadness during the spring only. There also seem to be a few individuals, who display a bimodal pattern with sadness at two times of the year interrupted by several months of well-being. In a recent study, almost one thousand people from Argentina, England, Saudi Arabia and Sweden were compared over a period of one year.[8] The results showed that the severity of sadness was about the same in England (52° N) and Sweden (56° N) and far exceeded the severity in Saudi Arabia (26° S) and Argentina (27° S). Almost half of the population in the two northern countries reported some degree of seasonal disorder, and serious symptoms were reported by between 7 and 8 per cent in Sweden and England, but by only 1 per cent in Argentina and Saudi Arabia.

The symptoms of SAD often begin as a more or less severe sleep disturbance. Insomnia is very common, and so is early awakening together with the inability to go back to sleep. After a few days this will result in extreme tiredness and lack of concentration during the daytime. The combination of tiredness and inability to sleep is very typical of a chronobiological disorder. This extreme tiredness often leads to inactivity coupled with social withdrawal as well as a gloomy mood, in some cases even to clinical depression. Some individuals respond with excessive overeating and an increase in body weight. When this pattern recurs during the same period over two or more consecutive years, we can be confident that we are dealing with a seasonal disorder.[9] The symptoms will become aggravated in windowless or otherwise dark indoor environments.

Mood

The study of human emotions is older than psychology itself. It was already of great interest to the ancient Greek philosophers, who used to classify people into four categories – the sanguine, choleric, phlegmatic and melancholic, according to their emotional disposition. My own field – environmental psychology – has generally taken a dimensional approach to the study of emotions. The idea is that every possible mood can be described in terms of its strength and hedonic tone. In my work over the past forty years I have identified four basic dimensions of emotions, and employed these in the study of many different kinds of environments (the Human-Environment Interaction model).[10] There is now considerable proof that the light and colour of interior spaces will influence a wide range of emotions, making people feel more, or less, alert, interested, happy and confident. For instance, in research on work environments our group has found an inverted U-shaped relationship between emotions, on one hand, and brightness, on the other.[11] Psychological mood was at its lowest when the lighting was experienced as much too dark. The mood then improved and reached its highest level when the lighting was experienced as just right, but when it became too bright the mood declined again. Perhaps somewhat amazingly, brightness assessed in subjective terms seems to be a better predictor of emotions than when the light is actually measured with a lux-meter. Of course, most lighting engineers nowadays are aware of the complexity inherent in any lighting situation and the need to consider also its qualitative aspects. A U-shaped relationship was found between emotions and the distance to the nearest window. There was one peak when the distance was 0 to 2 metres and another when the window was far away (more than 10 metres), actually so far that the workplace in practice was windowless. This latter peak might represent an adjustment to windowless environments.

The colour of the workspace also proved to be fairly important. Those who had the most colourful work environment, were generally in a better mood than those, who worked in places with little or no colour (Figure 27.2). Thus, it may seem that the brighter the colour, the better it is for those who work there. However, the majority of the environments were subdued or neutral, whereas only 5 per cent were experienced as very colourful. Results from laboratory studies reported elsewhere in this book indicate that it might not be a good idea to apply very strong colours abundantly in interior spaces, because strong, especially red, colours will put

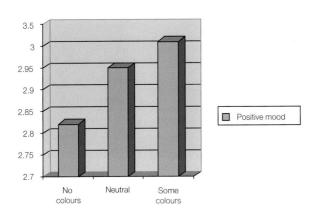

27.2 The average mood of office workers in four countries measured at five different occasions during one year. Obviously the presence of colours had a slight positive effect. Source: After Küller *et al.* (2006)

the brain into an excited state, sometimes to such an extent as to impair performance. I would still recommend an increased use of good colour design, since this will serve to improve the overall mood of people indoors.

Consequences

Light and colour are not only a matter of vision. They penetrate deeply into our minds and bodies, affecting us to an extent that is seldom realized. When waking up in the morning the ambient light will begin to influence our biological clock, tuning it into synchrony with the outside world, and making it possible for us to be in harmony with other people (actually, the small amount of light that passes through closed eyelids will have started this process even before we wake up). The transmission from the darkness of night to the lightness of dawn can be of immense importance for our mental and social adjustment and, in the long run, even for our health. Unfortunately, these aspects are seldom considered by those who design our homes and cities.

For that increasing section of the world's population who works indoors, later in the day light will continue to have an impact, but of a different kind. The distance to a window that provides daylight,

the lightness of the room itself and its interior colour and decoration, together will have a powerful influence on people's emotions. Feelings of alertness, interest and even happiness may be induced or inhibited. Most of you will have noticed the difference a sunny and a cloudy day can have on your spirit. It might actually be profitable to provide half-an-hour of outdoor time for people working long hours. The indoor lighting and decoration are just as important and will have consequences far beyond the purely aesthetic. Architects and interior designers are, indeed, powerful conductors of human life.

After a day that has probably been both hectic and stressful, most of us will retreat to our homes. There we will continue to be surrounded by light and colour, but in completely new constellations. Hopefully, these will serve to compensate and comfort us and prepare us for entering the nocturnal phase of sleep and recuperation. The decline should be gradual including the rituals of preparing a meal – here the light and colour of the kitchen are important. Later on, enjoying the evening alone or with the family, the light and colour of the living room becomes equally important. Watching television – as most of us do nowadays – there must be sufficient ambient lighting to prevent especially the early risers from falling asleep in the armchair. Finally, going to bed, the window curtains and bedside lamp, if well arranged, will help us enter into a good night's sleep and leave us refreshed the following morning.

All this considered, it seems to me that cats, with their highly flexible circadian rhythm, their independence of daylight and less than perfect colour vision, are much better off than we are.

6

PART 6 INTO
THE LIGHT

Dan Flavin and James Turrell are two American artists whose work with the medium of light places them outside the mainstream disciplines of painting and sculpture. Both embarked on decades-long explorations into the behaviour of coloured light – investigations that have become profoundly influential on architects. However, while Turrell's light installations often rely on his personal invention of new technologies, Flavin's minimalist pieces favour a low-tech hardware and confine themselves to light constructions involving off-the-shelf, utilitarian fluorescent tubes usually positioned against a wall and floor to articulate architectural space. Working with a limited palette of red, blue, green, pink, ultraviolet and four different whites, Flavin's work often challenges the preconceptions of viewers who are frequently surprised by the discovery of the properties of light. For example, while the admixture of hues across the pigment spectrum renders black, the blending of the colours of the light spectrum results in white light.

Turrell's lightworks sometimes uses a holographic process that the artist himself has developed; other installations utilize a computer-controlled colour array to generate light fields from a core of neon or LED lights which can subtly shift in colour over time. Many of Turrell's installations comprise walk-in colour spaces, some of which are built into museums and public spaces across America and beyond. To experience a Turrell colour-space is to enter a compelling world in which a three-dimensional colour is evenly and luminously distributed; in which materiality dissolves into a seeming boundless sea of coloured light. It induces an apparent infinity that is ultimately the product of our own perception; it is one in which we experience heightened levels of body awareness and consciousness in which we question our belief systems and habit of looking. This revelatory experience, known as a 'Ganzfeld',

is a visual phenomenon likened to a polar whiteout where depth cues remain absent and surface, colour and brightness all fuse to register an ethereal yet homogenous whole.

Turrell describes himself as an artist who traffics in light. He defines his approach as different from that, say, of the architect, because he immediately tries to subvert established rules. He also says that it is not the job of the artist to merely affirm the taste of the viewer; rather, it is to challenge that taste and, indeed, to change it. Because of his great interest in light he believes that there is too much emphasis in the design world on subtractive colour – and not enough emphasis on additive colour. For instance, when one subtractively mixes blue and yellow pigment, something approaching green is achieved, but when one additively mixes the same two colours in light, something close to white is achieved. Turrell emphasizes that we should remember that as we mix light, it becomes whiter and whiter, and that to achieve a particular coloured light means that other colours have been removed – with the consequence of less light. Turrell categorically also states that red is not warm and blue is not cool. Indeed, he maintains, this mythical association often exists as quite the opposite.

Obviously, the work of both Turrell and Flavin makes strong architectural references, a point that had not been lost on designers of the built environment. Recent advances in an LED technology have seen the birth of the 24-hour building and the animated building, that is, the 'chameleonic' envelope that can change colour either through sensors, computer-programming, temperature deviation, distance or angle of view. One such building is the Lehman Brothers' Building by architects Kohn Pedersen Fox Associates, situated on New York's 7th Avenue. This comprises a huge corporate installation near Times Square, a sequence of giant modular television screens that projects a constant day and night show of pictorial animation, information, weather, time of day and news and mood changes reflecting the state of the financial market. The exterior of the building is literally a giant television flat screen that, wrapping around bands of windows, stretches vertically from the third to the fifth floor while occupying two sides of the façade. By adapting the electronic billboard commonly attached to buildings in Times Square and Piccadilly Circus, the Lehman Brothers' building itself becomes an electronic sign. It heralds the arrival of a 'cinematic architecture' that creates an interface between the physical and the virtual. It recycles the didactic building, the 'talking building', to provide a modern digital update of the colour-washed Parthenon and the Gothic cathedral whose structural mass acted as host from which to project in pigment and gilding the ideas and images of contemporary belief systems. However, enshrined on these modern electronic 'temples' are new gods – the gods of commerce and consumerism. Their dynamic urban presence also represents the paradigm shift flagged in Chapter 3 by Jean-Philippe Lenclos, that is, our fascination with an interactive architecture and an environmental ambiguity. The current fascination with colour change and colour animation not only hints at a paradigm shift that strikes at the heart of traditional colour attitudes that see urban colour as part of the language of time, memory and place, but it also signals a shift from pigment to the effects of light. Bringing cinema into the street seems to reflect a 'black box' condition of modernity and a 'channel-surfing' state of flux. Coming as it does to displace the traditional roles of architectural colour, it also makes us rethink the values of contextualism and site specificity. This condition is summarized by Maria Palumbo when she writes:

One of the most surprising aspects of our modern world is that space, rather than being inhabited, seems to exist to be travelled through. Rather than establishing roots, societies are broken up, mixed, crossed and uprooted. There is an unending buzz of movement, telephone calls, and e-mails. We are in a contemporary world of nomadism, a restless existence on the move. We live on the net; we become what William Mitchell has prophesied – the electronic flâneur.[1]

This concluding Part opens with Peter Jones in Chapter 28 describing the inspiration behind the experience of his Colourscapes, that is, portable environmental works of art that provide settings in which participants become fully immersed in colour. Ensuing chapters include Mark Major's account of the approach and applications of the internationally recognized lighting architects, Speirs and Major Associates (Chapter 29). Lighting designer, Anne Militello follows in Chapter 30 with her description of the installation and later upgrade from incandescent to LED of her 'interactive' lighting project for Platt Byard Dovell's New 42nd Street in New York – one of the early proponents of the 24-hour façade which, after nightfall, switches to a new colour personality that pulsates in time with the heartbeat of the city.

Finally, Yann Kersalé, whose clients include Jean Nouvel, Helmut Jahn and Patrick Bouchain, is the foremost lighting artist with hundreds of experimental installations he calls 'Expéditions-Lumière' and realized projects to his credit. In Chapter 31, Kersalé describes his interventions on landmark buildings that choreograph this increasingly new experience of architecture – a luminous, nocturnal architecture of colour and light.

Being in Colour

Peter Jones

The more I work with colour, the less I understand colour. I just love colour. Colour never stays still. It cannot be pinned down. Colours continually modify the appearance and feeling of other colours near them. Most of our experience of colour is of light reflected from surfaces; from the surfaces of our living and working environments and the objects contained within them.

Inside Colourscapes, people are entirely surrounded by colour. This colour is transmitted from the inner surfaces as daylight filters through the plastic membrane from which Colourscape is made. There is no sense of colour applied to or separate from the surface. Visitors are immersed in colour. Colourscape with its pure translucent colours and subtle colour mixing is an intense experience, not normal.

Colourscapes are hand-tailored from flexible vinyl sheet, 0.25mm thick, coloured red, green, blue, yellow and opaque neutral grey,

specially made in collaboration with the industrial chemist of the manufacturing company. Panels are cut to shape and welded together using industrial high frequency machines and by hand using a liquid solvent. The finished structures are supported by air at low pressure, sufficient to maintain the shape of the lightweight material. Three or four aerofoil fans giving an air flow of 2/3 m3/second are used. The open entrance is shaped to control the pressure within. A large Colourscape occupying a site of about 3000m² would be constructed in three or four sections which are separated for transportation. When folded, each section can be handled by four people. A complete Colourscape weighs about 1,500 kg and can be moved from site to site in a medium-sized van. When shown in public places, Colourscapes are anchored to the ground for safe use (Figure 28.1).

In Colourscape, colour is used to make space active, to make ambiguous space beyond measurement. Colourscape can be described as a holon, simultaneously parts and wholes. The human scale space within contains nothing apart from other people. It is uncluttered and this unusual quality, for an architectural space, encourages exploration. Visitors to Colourscape choose the journeys they make within and feel that they are participating and not being controlled. Walking inside is a means of comprehending

28.1 Colourscape installation, Mirror Islands one, Aberystwyth (2002)

unfolding space, space which is infinitely dimensioned and where shifts are harmonious. As we walk we are aware of being in the world; a particular 'space' is turned into a 'place' by walking in it; foot leads eye and eye instructs foot. When we maintain the tension between foot and eye we embark on a holistic indirect approach to environment. Uninhibited by complicated form and by association to known things, Colourscape allows colour phenomena to be experienced more fully than normal. People become part of it, the colour they wear changes as they move, dynamically altering the space that others see. Visitors are simultaneously spectator and performer. Walking with strangers there are surprise meetings and often an exchange of smiles.

The awe that I feel with experiences of nature, especially as seen in sky, sea and weather remains the major inspiration for my work. To represent outward appearances is not my intention; it is the timeless inner quality I attempt to communicate. I hope that Colourscapes carry an echo of the wholeness of nature, nature in which we can participate in body, spirit and consciousness, nature where the shifting, and often elusive, elements of light and colour create living space.

An essential aspect of my art since 1963 is that people move within the work. The work in the 1960s was made with rigid materials, coloured with paint and lit by electric lighting. In 1970, I started to work with daylight and colour membranes. The early installation work within buildings and subsequent open-air structures independent of existing architecture were linked by my concept of three directions of space, related to human perceptions of gravity, horizon and forward movement. When limited portions of these spatial directions are measured as height, width and breadth, referred to as three dimensions, it is understandable that time can be designated the fourth dimension. But time as experienced is not fixed. The present moment can expand or contract according to our perception of space and action. Felt time is 'timeless', without dimension. Space can expand or contract within infinity. Infinity is not a linear extension of time or space but a shifting quality which is beyond measurement, but part of consciousness.

Early on, I became aware of how my colour space concerns were closely related to architecture. An influence on my artistic and social thinking was the work and writings of Theo van Doesburg and the 'de Stijl' group: 'Only a proper use of colour in space can produce the harmony for modern architecture. The problem of colour in space is the most important and difficult issue of our time' wrote Theo van Doesburg in 1924.[1] In his book *The Hidden Order of Art* (1967), Anton Ehrensweig writes about my 1960s 'space-place' installation and relates the way colour in this work affects the space of the room and how this is 'a reaction against the claustrophobia and fragmentation of modern architecture', and further states that 'This dynamic interior space grapples explicitly with the problem of enclosing and opening up architectural space mainly by making use of colour.'[2]

Linked to my shift from installations in rooms using electric light to being in the open air using daylight was the realization that showing work in the context of art galleries limited the possibility to communicate to a fully inclusive public. From then on I set up my work in public places. It was said by one commentator about an early Colourscape that: 'It is an experience not confined to a particular place or class of society. It is a work of art that you could wake up and find in your local park.' The form of Colourscape made possible its installation in public places and hence my colour work could be experienced by anyone in a safe context known to them. People's responses to the early Colourscapes in the 1970s were a real encouragement to me.

Peter Smith once wrote that colour in environment has a crucial role in keeping alive the connections between reason and emotion: 'When the wavelength profiles of colours perceived on different levels of the brain orchestrate into synchronous rhythms, the result is a special kind of experience, which in the old days was called beauty.'[3] The Colourscape environment offers visitors a chance to create their own experience from sense inputs stimulating personal feelings. The viewer plays an essential role as without cognitive interpretations by individuals there would be no reason for the work to exist. Colourscapes challenge perception of colour and space in such a way that the visitor's action is transformed from passive observation to participating consciousness (Figure 28.2). Artist, Masahiro Nakatani commented that 'Inside Colourscape colour is so all-encompassing that people seem to be swallowed up by it, and some primordial sensation is called up by the brilliance and changes of colour.'[4] Being completely surrounded by colour it is

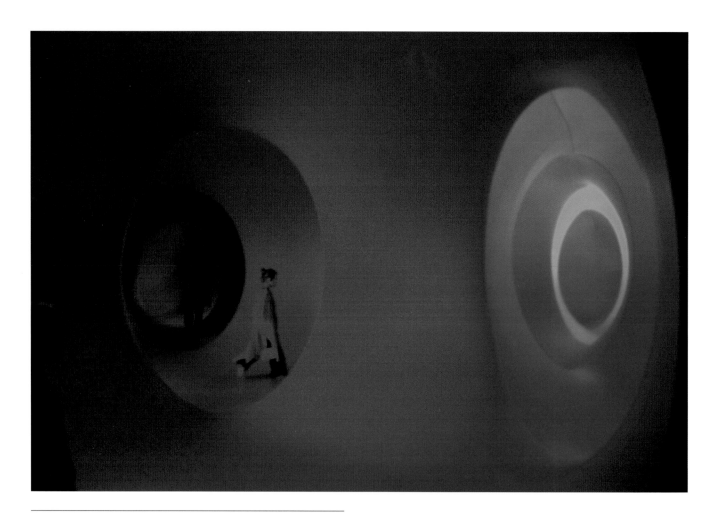

28.2 Colourscape interior, Mirror Islands two (2004)

impossible to step back from the active space created by colour/ form tensions and spatial ambiguities. Physical structure becomes less dominant and our perceptions are put into question. One visitor's written comment recorded: 'The feeling I have inside is excitement and joy being completely surrounded in any of the colours.'

Being surrounded by just one colour is a very intense sensation. Different colours provoke different reactions and the physical reactions can be measured as changes in heart rate and brain activity. Visitors are often surprised that when leaving Colourscape the light outside appears dull whereas the measured light level is actually lower inside. Of all the colours, red seems to become the most concentrated and its effect upon individuals is often commented on.

Film-maker Daniel Vernon wrote:

> The light within the chambers seemed like a mist, particularly the red chamber where the light had a thick granular-like texture that seemed almost tangible. I felt that the light had a definite presence that could be felt by your whole body – this quality of light has a mysterious yet soothing quality.[5]

With careful observation visitors notice that a colour changes by simultaneous contrast to an adjoining colour: complementary colours reinforce each other and where they meet there is a mix at the meeting edge caused by a spreading effect of the colours into each other. For example, where red meets green there is a yellow haze at the boundary. Sequential colour contrast takes place in Colourscape, as visitors move from colour to colour their colour perceptions are linked to their movement. Also the quality of a colour will change with the time spent surrounded by it. For instance, one visitor's comment described: 'The terrifying power of red – but, eventually, if you stand in the red it cools to orange and other colours become so intense.'

I have sometimes been asked how the light changes are controlled, by visitors unaware that it is their own movements that cause shifts in colour when mixing is viewed from different angles as they walk through the space. In Colourscape it can be seen how colour influences spatial depth and therefore apparent size. Space can contract or expand in an unexpected way, especially when observing the movement of other visitors. Sometimes the spatial depth is ambiguous as it appears to oscillate between expansion and contraction; but being entirely surrounded by colour integrates this 'odd' sensation into the whole colour space experience within Colourscape. Some visitors experience a shift in time linked to the unusual Colourscape perceptions they experience. 'I thought that I had been in there for just 10 minutes, but my watch said it was 50 minutes.'

Another phenomenon that can readily be experienced in Colourscape is that of after-images where intense colour stimulates its complementary which can be 'seen' by looking away or closing the eyes. Children are especially aware of this when blinking. Because after-images can be retained for some time, they can influence any subsequent colour perception. In a sense, we project the after-image colour onto other colours and modify them. With particularly intense colour sensations there can be intense after-images which in turn can cause secondary after-images, each after-image is not quite a true complementary to the colour of the original stimulus, but modified 'off centre'. This phenomenon, combined with colour shifts through simultaneous contrast and sequential contrast and time influence on surrounding colour, makes the colour perceptions experienced in Colourscape very complex. In addition to these experiences, certain colour sequences may also have a personal emotional significance for the individual. Also, most of us live with colour preferences, likes and dislikes, and colour associations with shape, sound, names, moods, feelings and other aspects of our lives. For some, these associations are particularly powerful, where two sense inputs interact in an apparently inseparable way, known as synaesthesia.

Group workshops in Colourscapes have explored colour associations to sound, shape and feelings and it is surprising how much agreement there is between individuals. Through ceremonies and habits, different cultures can influence how colours are seen, by that particular group. Also, it seems that the colours we see are most readily influenced by the words we use for them or the particular language we speak. The film-maker Stan Brakhage wrote: 'How many colours are there in a field of grass to a baby who is unaware of the word green?'[6] And the painter Wassily Kandinsky wrote: 'Words

are only hints; mere suggestions of colour. In this impossibility of expressing colour in words with the consequent need for some other mode of expression lies the opportunity for art in the future.'[7]

Added to the perceptual, and associative aspects of colour is the fact that colour can be perceived without eyes. The intense sensation of being surrounded by a single colour makes Colourscape an ideal place in which to test our ability to recognize differences of colours as felt by the body. Positive recognitions have been made by blindfolded persons and blind persons, demonstrating that being inside colour opens up a complex and rewarding experience. It is not difficult to understand that the power of colour when it can be felt in this direct way has the possibility of healing.

Inside Colourscape, we are enveloped in radiating colour which draws out the colour inside us. Colourscape can release our inner colours, allowing us to sense colour, not just with our eyes, with our whole being (Figure 28.3). As beings of light we are able to feel the inner colours. Human energy meets sun energy and the combination is necessary to make a whole being (if we do not live in a full spectrum of light we can suffer from SAD). Are the complementary after-images and the colours that trigger them a dialogue between inner and outer? Are auras projections of inner colours? In Colourscape this union of inner with outer colour makes one joyful and free to experience intense feelings, such as flying. We see others with bright eyes and this shared joy is communicated by smiles which connect people in a communal spirit. We can transcend our egos and the mundane with the help of being in colour.

Relaxing – exhilarating – therapeutic

'One of the most memorable experiences of my life. Relaxing and at the same time exhilarating.'
'I feel reborn. I feel calm for the first time in ages.'
'Tunnel of dreams. How I imagine heaven might be. I'm sure every visitor has had a health benefit from going through the colours – how subtle.' (95-year-old man)
'I really can't describe how I felt in there but left with a great sense of well-being and peace. The power of colour therapy!!'
'And close to what I imagine dying must be like – in the nicest possible sense.'

29

Architectural Light and Colour as a Source of Inspiration: an approach to the use of colour

Mark Major

Many years ago we at Speirs and Major Associates were invited by a young architect called Hugh Broughton to collaborate on an exhibition called 'Any Colour You Like' at the Building Centre in Store Street in Central London. The exhibition aimed to communicate ideas and approaches to the use of colour in architecture and included a wide range of exhibitors from the 'signature names' to the young and aspiring. We remember being surprised at the time that the contribution of our combined team was the only one which approached the subject through the use of 'lights' rather than 'pigments'.

Whether this demonstrated a limited perspective by the others or a wider cultural issue within architecture is difficult to say but it certainly underlined what we had already experienced in the field; the fact then when discussing colour in architecture that people rarely considered light as part of the solution and in some cases divorced it from the conversation altogether.

Of course, this flows out of what we often call the 'daytime view' of designing buildings – they are generally conceived with the sun as the source and to that end its is assumed that colour is to be viewed under natural lighting conditions. Not that there is anything wrong with that approach though the development of patterns of both work and leisure in the past century, and the evolution of all manner of spaces which do not benefit from natural light even during the daytime, mean that applied colour in the built environment is often seen under artificial lighting conditions – and in some cases for the majority of the time. Indeed, with some building types, the nocturnal image is far more important than that by day and in those cases the relationship between artificial light and colour is key, with light actually providing the colour in many instances.

As ever, there are exceptions to the rule and, as we will explore later in this chapter, the history of architecture is filled with fine examples of architects and artists who fully appreciated the opportunity afforded by the relationship between colour and light by both day

and night so that they employed both to elevate the buildings they created to the status of high art.

For us as lighting architects, colour is light and, as a result, our work not only explores the subtle tonal qualities of white light in all its forms but from time to time will employ saturated colour either to influence the perception of the viewer or simply create a sense of celebration. However, to do this, we need inspiration and we find this in many places.

Our starting point for the study and application of colour through light in the built environment is to look to nature itself and learn what we can from the effects of daylight and sunlight. Here we find an ever-changing relationship between the values of hues and their intensity and mix. We understand from looking at the effects of natural light not only the range of options that exist with respect to white light from the 'super cool' of the north sky to the warm flickering effect of firelight but also the magical effects of colour created by everything from the setting sun to the Aurora Borealis. Observing nature, in all its glory, can tell you pretty much everything you need to know about working with light and colour – it is largely a matter of learning to look.

One, of course, always has to remember a few 'basics' such as working with lights is 'additive' rather than 'subtractive' and that its primaries are red, green and blue. Understanding the principles of reflection and absorption is also helpful, for instance, learning to think of a red material being a 'blue-green' absorber may be a slightly protracted way of accepting that a surface is red but it not only helps to explain how the process works but can greatly inform the options available and the degree of control required to ensure that a surface ends up being rendered as desired.

Aside from the natural world, the roots of our work with colour also lie in an understanding of the essential relationship between light and architecture. Light has always played a key role within the 'Western tradition' whether it is the quest for the 'divine light' of Abbot Sugré and his French stonemasons during the development of the Gothic style in the thirteenth century or the spectacular gold and white interiors of Johannes Neumann, Johann Fischer and their counterparts during the evolution of the 'High Baroque' in Germany in the eighteenth century. In the modern era we see everything from the bright and colourful 'electric' displays of the great 'World Expositions' at the turn of the last century in France and the USA to the dazzling vision of Paul Scheerbart, Bruno Taut and the members of the Expressionist 'Glass Chain' in Germany in the 1920s (of a world constructed from light and coloured glass). In the late twentieth century we see such visions being realised through the work of architects such as Jean Nouvel and Toyo Ito, in which colour and light are seamlessly integrated into the architectural idea both inside and out through the use of advanced lighting technologies.

Other areas that inspire our work include the world of theatre and entertainment. Here we find breathtaking creations by artists who have considerable freedom to realise 'temporary solutions' ranging from the extremely subtle narrative of a 'National Theatre' production to the brash and dynamic extravagance of Broadway or rock and roll tours where lighting designers of considerable skill and vision invite us to share new experiences. In the world of 'theatre' we find internationally renowned designers such as Rick Fisher or Ken Billington developing extremely different approaches to working with colour and light while celebrities such as Luc La Fortune of Cirque du Soleil deliver dream-like sequences for travelling troupes and permanent shows from London to Las Vegas. Major recording artists such as U2 and the Rolling Stones employ talents such as Willie Williams and Patrick Woodroffe to create intense works using moving media and dynamic light that are exemplars of their form. Each of these artists and many more provide a constant source of imagery and reference for our work in the field of architecture and in many cases not just the techniques but also the technology cross the boundary from the world of the temporary show to that of permanent built form.

Alongside those who 'light to entertain' we also consider others who explore the full range of human experience through fine art. While there are a number of contemporary artists who are celebrated for their work, where light is the exclusive medium, we first turn to the more traditional world of painting as a point of reference. For us, it is worth remembering that man's origins lie in places where no natural light could reasonably enter; deep within cave systems such as Lascaux, where we find man's earliest surviving attempts at representing the natural world, pictures were created by firelight. We also see great artists such as Caravaggio and Rembrandt employing contrast in light and colour to create a range of emotions while Vermeer actually adopted optical techniques, such as the use of a pinhole camera, to replicate domestic scenes of Dutch life with a remarkable attention to detail, revealing the fine subtleties of diffuse coloured light and shade. Later the soft light of Turner leads the way to a fundamental exploration of light and colour through the work of the Impressionists, such as Monet and Cézanne. Each of these artists, and countless others, remind us of the power of light not only to evoke emotion but also the manner in which the eye and mind combine to create 'perception'. While moderns, such as Klee and Albers, provide us with a further insight into both the physical and psychological, it is 'light artists', such as the late Dan Flavin and James Turrell, who have guided us to new levels of perception in art. The work of the former used 'colour as light' to sub-divide space. He showed us how the mind can deceive as to what the eye beholds. Turrell, however, makes light actually 'occupy' space. He demonstrates its most remarkable properties to create works that go beyond accepted conventions. He truly shows us that light and colour may be made 'material'.

The handling of light and colour in film also deserves mention as it serves to provide us with common points of reference when discussing our work with clients. The legacy of the mood lighting of the great black and white epics such as Fritz Lang's *Metropolis* and Alexander Korda's *Shape of Things*, the latter of which includes some incredible sequences from Laszlo Moholy-Nagy's innovative 'Light Space Modulator' remain with us today. And while a generation of architects have been undoubtedly influenced by the dark rain-soaked backgrounds cut with light and media of Ridley Scott's *Blade Runner*, or the stark whiteness of George Lucas's *THX1138*, it is sometimes in the simpler more direct approach of television that we find both the mood and imagery that can form a common language between ourselves and clients. The direct but dramatic lighting in all manner of TV programmes shows how light and colour can be used to change everyday environments into 'special places'. Just watch any good show for its lighting (and not its action) and you will see what we mean!

A further source of inspiration as well as a critical means of communication is the spoken and written word. This may seem obvious but light is very difficult to describe, and even more difficult to represent. At the early stages of any project we perhaps rely on words more than many other designers working with the built environment. They can quickly sketch the form while we must 'paint' the full picture. When discussing our work, we aim to clearly communicate the quality, quantity, colour, direction and effect of the light, and while we will often employ 'borrowed' imagery to approximate to the result, we will generally supplement that with words. In some cases the 'language of light' may be derived from works of literature in the form of 'light quotes' that help to convey the spirit of the scheme. The pool of choice is infinitely wide but in selecting words carefully we can refer to a colour or an effect quite precisely. For example, we could describe lighting a space by saying: 'It will be illuminated with a low level of cool white light' but this leaves the effect wide open to a range of interpretations. However, if we say: 'It will be moonlit with a soft wash of pale blue light', this not only implies an effect but also an atmosphere.

While there are many areas of both art and physics that can inspire and delight, for us the bridge between the idea and the actuality is the technology. While we strictly adhere to the principle of designing the light first and only then selecting the tools that will deliver the effect, we often look to the cutting edge of lighting technology to assist with our ideas.

There is a long history of man's use of artificial light from fire, through burning tallow, wax, oil and gas but it is electric light that has served to emancipate the relationship between light and colour after dark. And yet this form of light has a relatively short history. While some dispute still exists as to 'who invented the light bulb' at the end of the nineteenth century – Joseph Swan or Thomas Alvar Edison – it was the latter who at least ensured that not only was a new and convenient source readily provided but also that the means to power it became available and affordable. In that sense, Edison must be seen as the pioneer who established electric lighting as a useful and workable system within the built environment. This development was to have a profound effect not only by extending the day and, thereby, changing patterns of work and leisure throughout the world, but also enabling architects to fully integrate artificial light into the design of their buildings. While the history of all that is too long to dwell upon here, the gradual introduction of new and exciting electric lighting technologies not only provided all manner of 'whites' but also pure saturated colour as an available extension to the lighting palette.

And while coloured light had always been available to architects from the 10th century by allowing natural light to pass through a dyed medium, such as stained glass, or through vessels filled with coloured fluids, such as were experimented with by Brunelleschi during the Renaissance, it was not until a Frenchman, Georges Claude developed neon in the 1920s that coloured light became available not only as a source but also as a highly flexible tool.

However, once Claude and others had perfected the technique of employing different colours by using different gases and coatings on his glowing glass discharge tubes, the idea that electric light could readily produce colour, and to the artist's or designer's requirements, created all sorts of new possibilities. While these were taken up with enthusiasm, not only by advertisers in both the USA and Europe, the technology also found its way into architecture during the 1920s and 1930s and in a highly integrated manner. Indeed, cold cathode (as neon is more commonly referred to by lighting designers) is still used extensively, not only for the production of signs from Las Vegas to London, but also to create a wide variety of architectural effects – its bespoke nature and long life being seen as considerable advantages. Its main limitation these days is its energy-hungry nature and its cost.

Beyond the use of this material and the odd development in coloured lamps, which still generally relied on the glass bulb being dyed thereby subtracting valuable light, it was not until the late 1970s that new and exciting developments came about. These introduced the idea of single sources of light that rapidly and precisely changed colour based on a specific instruction or cue. Interestingly, such developments largely flowed out of the rock and roll industry. Up until that time designers working in the rapidly developing field of live concerts and events had employed the same tools as their counterparts in the theatre, namely 'cans' which held not only a high intensity sealed beam lamp but also colour filters and other accessories that could modify the light to create the desired effect. As shows grew in ambition the number of lighting instruments required and the labour associated with transporting them and rigging them became increasingly onerous – witness the almost clichéd image of heavy metal bands of the late 1970s with hundreds of lanterns above the stage on huge rigs, the coloured beams of light picked out in the fog of dry ice! At the height of their powers, the UK rock band Genesis worked with the US Company Varilite to develop the first fully-functioning and reliable moving head colour change projector. These tools not only revolutionised the rock and roll industry by allowing designers almost limitless freedom to choreograph light and colour in a manner never witnessed before but also spawned a generation of copycat fittings that eventually found their way into the field of environmental design. The significance of this was not lost on a developing group of professional architectural lighting designers, including ourselves, who readily realised the possibilities that such technology could bring to architecture. No longer was the use of colour limited to choosing the hue and its saturation of a source and sticking to It. We could now colour an interior or exterior space as we wished and when we wished on a fully automated basis.

Of course, the idea of 'colour change' in the built environment was nothing new. The use of multiple coloured tungsten lamps dimmed on different circuits was seen as early as 1905 at the Louisiana Purchase Exposition and Joseph Emberton's famous 'Simpson of Piccadilly' in London. This was created with a fully integrated RGB cold cathode lighting system as early as 1926 which allowed the main façade to be rendered in a choice of colours – and here was a technology that not only delivered millions of colours of pure saturated light, but it emanated from a single source. The only issue with the successors to Varilite had been cost and reliability and, most importantly, a lack of creative ability in those who employ them in the built environment. The rock and roll lighting designers and their colleagues in theatre who also adopted such tools for their purposes, tended to use them with clarity of purpose, whereas in architecture there often seemed no clear understanding as to why the environment should be coloured in the first place, let alone why it should change. It therefore became a case of the tail wagging the dog – because the technology existed it was used – as a result, the idea of 'colour change' has become somewhat discredited in architectural lighting in recent years.

The next new technology to come along represented a more substantial revolution. The beginning of the 1990s saw architectural lighting designers begin to employ light emitting diodes (LEDs) for decorative purposes. These low energy long-life solid state devices offered the opportunity to create points of intense, coloured light, albeit limited to red, amber and green in the early days that could even be seen in daylight. While early versions did not offer useful light other than visual brightness, it was the start of a revolution that history will be as fundamental to the development of lighting as Edison's pioneering work. While LEDs had originally been employed by the aviation and automotive industry in instrumentation panels, and appeared in a variety of consumer goods as indicator lights, the move towards developing this source for environmental lighting purposes was to prove profound, especially in an age where saving energy was becoming of paramount concern. It also saw the introduction of unfamiliar names such as 'Panasonic', 'Hewlett Packard' and other silicone industry giants into the field, thereby providing a financial and R&D base previously often lacking in the lighting industry. As a result, developments accelerated rapidly with

blue and then white LEDs becoming available, rapidly followed by an increase in output that made them be viable for lighting applications where low levels of illumination would suffice. In respect of colour, however, the development of LED-based screen technologies that allowed the creation of large surfaces that did not simply change colour but could also support an image in a manner similar to cathode rays tubes, TFT, plasma, LCD and other screen technologies led to the introduction of RGB-based systems that could colour whole environments with intense and saturated hues with total control and relatively low expenditure in respect of energy. The other key to the success of LEDs, beyond their low energy consumption and long life, is the ability to clearly see this source in daylight. This was the first time such a possibility had really existed and, in the case of screen technologies used for commercial purposes, made sense of the economics. Today we are still in the midst of this revolution that provides us with new and dynamic ways of colouring our environment, if we so choose.

Which brings us neatly to the point where we can take on board these sources of inspiration plus the seemingly infinite flexibility provided by the new generation of tools which allow lighting designers, architects and artists to approach the use of colour in architecture in a progressive manner (Figure 29.1).

For our part, we have developed an approach to our work in which we have a clear idea about how colour through light in architecture may be handled. It is only one view but it perhaps gives clues to the fact that given the often highly public nature of using coloured light in the built environment and its psychological and even physiological effect that any hue beyond the 'natural' state of the broad spectrum of white light must be handled with extreme caution – and by 'broad spectrum' we refer to every version of white from the warm intensity of ambers and oranges that reflect firelight to the cool intensity of the blue light of the twilight sky. Indeed, it is our belief that the predominant use of warm orange light and increasing presence of cool blue light in our cities, and the broad acceptance of such colours, is due to the perception that they are simply an extension of the palette of 'natural white light' (Figure 29.2).

While most of our work centres on the use of white light, we will occasionally employ other colours to reinforce a particular idea. For instance, our lighting scheme for Zollverein Kokerei near Essen employs a low level of 'rusty' red light not only to suggest decay but also new life as part of its renewal as a nocturnal urban park (Figure

29.1 Original lighting concept to develop a new night-time skyline for the People's Playground, Blackpool, UK

29.2 St Paul's Cathedral, London. It is generally most appropriate to reveal architecture with white light

29.3 Light is used to articulate new interpretations of an industrial complex, in this case, the Zollverein Kokerei industrial complex in Gelsenkirchen, Germany

29.4 Sequenced blue light against the rusty red light in the main space of Magna, a Science Adventure Centre set in a defunct steel mill near Rotherham

29.5 The lighting concept for the Burj Al Arab tower in Dubai,
UAE, employs computer-controlled colour-changing luminaires,
programmable stroboscopes and moving head skytrackers to provide
a sequence of slow rippling light changes after dark

29.3). Similarly, the strong use of red, blue, turquoise and yellow light at the Magna Science and Adventure Centre in Rotherham reinforces the different character areas of the exhibits that examine the role of fire, air, water and earth in the steelmaking process (Figure 29.4). Such symbolic use of coloured light, while direct, almost clichéd, always relates strongly to an idea which evolves as a central part of the lighting concept and in such instances the selection is neither random nor arbitrary.

Another approach we have taken in the past is to use coloured light to discriminate between different actions over time. Such use generally relates to the occasions when we engage in 'visual narrative', that is, when different colours represent different times of the day, week and even season (Figure 29.5).

New 42nd Street, New York

Anne Militello

The New 42nd Street is a performing arts centre designed by the Manhattan-based practice of Platt Byard Dovell. Situated within and inspired by the buzz of Times Square, and audaciously created before the explosion of new lighting technologies, the concept for an all-singing, all-dancing façade was born – the architects inviting the lighting designer, Anne Militello to collaborate on the project. Operating out of Los Angeles and New York City, Militello's installation is interesting because it represents one of the early proponents in the interactive life of the 24-hour building, that is, a building which projects one character in daylight and quite a different character after dark. However, this is no Jekyll and Hyde experience for, at nightfall, the building transforms into a pulsating symphony of changing coloured light that chromatically throbs in tune with the heartbeat of the city. What follows is Anne Militello's approach to the project and its transformation from incandescent to LED lighting.

The challenge for this project involved the creation of a permanent lighting installation to advertise in an abstract manner the creative process of the theatrical rehearsals taking place within the building studios.

By day, the materials used by the architects are quite alive – reflective metals, dichroic glass and dimensional structure. The lights at night had to be just as dynamic, therefore our goal as a team was to use light to interpret the spirit of the performing arts at night. As a lighting designer for the stage as well as architecture, I endeavored to create a moving visual art piece that would constantly change, reflect the function of the interior spaces of the building and, while drawing from the energy of Times Square, give the building a sense of place on the street.

Using a combination of theatrical lights modified for architecture with sophisticated control, I designed a system that allowed the lights to have seemingly infinite programming, creating dynamic color shifts and movements that appear to dance and shimmer across the steel blades of the armature, as chromatic symphonies of flowing colour and blurred images.

Working closely with the architects, Platt Byard Dovell, for over two years, several experimental mockups were constructed which determined the right materials for the 'blades' and the most appropriate lights. The challenges of this unique project involved designing dichroic color filter holders that could both withstand the acid rain and New York City's extreme temperature shifts; it also meant finding extra strength filaments for the halogen lamps that could endure the imperceptible but constant and potentially damaging vibrations of the New York City subway below.

Enlisting light sources comprising halogen, metal halide and fluorescent lights fitted with dichroic filters and heavy duty theatrical gel, and composed of the widest possible spectrum available at the time, I could carefully choose individual hues and precisely sequence and time their changing combinations. There are also several computer-controlled intelligent lights, a modified theatrical light – the first to be developed for architectural use, which, as well as the blades, illuminate the 200 ft lightpipe structure that runs up the side of the façade.

Many of the lights on the façade are halogen sources on dimming control which enables them to be programmed to crossfade slowly or very rapidly. The palette of these lights is broken into three secondary colours that can combine to create multicolor hues. The intentional scratches on the steel blades help to break up the light into minute slashes and dots, causing a mosaic fusion phenomena, allowing the eye to blend colors more easily from a distance. Each light is on its own circuit, enabling the creation of seemingly endless combinations. Colours can traverse vertically, horizontally, diagonally, or blend together in pools. There are some metal halide and fluorescent fixtures that have a deep primary blue colour which snap on and off in certain sequences, adding depth. The lights exist on three architectural layers – one layer behind the glass curtain wall which consists of fluorescent wall washers in blue, lighting a translucent scrim, a second layer of lights outside and behind the blades, mounted on catwalks at each floor designed by the architects and construction manager Christopher Buckley, and an outer, frontal layer emanating from intelligent light sources placed at the base of the façade grazing the outer edges of the steel.

A further consideration was that the installation had to be designed from the perspective of the majority of viewers, which was a viewpoint from the sidewalk across the street. In 1999, when we began testing the programming, virtual technology was not yet available. Consequently, this had to be done live. To do so, I enlisted the help of lighting programmer, Ryan O'Gara. However, 42nd Street at that time was too dangerous to set up the computer in the street at night, so consequently we gained permission for him to be positioned in a third floor window across the street – a vantage point affording a direct view of the façade. We used a radio control that transmitted across 42nd Street in order that the lighting control computer could interface with the dimming system installed in the New 42 building. I had stationed myself on a folding chair on the street below using a wireless headset to communicate with the programmer.

30.1 Anne Militello's pulsating light on the New 42nd Street building is programmed to reflect both the tempo of dance – the function of the building – and also coincide with the throb of city life

The eventual design for the sequence and tempo of the light show resulted from my sitting on the street every night for six weeks. This allowed me to tune into the energy and vitality of 42nd Street which inspired this creative process. By directly rehearsing the changing colour and pattern combinations on the building, I was able to create this visual streetscape in a hands-on manner. The computer and its astronomical time-clock allowed for the ability for any timing movements at any speed and to decide the nights and times during the night, that certain looks could be seen.

I was often alone, with just a clipboard and a wireless headset hidden under my hair. Sitting between the incense sellers and street hawkers and apparently talking to myself, I was often mistaken for a demented person. Sometimes passers-by approached: plainclothes police, partygoers, sailors on leave, Broadway theatergoers, etc., and I shared with them my craft and would listen to their suggestions as I 'wove', my colors. On one occasion I was almost assaulted by a gang of hoodlums, but was able to escape a beating by talking into my invisible, headset and, with a wave of my hand, apparently and magically transforming the colors of the façade across the street. A building whose façade could change color like that had yet not been seen in New York, so this was my saving grace – and, maybe to these crooks who were probably under the influence of drugs or alcohol, I really did seem to be a magician!

As the pulse of 42nd Street changed from the beginning to the end of the week, the tempo of the lights were programmed accordingly, with Sunday and Monday being the quietest nights and then increasing to a cascading frenzy by Saturday night. The light installation is a nightly interactive tribute to the activity of one of the most famous streets in the world. While it continues to reflect the vibrance of the street below and the dynamic world of the performers who rehearse within its studios, it doesn't overpower the rest of the chaotic street.

In late September 2007, I returned to New 42nd Street to implement a new retrofitted design of the façade. This resulted from the client's request for a solution to lower the power bill and minimize maintenance. Consequently, I replaced all the halogen and metal halide lighting with LED fixtures and replaced the control with a state of the art lighting integration system that allowed me to feed video clips which projected abstractly across the façade. The quality of light is now much brighter, bolder and more dynamic while reducing the power consumption by one-sixth. It was a challenge to try to soften the light through programming and control while attempting to use this technology to its fullest extent. I recreated some of the movements from the former design while adding more colors and textures. I composed abstract light videos and fed them in between composed looks and created a new symphony, so to speak. It took a quarter of the time to program with the new system, especially since I had the ability to create some of the looks on a virtual program before arriving on site (Figure 30.1).

There is no substitute for the human eye, so therefore tweaking the cues had to be done again on the street. The dynamics of the street had changed in the last seven years, and therefore the lighting had to reflect this new energy. I look forward to its next incarnation and the excitement of the unknown future of 42nd Street.

The Fisherman of Light

Yann Kersalé

During my art student days at the Quimper Ecole des Beaux Arts in Brittany in the west of France, I studied engraving. However, although gravure is still important to me, light is my chosen medium. This is because of its complexity; it offers an unlimited field of research, and one in which an individual lifetime will not be enough to explore all the questions. While studying engraving I was quickly drawn to light and luminosity, attempting to discover it in the interplay between engraving, ink and printing. This is perhaps due to its working method, because while etching a copper plate and working with ink, one is always looking for light. There was also my insatiable desire to simultaneously experience all the fine art disciplines: printmaking, painting and sculpture. This obsession became synthesized in my final year student project which became

prototypical of the future direction of my work. It involved a 6m-diameter light-emitting jellyfish form that received light projections on to its envelope, causing its translucent form to pulsate like a living organism (Figure 31.1). This work involved much experimentation with the projection of images which, by the way, were not figurative images but abstract images of materials.

Among my first environmental projects was a study commissioned in 1989 by Joel Batteux, the far-sighted mayor of Saint-Nazaire and its dock area, whose perseverance, despite initial reluctance from the port authority and a gamut of related agencies, managed, following the presentation of mock-ups, to gain tacit overall approval for my proposal – a process that took three years. For many years I had been dreaming of such a dock environment for a project. The docks at Saint-Nazaire, with its paraphenalia of grain elevators, mobile cranes, swingbridges, turnbridges and drawbridges, etc., also house the infamous and indestructible submarine pens which remain as a haunting reminder of the war (Figure 31.2). Apart from the submarine pens which were washed in blue, the concept

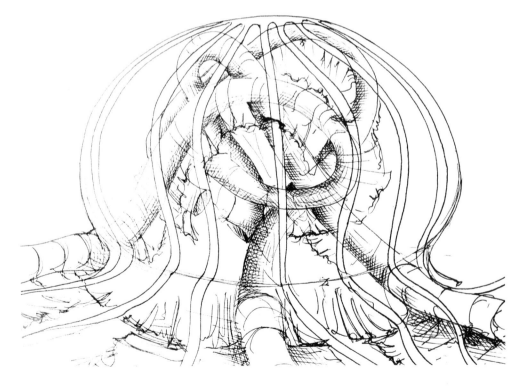

31.1 Yann Kersalé's sketch of his graduate student project, a 'habitable' marine form fabricated in PVC that pulsates with back- and front-projected images

for this installation used a static white light for the mobile struc-tures, such as the cranes and bridges, which, when activated and in full swing, caused luminous pulsations. Meanwhile, to echo the light beacons that signal the harbour entrance, all bulkhead struc-tures are equipped with small red lights on the port side and green lights on their starboard side. This installation was a revelation as it appeared to rekindle an appreciation in the powers that be of the beauty of their industrial heritage. Indeed, roads soon were resur-faced, buildings repaired and repainted. For me, this public work of art seems to have become an extraordinary public relations tool and to have reconciled the town of Saint-Nazaire with its port.

Whether the subject is a building, a tree or an object in an industrial landscape, my approach to a lighting composition can be com-pared with the creation of a movie storyboard or the scenario of a play; it simply tells a story. For instance, in early thrillers, film direc-tors and their directors of photography have long made the point that light is an important dimension in sustaining narrative. Light is an essential ingredient in film writing. However, when I speak of light in terms of narration, this is not in the sense of subjective writing but in terms of framework, project and structure. The aim remains constant, that is, to reveal the object at all levels of our sensibility. It is here that I believe there is a frontier between art and architecture, a real possibility to create sculpture with light.

Obviously, this approach is diametrically opposed to the banality of city illumination and its pervading sodium lighting that brutalizes and disfigures our perception of architectural monuments by night. What a shame that one can badly light the object. Today one finds too many examples of what I call 'pâtisserie-type' luminous decorations, that is, light that is too baroque, too heavy. Introduced into the night, such lighting tarnishes sensitivity; it is meaningless, insignificant and worthless. Soon I will have spent thirty years working with light and its artistic intervention in urban space and during this time I have seen other groups of people, such as engineers and publicity people making what I call a hostile takeover of the night. It makes me very angry because light has much more to say, far more to tell.

When I began working with light, there was no one else working on objects in the nocturnal architectural setting and, especially, in the industrial environment. There had been installations in the 1900s – the lighting of pavilions for World Fairs and the lighting of the Eiffel Tower – but these were early experiments celebrating the invention of electricity and showing off garlands of Edison's incandescent bulbs. There were artists such as Victor Vasarely and the associated kinetic movement, and also Julio le Parc, who made light experiments, but, like Dan Flavin's fluorescent tubes, these were art pieces destined for museums and created to be viewed in a particular way and often from predetermined vantage points. And, of course, one cannot talk about light without mentioning the name of James Turrell. There is also Walter de Maria – who had created an installation involving lightning rods in a desert which are experienced only in the event of a storm. In the early days, there was no one else. Before I made my first light installations there were no artists working on the architectural environment, on objects in the night. There was no artistic light in New York, none in Tokyo, nor London; the first experiments were in France.

As a student, I studied all the experiments of artists of this older generation and although I recognized in their work a sort of kinship, a kind of fraternal rapport with light, I cannot say that they had a profound influence on my work. Here, I should mention that I don't simply flood light on objects at night, I create a dynamic work with light – I create journeys. Gilles Deleuze once wrote that philosophers invent concepts and artists create percepts. It is here that I can develop a parallel with the work of James Turrell and the percepts that he created. However, while Turrell's work is physio-sensory, mine is not; it is more a work of nocturnal deambulation – a game which is sensitive to the journey of the individual, of the spectator. It is a work that I transpose at night into another quite different visual experience from what is seen in a particular way during the day. While the works of light artists summon the spectator for a controlled viewing, I summon the spectator to travel, to be free to move at will and to find his or her own viewpoints.

What interests me is penetrating the heart of an object, capturing the resonance that emanates from its quintessential existence. While the sun functions as a natural cleanser that indiscriminately washes objects from dawn to dusk, the whole duration of the night-time is free – when the intervention of a light composition can accentuate certain elements and relegate others to the shadows. Such work not only brings a dramatic counterpoint to our daytime perception but it also demands the invention of new lighting concepts – poetic concepts that, using night as the 'canvas' can pulsate rhythmic components, deform edge and surface, dematerialize physical mass and make it appear weightless and make references to the city or to the temporal function of the building itself. And this is the second part of my theory and research in the quest for a percept. Wherever I make an intervention, I seek meaning within the location in order to introduce a specific idea. When the introduced light is dynamic, it is not so for its own sake; it is because it tells a story.

An example of this is when I worked with Jean Nouvel on his amazing superstructure atop Lyons Opera House – a glass curved barrel roof which not only tripled the audience capacity but was installed without touching the walls of the historic building. My concept focused on red to symbolize the fire that had destroyed the original roof, the velvet of the stage curtains and the passions being theatrically played out within the auditorium. Diffused by the metallic louvres as the huge roof curves upward and away from the viewer, the red gradually fades into a pink magenta (Figure 31.3). The red theme continues on the colour-washed caryatides on the main façade as are the suspended glass lights at ground level that mark the arches of the arcade (Figure 31.4).

However, the dynamic of the light relates to a narrative that sees the building as having three lives: one when there is a performance and inhabited by technicians, costume-makers, make-up artists, performers and audience; another when there are rehearsals, and a third life when, apart from security people, the theatre is empty. Consequently, the installation dynamically and differentially reflects each of these conditions; in this project, light functions to describe a narrative of what is going on inside the building that can't be seen from outside. The light sequence is controlled by a bank of sensors that monitor occupancy of the building which causes the neon-lit barrel roof to differentially shimmer, throb and ripple in response to backstage and front of house activity. When the theatre is fully operational and a production is on stage, the roof is fully animated – pulsing like a person breathing; when there is no performance, the neon tubes ripple into waves that sweep up and over the roof. When the building is empty, the roof goes to sleep, save for two lower lines of neon that remain lit to glow like embers. However, deep into the night, the presence of a nightwatchman, with a wave of his arm, can, momentarily, reawaken and reactivate the chromatic display.

This function of light is very different from that on, say, a pharmacy or a nightclub where colours change for no reason. I use colour always with the idea of transmitting an idea to the spectator and inviting them to share in this idea.

I feel it vital to thoroughly investigate the site, to live it out, to extract the constraints and approach them, not as obstacles, but as ingredients that are fully a part of the creative process. The initial phase of this approach involves the establishment of storyline – the formation of a scenario that draws together, synthesizes and gives expression to all the various mental concepts. The process is dual, that is, on the one hand, made up of the visual materiality of the object and, on the other, by the introduction of the concept. At this point, light weaves connections that become incorporated in the object. This process involves intense amalgamation with the support of, and also implicates the complicity of, the architect – the designer of the building – and a deep understanding before, during and after the implementation of the building and its lighting. However, inextricably bound as I am to architecture, I attempt to remain as independent as possible, to offer an entirely new perceptual point of view, a different visual concept. In spite of existing as the identical twin of the diurnal object, the ultimate realization of a nocturnal object is nevertheless fundamentally different.

For instance, my work for Jean Nouvel on his Agbar Tower in Barcelona, dealt with a building that exhibits one polychromatic personality during the daytime and another by night. Headquarters of

31.3 (left) Detail of Yann Kersalé's pulsating barrel roof on Jean Nouvel's Lyons Opera House

31.4 (above) Yann Kersalé's collaboration with Nouvel on his Lyons Opera House uses an interactive red illumination programmed to create an ever-changing nocturnal experience

the city's water utilities, the tower is a huge bullet-shaped, phallus form situated in one of Barcelona's circular squares on which millions of suspended, slightly angled strips of glass appear as an outer screen and set forward from the inner painted concrete structure. Between them is not a terrace but a gangway for window cleaners. The potential of the visual interplay between the intricate painted zones of reds, blues and oranges on the inner wall and the glass outer screen was to cause a kind of moiré illusion – a shimmer effect that reflects the liquidity of the vibrating heat haze that rises from the city on extremely hot summer days (Figure 31.5).

Following a long period exchanging ideas with Jean, I began a series of experiments. Initially I considered matching these painted colours with corresponding hues in light but ultimately decided to recreate the subtle colouring of a nocturnal 'sunlight' by projecting white light upward on to the glass fins so that it reflected back to colours of the inner wall, and varying its intensity at each successive storey (Figure 31.6). The similarity between the Agbar Tower and another of my projects, Tour Sans Fin, is the impression of immateriality – an indistinct, illusive quality of surface that has been

described by Jean Nouvel as 'suggesting water, smoothness, continuity, vibration and transparency'. However, whereas the latter was created to visually melt into space, the dematerialization of the Agbar Tower is arrested by its 'ice cap' glass dome – a reference to the Montserrat rock, near Barcelona, that so inspired Anton Gaudí for his Sagrada Familia (Figure 31.7).

I have also realized several collaborative works with the Chicago-based architect, Helmut Jahn. One such project is my installation for his Sony Centre complex situated close to the Potsdamer Platz in Berlin. The complex comprises a tower block accommodating offices, housing and a hotel that encloses a 4000 m² oval forum filled with theatres, cinemas, restaurants and bars. High above the Forum and the after-dark vibrancy of its nightlife is a large dome designed by Ove Arup + Partners. Its form, seen from inside as an enormous marquee or, from the city at large, as a translucent volcano, is created by sheets of glass under which drapes of diaphanous material are stretched corolla fashion using a system of cables (Figure 31.8). When invited by Jahn to conceive the lighting of the Forum, I proposed that it should emanate from within the space (and not from outside as

others had previously proposed) and involve a pulsation that would at once radiate light to reflect the intensity of nocturnal activity as well as send out signals. Apart from internally lighting the Forum using a cyclical phasing of colour, a further intervention involved the location of blue neon lights at the corners of the building to signal the many entrances into the space and also to anchor what I saw as a huge 'jellyfish' to the ground. Remaining white until nightfall, the huge marquee moves into its spectral cycle, from magenta to cyan – with the exception of yellow. When, in the early hours, the Forum closes, the dome transforms into an intense blue which, by dawn, subsides before fading back into white (Figure 31.9).

Until now, I have not based my work on any natural light phenomena but, more recently, using digital cameras, I have been developing methods of capturing natural lights, such as the play of light on water, and transporting them far from their place of origin. Moreover, the constant subtext in my work: liquidity, shimmer, transparency, the ripple of sunlight on the ocean, aquatic creatures, anchoring, etc., may have something to do with the fact that I spent my boyhood on the coast of Brittany where I continued to work as a fisherman while an art student. Consequently, I suppose that you might call me a 'fisherman of light'.

31.7 (left) One of Yann Kersalé's concept drawings showing the 'ice cap' on the Agbar Tower

31.8 (below) Yann Kersale's drawing showing his concept for the glass 'volcano' to be seen from the city

I am constantly thinking about the future. I predict that in the future the difference between functional and narrative, or allegorical lighting, will become one and the same. There will also be opportunities to interact – light being a living entity with the object. I think that in future architectural objects will be increasingly bound to light – light will be intrinsic to the object. I am impatient for the time when light can be produced without electricity. It will happen soon. With LEDs, it's fantastic, ten years ago I couldn't create the projects I do today!

31.9 Yann Kersale's cyclical phasing of colour which sees the Forum in Helmut Jahn's Sony Centre, Berlin, as a huge 'jellyfish' programmed to change from white during the day to a night-time spectral cycle

Notes

Introduction

1   Batchelor, D. (2000) *Chromophobia*, London: Reaktion Books.

Part 1: Why and How We See Colour

Chapter 1: The Colour Currency of Nature

1   Humphrey, N.K. (1972) 'Interest and pleasure: two determinants of a monkey's visual preferences', *Perception*, 1: 395–416.
2   Humphrey, N.K. and Keeble, G. (1974) 'The reactions of monkeys to "fearsome" pictures', *Nature*, 500–2.
3   Porter, T. (1973) 'An investigation into colour preferences', *Designer*, September: 12–14.
4   Gerard, R.M., quoted by J.M. Fitch (1968) 'The control of the luminous environment', *Scientific American*, 219: 190.
5   Goldstein, K. (1942) 'Some experimental observations concerning the influence of colors on the function of the organism', *Occupational Therapy,* 21: 147; Halpern, L. (1956) 'Additional contributions to the sensorimotor induction syndrome in unilateral disequilibrium with special reference to the effect of colors', *Journal of Nervous and Mental Diseases*, 123: 334.
6   Wright, B. and Rainwater, L. (1962) 'The meanings of color', *Journal of General Psychology*, 67: 88–9.
7   Pinkerton, E. and Humphrey, N.K. (1974) 'The apparent heaviness of colours', *Nature*, 250: 164–65.
8   Berlin, B. and Kay, P. (1969) *Basic Color Terms*, Los Angeles: University of Los Angeles Press.
9   Brown, W.P. (1972) 'Studies of word listing', *Irish Journal of Psychology*, 3: 117–59.
10 Goldstein, op. cit.
11 Humphrey, N.K. and Keeble, G. (1978) 'Effects of red light and loud noise on the rate at which monkeys sample their sensory environment', *Perception*, 7: 343.
12 Turner, V. (1966) 'Colour classification in Ndembu ritual', in M. Banton (ed.) *Anthropological Approaches to the Study of Religion*, London: Tavistock.

13 Humphrey, N.K. (2006) *Seeing Red: A Study of Consciousness*, Cambridge, MA: Harvard University Press.

Chapter 2: Seeing Colours

1   Gregory, R.L. (2005) *Eye and Brain: The Psychology of Seeing*, Oxford: Oxford University Press.
2   Newton, I. (1704) *Opticks*, London: Smith & Walford.
3   Young, T. (1807) *A Course of Lectures in Natural Philosophy*, London: Johnson.
4   Helmholtz, H. von (1856) *Handbuch der physiologischen Optik*, Leipzig: Voss.
5   Munsell, A.H. (1905) *A Color Notation*, Boston: Ellis.
6   Ostwald, W. (1916) *Die Farbenfibel*, Leipzig: Unesma.
7   Ladd-Franklin, C. (1929) *Color and Color Theories*, New York: Harcourt Brace.
8   Hering, E. (1878) *Zur Lehre vom Lichtsinne*, Vienna: Gerold.
9   Rushton, W.A.H. (1962) *Visual Pigments in Man*, Springfield, IL: Thomas.
10 Purves, D. and Lotto, R.B. (2003) *Why We See What We Do*, Sunderland, MA: Sinauer Associates.
11 Ibid.
12 Land, E. (1977) 'The retinex theory of colour vision', *Scientific American*, 237: 108–28.
13 Gregory, op. cit., p. 121.

Chapter 3: The Dynamics of Colour

1   Glancey, J. (2000) 'Do architects have a future?', the *Guardian*, 26 June.
2   Manley Hopkins, G. (2006) *Collected Works of Gerard Manley Hopkins*, vol. IV, Oxford: Oxford University Press.
3   Berlyne, D. (1971) *Architecture and Psycho-biology*, New York: Appleton Century Crofts.
4   Lawton, G. (1974) 'A brain of two halves', *New Scientist*, 22 Sept., p. 38.
5   Lewin, R. (1974) 'The brain's other half', *New Scientist*, 6 June.
6   Jung-Beeman, M., Bowman, E. and Kunios, J. (2004) *Biology Today*, April.
7   Chomsky, N. (1972) *Language and Mind*, New York, Harcourt, Bruce, Jovanovich.
8   Lumsden, C.J. and Wilson, E.O. (1982) *Genes, Mind and Culture*, Cambridge, MA: Harvard University Press, p. 89.
9   Smith, P.F. (2003) *The Dynamics of Delight*, London: Routledge.
10 Porter, T. and Mikellides, B. (1976) *Colour for Architecture*, London: Studio Vista, p. 99.

Part 2: Colour Mapping: colour at the city scale

Chapter 4: Light, Locale and the Color of Cities

1 Swirnoff, L. (2003) 'The geometry of brightness and the perception of form', in *Dimensional Color*, 2nd edn, New York: W.W. Norton.

2 Swirnoff, L. (2003) 'Chiaro e scuro inverted', in *Dimensional Color*, 2nd edn, New York: W.W. Norton.

Chapter 5: Italian City Colour Plans (1978–2007)

1 Symcox, J. (1983) *Victor Amadeus II: Absolutism in the Savoyard State, 1675–1730*, London: Thames & Hudson.

2 Brino, G. and Rosso, F. (1980) *Colore e Citta. Il Piano del Colore di Torino, 1800–1850*, Milan: Idea Books.

3 Brino, G. (1991) *Colori di Liguria*, Genoa: Sagep Editrice.

4 Brino, G. and Rosso, F. (1972) 'La Casa dell'Architetto Alessandro Antonelli in Torino', in *Atti e Rassegna Tecnica della Società degli Ingegneri e Architetti in Torino*, July–August, 7–8.

5 Brino, G. (1995) *Crystal Palace: cronaca di un'avventura progettuale*, Genoa: Sagep Editrice.

6 Brino, G. (1989) 'Il laboratorio mobile per il restauro delle facciate', *Italia Nostra*, no. 266.

Chapter 8: Digital Colour Mapping

1 Lenclos, J.P. (1977) 'Living in colour', in T. Porter and B. Mikellides (eds), *Colour for Architecture*, London: Studio Vista; Foote, K.E. (1983) *Color in Public Spaces: Toward a Communication-based Theory of the Urban Built Environment*, Chicago: University of Chicago Press; and Iijima, S. (1995) *Study on the Relationship between Local Colour Attributes of Streetscape and Climatic Elements*, City Planning Report No. 30, Northern Japan: Okayama Shoka University, pp. 271–6; Iijima, S. (1997) 'Cross-cultural color differences of commercial facility between Great Britain and Japan', *Bulletin of Okayama Marketing University*, 33(2): 39–51.

2 Hong, G., Ronnier Luo, M. and Rhodes, P.A. (2001) 'A study of digital camera colorimetric characterization based on polynomial modeling', *Color Research and Application*, 26(1): 74-84; Morovic, J. and Morovic, P. (2003) 'Determining colour gamuts of digital cameras and scanners', *Color Research and Application*, 28(1): 59–68.

Part 3: The NCS (Natural Color System) and Research Applications

Chapter 9: NCS – The Natural Color System for the Denotation of Colour

1 Berlin, B. and Kay, P. (1969) *Basic Color Terms*, Los Angeles: University of Los Angeles Press.

2 Hård, A. and Sivik, L. (1981) 'NCS – Natural Color System: a Swedish standard for color notation', *Color Research and Application* 6(3).

Chapter 11: Seven Kinds of Colour

1 Kuehni, R. (2003) *Color Space and Its Divisions*, Hoboken, NJ: John Wiley & Sons, Inc., p. 15.

2 Maund, B. (2001) 'The pluralist framework for colours', in *AIC 2001 – The Ninth Congress of the International Colour Association*, SPIE – The International Society for Optical Engineering, Rochester, New York.

3 Farrant, P. (1999) *Colour in Nature*, London: Blandford, p. 90.

4 Ball, P. (2002) *Bright Earth*, Harmondsworth: Penguin Books, p. 85.

5 Fergusson, R., Manser, M. *et al.* (2000) *The New Penguin Thesaurus*, Harmondsworth: Penguin Books, p. 485.

6 Garfield, S. (2000) *Mauve*, London: Faber and Faber.

7 Fridell Anter, K. (2000) *What Colour is the Red House?*, Stockholm: Department of Architectural Forms, Royal Institute of Technology, p. 338.

8 Billger, M. (1999) *Colour in Enclosed Space*, Gothenburg: Department of Building Design – Theoretical and Applied Aesthetics, Chalmers University of Technology, p. 11.

9 Hård, A. and Sivik, L. (1981) 'NCS – Natural Color System: a Swedish standard for color notation', *Color Research and Application* 6(3).

Chapter 12: Daylight Influence on Indoor Colour Design

1 Honkonen, V. (2003) In Visullavarldar2, G Vessel. Available at: http://www.visuellavarldar2.se.

2 Hårleman, M. (2007) *Daylight Influence on Colour Design: Empirical Study on Perceived Colour and Colour Experience Indoors*, Stockholm: KTH, AxlBooks.

Part 4: Architects and Colour at the Building Scale

Chapter 14: Color Structure: a perceptual techtonic
1 Swirnoff, L. (2003) *Dimensional Color*, 2nd edn, New York: W.W. Norton.

Chapter 17: On Colour and Space
1 Batchelor, D. (2000) *Chromophobia*, London: Reaktion Books, p. 52.
2 Ibid., pp. 66–7.
3 Ibid., pp. 22–3.
4 Ibid.
5 Goethe, J.W. (1810) 'Farbenlehre'.
6 Semper, G. (1860) 'Der Stil'.
7 Ibid.
8 Gideon, S. in A. Rüegg (1994) 'Colour concepts and colour scales in modernism', Berlin: *Daidalos*, No. 51, p. 68.
9 Le Corbusier (1922–33) *L'Architecture Vivante*, ed. J. Badovici, Paris: A. Morancé.
10 Ibid.
11 Taut, B. (1938) in O. Putz (1984) 'Über das verhaltnis von farbe und architektur am beispiel Bruno Taut', *Österreichische Gesellschaft für Architektur*, Wien: UMBAU Akademie, p. 38.
12 Ibid.
13 Albers, J. ([1963] 1971) *Interaction of Color*, New Haven, CT: Yale University Press.
14 Ibid.
15 Ibid.

Part 5: Colour Psychology and Colour Aesthetics
1 Casson, H. (1976) Preface, in T. Porter and B. Mikellides (eds) *Colour for Architecture*, London: Studio Vista, pp. 8–9.

Chapter 23: Colour Preference: the longitudinal perspective
1 Humphrey, N. (1972) 'Interest and pleasure: two determinants of monkeys' visual preferences', *Perception*, 1: 395–416.
2 Humphrey, N. and Keeble, G. (1978) 'Effects of red light and loud noise on the rate at which monkeys sample their sensory environment', *Perception*, 7: 343.
3 Bergström, B. (2008) 'Colour effects and affects', in *AIC 2008 Proceedings*, Stockholm: Farginstitutet.
4 Eysenck, H. (1941) 'A critical and experimental study of colour preferences', *American Journal of Psychology*, 54: 385–94.
5 Porter, T. (1973) *Synthesis 2*, pp. 2–5.
6 Oberascher, L. 'Simulating real world complexity', in L. Sivik (ed.) *Colour Report F50*, Stockholm: Farginstitutet, pp. 45–9.
7 Porter, T. and Mikellides, B. (1976) *Colour for Architecture*, London: Studio Vista.
8 Whitfield, T.W.A. and Slatten, R. (1979) 'The effects of categorization and prototypicality on aesthetic choice in a furniture selection task', *British Journal of Psychology*, 70: 65–75.
9 Taft, C. and Sivik, L. (1996) 'Colour meaning and context', in L. Sivik (ed.), *Colour Report F50*, Stockholm: Farginstitutet.
10 Janssens, J. (1992) 'Individual and contextual factors in urban colour perception', in L. Sivik (ed.), *Colour Report F50*, Stockholm: Farginstitutet.
11 Sivik, L. (1976) 'The language of colour', in T. Porter and B. Mikellides (eds), *Colour for Architecture*, London: Studio Vista.
12 Küller, R. (1980) 'Architecture and emotions', in B. Mikellides (ed.), *Architecture for People*, London: Studio Vista, pp. 123–39.
13 Hulbert, A.C. and Ling, Y. (2007) 'Biological components of sex differences in colour preference', *Current Biology*, 17(16): 623–5.

Chapter 24: Preferences for Colours on Buildings
1 Küller, R. (1981) *Non-Visual Effects of Light and Colour: Annotated Bibliography*, Stockholm: Swedish Council for Building Research.
2 Eysenck, H. (1941) 'A critical and experimental study of colour preferences', *American Journal of Psychology*, 54: 385–94.
3 Sivik, L. (1974) *Color Meaning and Perceptual Color Dimensions: A Study of Exterior Colors*, Göteborg Psychological Reports, 4, No. 11, Gothenburg: Gothenburg University.
4 Janssens, J. (2001) 'Facade colours not just a matter of personal taste', *Nordic Journal of Architectural Research,* 14: 17–21, 34.
5 Küller, R., Mikellides, B. and Janssens, J. (2008) 'Colour, arousal and performance: a comparison of three experiments', accepted for publication in *Color Research and Application*.

Chapter 25: Colour, Arousal, Hue-Heat and Time Estimation

1   Sivik, L. (1996) 'Colour report, F50', Stockholm, Farginstitutet.

2   Bayes, K. (1967) *The Therapeutic Effect of Environment on Emotionally Disturbed and Mentally Sub-Normal Children*, Surrey: Unwin Brothers Ltd.

3   Gerard, R.M. (1958) 'Differential effects of colored lights on psychophysiological functions', doctoral dissertation, University of California, Los Angeles.

4   Ali, M.R. (1972) 'Pattern of EEF recovery under photic stimulation by light of different colors', *Electroencephalography and Clinical Neurophysiology*, 33: 332–5.

5   Sivik, L. (1976) 'The language of colour', in T. Porter and B. Mikellides (eds), *Colour for Architecture*, London: Studio Vista.

6   Acking, C.A. and Küller, R. (1976) 'Interior space and colour', in T. Porter and B. Mikellides (eds), *Colour for Architecture*, London: Studio Vista.

7   Sivik, L. and Hård, A. (1984) 'Namn Pa Farger', in *Colour Report F24*, Stockholm: Scandinavian Colour Centre.

8   Mikellides, B. (1990) 'Colour and physiological arousal', *Journal of Architectural and Planning Research*, 7(1): 13–20.

9   Mikellides, B. (1979) 'Conflicting experiences of space', in J. G. Simon (ed.), *Conflicting Experiences of Space*, vol. 11, Louvain: Catholic University of Louvain Press.

10 Jacobs, K.W. and Hustmeyer, F.E. (1974) 'Effects of four psychological primary colours on GSR, heart rate, and respiration rate', *Perceptual and Motor Skills*, 38: 763–6; Wilson, G.D. (1966) 'Arousal properties of red versus green', *Perceptual and Motor Skills*, 23: 947–9.

11 Küller, R. (1976) 'The use of space: some physiological and philosophical aspects', in P. Korosec-Serfaty (ed.), *Appropriation of Space* (Proceedings of the Strasbourg conference), pp.154–63.

12 Lacy, J.I. and Lacy, B.C. (1970) 'Some autonomic and central nervous system interrelationships', in P. Black (ed.), *Physiological Correlates of Emotion*, New York: Academy Press.

13 Mongersen, M.F. and English, H.B. (1926) 'The apparent warmth of colours', *American Journal of Psychology*, 37: 427–8l; Sivik, L. (1974) 'Color meaning and perceptual color dimensions: a study of exterior colors', *Göteborg Psychological Reports* 4, No. 11, Gothenburg: Gothenburg University; Hogg, P. *et al.* (1979) 'Dimensions and determinants of judgements of colour samples', *British Journal of Psychology*, 70: 231–42; Küller, R. and Mikellides, B. (1993) 'Simulated studies of color, arousal and comfort', in R.W. Marans and D. Stokols (eds), *Environmental Stimulation*, London: Sage.

14 Berry, P.C. (1961) 'Effect of colour illumination upon perceived temperature', *Journal of Applied Psychology*, 45(4): 248–50; Bennett, C.A. and Ray, P. (1972) 'What's so hot about red?' *Human Factors*, 14: 1949–50; Fanger, P.O., Breum, N.O. and Jerking, E. (1977) 'Can colour and noise influence man's human comfort?', *Ergonomics*, 20: 11–18; Green, T.C. and Bell, P.A. (1980) 'Additional considerations concerning the effect of "warm" and "cool" colours on energy conservation', *Ergonomics*, 23: 949–54; Mikellides, B. (1996) 'Emotional and behavioural reactions to colour in colour and psychology', in L. Sivik (ed.), *Colour Report*, Stockholm: Farginstitutet.

15 Fanger *et al.*, op. cit.

16 Mikellides, 'Emotional and behavioural reactions', op. cit.

17 Gregory, R.L. (2005) *Eye and Brain: The Psychology of Seeing*, Oxford: Oxford University Press.

18 Mikellides, 'Emotional and behavioural reactions', op. cit.

19 Caldwell, J.L. and Jones, G.E. (1985) 'The effects of exposure to red and blue light on physiological indices and time estimation', *Perception*, 14, 19–29.

20 Mikellides, B. (1979) 'Conflicting experiences of colour space', in J.G. Simon (ed.), *Conflicting Experiences of Space*, vol. II, Louvain: Catholic University of Louvain Press.

21 Humphrey, N. and Keeble, G. (1978) 'Effects of red light and loud noise on the rate at which monkeys sample their sensory environment', *Perception*, 7: 343.

22 Smets, G. (1969) 'Time expression of red and blue', *Perceptual and Motor Skills*, 29: 511–14; Humphrey and Keeble, op. cit.

23 Porter, T. and Mikellides, B. (eds), *Colour for Architecture*, London: Studio Vista.

Chapter 27: Light, Mood and Seasonal Disorders

1   Arendt, J. (1998) 'Biological rhythms: the science of chronobiology', *Journal of the Royal College of Physicians of London*, 32: 27–35; Brainard, G.C. and Hanifin, J.P. (2005) 'Photons, clocks, and consciousness', *Journal of Biological Rhythms*, 20: 314–25; Küller, R. (2002) 'The influence of

light on circarhythms in humans', *Journal of Physiological Anthropology and Applied Human Science*, 21: 87–91; Küller, R. and Küller, M. (2001) *The Influence of Daylight and Artificial Light on Diurnal and Seasonal Variations in Humans: A Bibliography*, Technical Report of CIE No. 139, Vienna: International Commission on Illumination.

2 Brainard and Hanifin, op. cit.

3 Arendt, op. cit.

4 Küller, R. and Wetterberg, L. (1993) 'Melatonin, cortisol, EEG, ECG and subjective comfort in healthy humans: Impact of two fluorescent lamp types at two light intensities', *Lighting Research and Technology*, 25: 71–81; Küller, R. and Wetterberg, L. (1996) 'The subterranean work environment: impact on well-being and health', *Environment International*, 22: 33–52.

5 Brainard and Hanifin, op. cit.

6 Küller, R. and Lindsten, C. (1992) 'Health and behavior of children in classrooms with and without windows', *Journal of Environmental Psychology*, 12: 305–17.

7 Küller, R. and Wetterberg, 'Melatonin', op. cit.

8 Küller, R., Ballal, S.G., Laike, T., Mikellides, B. and Tonello, G. (2001) 'The prevalence of seasonal affective disorder symptoms in working populations in Argentina, England, Saudi-Arabia and Sweden', in G. Tonello (ed.), *Lighting, Mood, and Seasonal Fatigue in Northern Argentina: Comparison to Countries Close to and Further from the Equator*, doctoral dissertation, Lund University, Lund. pp. 81–110.

9 Rosenthal, N.E. (1998) *Winter Blues. Seasonal Affective Disorder: What It Is and How to Overcome It,* New York: The Guilford Press.

10 Küller, R. (1991) 'Environmental assessment from a neuropsychological perspective', in T. Gärling and G.W. Evans (eds), *Environment, Cognition, and Action: An Integrated Approach*, New York: Oxford University Press, pp. 111–47.

11 Küller, R., Ballal, S., Laike, T., Mikellides, B. and Tonello, G. (2006) 'The impact of light and colour on psychological mood: a cross-cultural study of indoor work environments', *Ergonomics*, 49: 1496–507.

Part 6: Into the Light

1 Palumbo, M. (2000) *New Wombs: Electronic Bodies and Architectural Disorders*, Basel: Birkhauser.

Chapter 28: Being in Colour

1 Doesburg, T. van (1924) 'Towards a plastic architecture', Rotterdam: *de Stijl*, No. 12.

2 Ehrensweig, A. (1967) *The Hidden Order of Art*, Berkeley, CA: University of California Press.

3 Smith, P. (1976) 'The dialectics of colour', in T. Porter and B. Mikellides (eds), *Colour for Architecture*, London: Studio Vista.

4 Kakatami, M. (2002) London: *Xebec Sound Arts*, No. 12.

5 Vernon, D. (1997) 'The artistic manipulation of light', PhD dissertation, University of Brighton.

6 Brakhage, S. (1963) 'Metaphors of vision', New York: *Film Culture*, No. 30.

7 Kandinsky, W. (1977) *Concerning the Spiritual in Art*, New York: Dover Publishing Inc.

Index

Page numbers in italics refer to illustrations

Image credits

The authors and publishers would like to thank the following individuals and institutions for giving permission to reproduce illustrations. We have made every effort to contact copyright holders, but if any errors have been made we would be happy to correct them at a later printing.

Archivio Storico Città di Torino: 5.1
Bergström, Berit: 10.1
bitterbredt.de: 17.2–17.4
Daria Scagliola and Stijn Brakkee: 19.1; 19.2
Gonzales, Juan Antonio: 6.1–6.4
Kaplan, Todd: 30.1
©Kersalé, Yann: 31.1–31.9
Kisling, Annette: 17.1
Legorreta, Lourdes: 21.1
Lenclos, Jean Philippe: 7.1–7.4; 15.1; 15.2
©Niall McLaughlin Architects: 20.1; 20.2
NCS – Natural Color System®© property of Scandinavian Colour Institute AB, Stockholm 2008. References to NCS®© in this publication are used with permission from the Scandinavian Colour Institute AB: 9.1–9.8
Renzo, Gianni di: 5.3
Ruault, Philippe: 16.1; 16.2; 16.3; 16.6
Schaewen, Deidi von: 16.4; 16.5
Speirs and Major Associates/Bryan F. Peterson: 29.5
Speirs and Major Associates/Colin Ball: 29.4
Speirs and Major Associates/LDA Design: 29.1
Speirs and Major Associates/Tim Soar: 29.2
Speirs and Major Associates/Werner J. Hannappel: 29.3
Swirnoff, Lois: 4.1; 4.2